BLACKS FOUND IN THE DEEDS

OF

LAURENS & NEWBERRY COUNTIES, SC :

1785 to 1827

❖

Listed in

Deeds of Gift, Deeds of Sale,

Mortgages, Born Free and Freed

Abstracted from
Laurens County, SC
Deed Books A - L
and
Newberry County, SC
Deed Books A - G

Abstracted by
Margaret Peckham Motes

CLEARFIELD

Printed for
Clearfield Company, Inc. by
Genealogical Publishing Co., Inc.
Baltimore, Maryland
2002

International Standard Book Number: 0-8063-5156-X

Made in the United States of America

Contents

Preface

In my previous book, *Free Blacks and Mulattos in South Carolina; 1850 Census*, I demonstrated the extent to which records are available for a large population of free blacks and mulattos in South Carolina. In this new work, *Blacks Found in the Deeds of Laurens & Newberry Counties, SC: 1785 to 1827*, Laurens and Newberry Counties were selected to continue work on this subject.

Laurens and Newberry counties were formed in 1785. These two counties had been a part of the Ninety-Six District. The material in this present work is drawn from the Deed Books of Laurens County, 1785-1827 and Newbury County, 1785-1805. Prior to1785 deeds were recorded in Charleston, SC.

These deeds cover a span of forty-two years. They contain the names of blacks and mulattos in bills of sale, marriage contracts, settlements and separations, estate settlements, deeds of gift, mortgages, and emancipations. Twenty-six types of deeds are listed, see index page 204.

Negro slaves were property, deeds list them by name and age along with the household belongings, kitchen utensils, farm tools and livestock. It was important for their owners to have their provenance recorded.

Important information is found in deeds, which consisted of: from whom they were purchased; in some instances, from which state they came; their age; and the number of children. Some children are listed with the name of their parent or parents. Deeds also list married Negroes and their children. Some last names are listed for free blacks; occupation may be included. Actual dates of birth are found in some records. Information in the deeds also note if free born, tendency to be a run away, aged, maimed, country born, color if very black, or, if a mulatto, the coloration of their skin.

These deeds can also be used to help put together the relationship of the white families in these two counties. By using these types of records, researchers can trace the transaction of certain Negroes through the last will and testament, or deed of gift from an owner, to a later sale of the individual.

In the Name Index (Black), each child who has a parent is listed to that parent; couples are also listed as man and wife.

Some films were difficult to read, and there is the possible omission of some records. Every effort was been made to locate and record all of the different deeds in which blacks and mulattos are found, so they could be grouped together to help those working on their ancestral roots.

Variations occur in the spelling of some first and last names, and due to the poor quality of some microcopy the text is often difficult to read. When using these records for research, if you have any questions, it is always best to review the source documents to recheck the information.

Margaret P. Motes
Newburyport, Massachusetts

Sources

Deeds abstracts were noted principally from:

Microcopy of Deeds:
Laurens County, South Carolina, Deed Books A-L
Newberry County, South Carolina , Deed Books A-G

Ellen L. Aull, compiler; Works Project Administration, Project No. 465-33-33-14 and Project 165-333-7999 Newberry County (South Carolina) Deed Books A, B, C, D, D-2, E, F, G. Sponsored by University of South Carolina. Supervised by Miss Flora B. Surles, pub. 1937.*

Sara M. Nash, Abstracts of Early Records of Laurens County, South Carolina 1785-1820 (Fountain Inn, South Carolina: Priv. pub., 1982).*

*Information from these sources helped to locate information, which then was abstracted from microcopy of the deed books of these two counties.

LAURENS COUNTY, SOUTH CAROLINA

DEED BOOK A: 1785 - 1786

Deed Book A: 134
April 7, 1785. Deed of Gift. Alexander Deale unto his sons Clement and Alexander Deale, all residents, of the State of South Carolina and District of 96; for and in consideration of the Natural Love and Affection I bare unto my two sons Clement and Alexander Deale, and for good causes....have and by these presents do make a Free Deed of Gift of all my property, in manner following.
Namely after my decease, I give unto my son Clement Deale a tract of land containing 150 acres on which I now live in the forks of Banks Creek, likewise a negro wench called Pegg, one negro wench called Grace and their increase, also a negro boy called Ceaser and no more. Likewise I give unto my son Alexander Deale, Junr. land containing 200 acres joining land on which I now live called new Survey; a negro winch called Zilphia and her child named Joe and Zilpheas increase and no more... signed 7 April 1785 Alexander Deale. Test. Josa Roea, John Meek, Thomas Forkes. Recorded Jan 19, 1786.

Deed Book A: 139
January 20, 1786. Bill of Sale. Charles Saxon, of the State of South Carolina and County of Laurens to Lewis Saxon of the State and County aforesaid for the sum of £100; have sold one certain Negroes man named Prince, between 18 and 20 years old to be his lawful right and property. ..Set his hand 7 August 1785 Charles Saxon. Test. Joshua Saxon.

Deed Book A: 281
February 17, 1786. Bill of Sale. Know all man by these presents that we Hans and Berk of Charleston, Merchants and James Tinker of New York, Master of the Sloop Maria, for and in consideration of the sum of £38; 12 shillings and one penny paid by Mr. Lewis Saxon, sell unto the said Lewis Saxon a Negro wench named Hannah about 16 years old.. Signed Hans and Berk, James Tinker. Wit. John Hunter, Silvanus Walker. Recorded July 19, 1786.

DEED BOOK B - 1787 - 1790

Deed Book B: 275
November 5, 1787.Deed of Gift: I John Falkoner of Laurens County, 96
District, State of Couth Carolina, send greets know that I the said John
Falkoner as well for and in consideration of the Natural Love and Affection
which I have and bare to my well beloved friend Nathaniel Hall, Sr. for
divers other goods and consideration here unto I give and grant unto the said
Nathaniel Hall, his heirs after my decease and after my now living wife
Elizabeth's decease; all my Negroes to wit. My Negro woman Priscilla,
George, Juda, Ephraim, Milley and off there increase... signed John
Falkoner. Wit. Robert Hall, Hannah Clardy, John Hall. Proved by John
Hall and Hannah Clardy before James Mayson, J.P. 4 April 1788.

Deed Book B: 340
February 9, 1788. James McNees of the District of 96, Laurens County,
State of South Carolina. Greetings. Where as I the said James McNees by
bond or obligation baring date with these presents became held and firmly
found into Robert McNees of the said County and State aforesaid in the
penal sum of £100 Sterling money of South Carolina, deliver to the said
Robert McNees a likely Negro goy or girl between the year of 14 and 20 on
or before 25 December....
Know ye that I the said James McNees for the better serving the payment of
the said sum of £50 or the Negro boy or girl as above mentions that the sais
Robert McNees his heirs, executors, administrators, assigned have
bargained and sold to said Robert McNees a tract of land containing 160
acres .... James McNees. Wit. Wm. Jones, Andrew Rodgers.

Deed Book B: 354
April 4, 1788. Laurens County, South Carolina. Know ye that we Reuben
Pyles and wife S.E Pyles, his wife, in consideration of the sum of £75 to us
in hand paid at and before the sealing and delivery of these presents by
Lewis Saxon, to bargain and sold unto the said Lewis Saxon a negro woman
named Aimoy about 21 years old, also her negro boy child names Samson
about 5 months old... Reuben Pyles, S.E. Pyles. Wit. Lydall Allin, John
Pyles. Proved by Lydall Allin before Jonathan Downs, J.P. 4 April 1788.

Deed Book B: 358
January 1, 1787. Deed of Gift: Laurens County, South Carolina. Indenture
made 1 January 1787 between Mary Williams, Executrix to the late Col.
James Williams deceased of the County and State aforesaid, and Elizabeth
Tindsley of the same place. That the said Mary Williams in consideration of

the Natural Love and Affection which she hath and bequest unto her beloved daughter Elizabeth Tindsley, also the sum of £1 Sterling to her paid....returned back again from when it came to be equally divided among the Col. Williams' children then alive, Viz., one Negro man slave names Peter, one negro woman slave named Tina, one Negro boy slave named Fell, one negro girl slave named Easter, one Negro girl slave named Marian, and one hundred and fifty acres of land. Granted unto Joseph Hutcheson on 6 Mar. 1770 lying upon Mudlick Creek.... Mary Williams. Wit. John Williams Junr., Robt. Sayer, Anthony Golden, As. Criswell, Prestings Tindsley. Recorded 24 June 1788.

Deed Book B: 359.
May 14, 1788. Deed of Gift: Laurens County, South Carolina. Indenture made 14 May 1788 between Joseph Griffin and Mary his wife of the State and County aforesaid and James Williams and Washington Williams of the same place. Witness that the said Joseph Griffin and Mary his wife as well for the Natural Love and Affection which they hath bequest unto their beloved {?} William Washington, [also lists Negro slaves - copy very poor to read] Recorded June 25, 1788.

Deed Book B: 360
January 26, 1787. Deed of Gift: Laurens County, South Carolina. Indenture 1 April 1788 between Joseph Griffin and Mary his wife of the State and Country aforesaid for Love and Affection they have to their beloved daughter Sarah Griffin £ 270, also one Negro woman slave named Polly, one Negro boy slave named Phillis, one mulatto boy slave named Nath'l, one Negro boy slave named Cato, one Negro girl slave named Molly, one feather bed and furniture....signed Joseph Griffin, Mary Griffin. Wit. Arche Siers, John Neely. May 13, 1788. Recd of the within mentioned Sarah Griffin by the hand of her husband John Griffin the sum of £ 270 Sterling - if being the full of the consideration money mention in the within deed. Recorded June 26, 1788.

Deed Book B: 375.
January 29, 1787. Mary Williams to James Atwood Williams. Mention of Slaves - very poor microfilm copy. Recorded June 30, 1788.

Deed Book B: 408.
April 24, 1788. Mortgage. William Rucks to Jonathan Johnson, merchant - mortgage on Negro. [very poor microfilm copy.] Recorded Sept. 19, 1788.

Deed Book B: 412
May 3, 1788 - Deed of Gift. I John O'Neil of Laurens County, South
Carolina. In consideration of natural affection and for divers good causes
and considerations have given and granted unto my son in law Wm.
Shanley, a negro girl Milley. Wit. Angus Campbell, Margret Scott, Jno.
Cook. Recorded Sept. 19, 1788. {film very poor}

Deed Book B: 463
August 4, 1789. Mortgage. Wm. Thomason to Nathan Austin a mortgage on
two negroes. Wit. Charles Sullivant, Benj. Camp. Jonathan Downs, J.P..
Recorded November 24, 1789. {film very poor}

DEED BOOK C - 1789 - 1791

Deed Book C: 21.
May 3, 1788. Deed of Gift.   John O'Neal, of the State of South Carolina,
Laurens County. For and in consideration of the natural affection and for
divers other good causes and consideration here unto moving have given
and granted unto my son in law William Shanley, one Negro girl named
Milley.. May 3, 1788. Signed John O'Neal. Wit. {A}ngus Campbell, J.P.
{M}argaret Scott, {torn} Cook. Proved 19 June 1789.

Deed Book C: 30.
October 27, 1788. Bill of Sale. John Edward and wife Mary of Newberry
County, South Carolina to John Brison of the State aforesaid for the sum of
£45 sell unto John Brison one Negro wench named Clary about 26 years of
age and her increase... signed John Edwards, Mary Edwards (mark) 9
October 1788. Wit. Mikle Abney, James Brison. Wit. Proved James Brison
1 Nov. 1788 before Silvanus Walker J.P.. Recorded June 23, 1789.

Deed Book C: 80.
November 27, 1789. Deed of Gift: Know ye that I the said Shadrack
Martin, of the State of South Carolina and Laurens County Little River
Settlement freeholder and planter for and in consideration of the love
goodwill and affection which I also have toward my loving daughter Jean
Martin of the same County and State and settlement have given and granted
unto said Jean Martin, one bay horse, give years old, one white hind foot.
Also one good feather bed and furniture. Also to my living daughter
Margaret Martin her heirs, executors, administrators. One negro fellow
named Isaac, also one Negro wench named Bett with all my goods and
chattels... 27 Nov. 1789.

4

Shadrack Martin. Wit. Ezekiel Rolands, Joshua Downs. Wm. Mitchussen? J.P. Recorded November 27, 1789.

Deed Book C: 103
April 26, 1789. Mortgage. Indenture made 26 April 1789 between Joshua Roberts and Sarah his wife, of the State of South Carolina, Laurens District and John Simpson, merchant, of said County mortgage on a Negro girl named Bark..... Signed Joshua Roberts (mark) and Sarah Roberts (mark). Wit. Andrew Smith, James Simpson. Proved by James Simpson 5 June 1789 before John Hunter, J.P. Recorded January 2, 1790.

Deed Book C: 158
No date. © 1769) Affidavit. Laurens County, South Carolina. Personally came unto court Jeremiah Searcy and made oath that sometime in the year of 1769 he was personally present at a plantation formally called Michael Willsons on Simons Creek and saw Samuel Henderson pay Michael Willson, Senior a negro man named Dave, in consideration fo said land and plantation which said Herderson had purchased of said Willson and then resided on and was in possession of said land. Jeremiah Searcy, before John Hunter, J.P. Recorded April 27. 1790

Deed Book C: 167
December 4, 1789. Bill of Sale. Know all men by these presents that I David Bailey of Laurens County, Blacksmith, of the State of South Carolina for the sum of £ 27, 10 shillings and 6 3/4 Sterling money of the State aforesaid sell to Thomas Wasdsworth and William Turpin, otherwise Wadsworth and Turpin, merchants of the County and State aforesaid a certain Negro man named Joe about 5 ft six inches high, about 27 years of age.....signed 24 December 1789 David Bailey (D). Wit. John Trotter, John Cargill, Junr. Proved by John Trotter March 11, 1790 before Silvanus Walker, J.P. Recorded April 29, 1790.

Deed Book C: 207
January 11, 1790. Bill of Sale. Know all men by these presents that we Sarah Cleary and Cornilius Cargill of the State aforesaid for the sum of £75 Sterling; sell to Patrick Cunningham one Negro woman named Hannah about 25 years old and one Negro child named Lewis about 16 months old to have and to hold the said Negro woman and said Negroes child until the said Patrick Cunningham his heirs, Executors, Administrators....forever. 27 January 1790. Signed Sarah (S) Cleary , Cornelius Cargill. Wit. Menusant Walker, Richard Duty. Proved by Hardy Conant 9 March 1790 be3fore Jonathan Downs, J.P. Recorded June 21, 1790.

Deed Book C: 214
October 5, 1789. Mortgage. Laurens County, South Carolina. Wm.
Thomason, Sr. of the State and County aforesaid am held and firmly bound
unto Thomas Cuningham of the State and County aforesaid in the full and
just sum of £ 6, 5 shilling and 9 pence. I do pledge by way of mortgage unto
the said Thomas Cuningham a Negro girl about 3 years old named Lede,
now my own right an property which I never bargained nor sold to any
person or persons whatsoever nor neither have I parted from her as my
property by way of Deed of Gift... 5 October 1789 Wm. Thomason, Sr. Wit.
Isaac James, Jno. McCambridge. Proved by John McCambridge 7 October
1789 before Joseph Downs., J.P.   Recorded August 3, 1790.

Deed Book C: 272
March 15, 1789. State of South Carolina, Know all men by these presents
that I Duke Williams have sold unto my father John Williams a certain
Negroes girl named Rose about 10 or 12 years old for the sum of £25
Sterling... 18 March 1789 Duke Williams. Wit. Jonathan Johnston, Wm. T.
Johnson. Proved by Angus Campbell, J.P. March 15, 1790. Recorded
September 30, 1790.

Deed Book C: 312
March 16, 1790. Bill of Sale. Joseph Griffin of Laurens County, State of
South Caroling for the sum of £35 lawful money of the state aforesaid to
James Goodman of Newberry County State aforesaid a certain Negroes man
named Will about 35 years of age a native of Africa about 5 feet four or five
inches high well set... 15 Mary 1790 signed Joseph Griffen. Wit. John
Trotter, Thomas Wadsworth. Proved by John Trotter August 1790 before
John Hunter, J.P. Recorded March 9, 1790.

Deed Book C: 338
March 10, 1791. Bond. Laurens County, South Carolina. Indenture made
between William Milwee of one part and Messrs. John and A. Simpson.
That the said William Millwee standith justly indebted to the said John and
Alexander Simpson in the sum of £27, 15 shillings and 8 pence by notes
and bonds and as usual for the better securing and payment of the sum
William Millwee hath granted, bargained and sold and assigns a negro man
named Frank unto said Messrs. Simpsons. William Millwee. Wit. John
Hunter, David Spears. Proved by David Spears 10 March 1791 before John
Hunter, J.P. Recorded March 14, 1791..

Deed Book C: 359
October 17, 1787. Bond. Know all men by these presents that I Silvanus
Walker of Laurens County and State of South Carolina am held and firmly

bound unto John Faloner of the County and State aforesaid in the full and just sum of 2000 £ 17 October. 1789.
The Condition of the above obligation is such that whereas the aforesaid John Falconer bath through proper to give unto the above named Silvanus Walker and his heirs forever five Negroes, Viz., Priscilla, George, Judith, Ephraim and Milley and their increase... Signed Silvanus Walker, Wit. Cornelius Dendy, John Dendy, Armistead E. Stokes. Proved 22 March 1791 by John Dendy before Charles Saxon, J.P. Recorded March 23, 1791.

DEED BOOK D: 1791 - 1793

Deed Book D: 39
April 23, 1791. Charles Saxon, Esqr. Of Lauren County, South Carolina in consideration of the sum of £ 41, 10 shillings Sterling paid by Samuel Saxon have sold unto said Samuel Saxon a negro boy named Jesse. Charles Saxon (seal). Wit. William Barksdale, Ann Craddock, Mary (mark) Barksdale. Proved by William Barksdale 16 August 1791 before George Anderson, J.P. Recorded August 18, 1791.

Deed Book D: 53
July 13, 1790. Mortgage. Thomas Garner of Laurens County, South Carolina to Benjamin Camp of the same place, have firmly bound unto Benjamin Camp for the sum of £100 Sterling payable the 25 December next, one likely negro boy between 15 and 20 years of age, clear of sickness or disorders and not known to be a negro Practis'd to running away... I pledge by way of mortgage unto the said Benjamin Camp my plantation whereon I now live together with the mill and tract of land containing 198 acres. Thomas Garner. Wit. Jonathan Downs, J.F. Wolff. Proved by Jonathan Downs Esq. 19 July 1791 before Joseph Downs. Recorded October 6, 1791.

Deed Book D: 69
November 18, 1790. Bill of Sale. I Edward Mitchersson of Laurens County in consideration of £800 Sterling paid by Wm. Metehersson of the County aforesaid have bargained, sold and delivered 14 head of Negroes named Nearon?, January, Tae_?, Tony, Hager, Benn, Pompy, Class, Dener, Bet, Bety, Nell, Judith. Edwd. Mitchersson. Wit. Elizah Stevens, Benj. (B) Norwood, James (mark) Satterfield. Proved 9 October 1791 by Eliza Stevens before Charles Saxon, J.P. Recorded October 21, 1791.

Deed Book D: 83.
April 4, 1791. Gift In Trust. Wm. Burton, of Laurens District, South
Carolina in consideration of the sum of £10 paid by Joshua Saxon to sell
unto said Joshua Saxon one negro child Patt it being a girl child in trust for
Clarinda Saxon unto the said Clarinda Saxon shall come to the years of 16
and then to her heirs. Wm. Burton. Wit. Joshua Downs. Proved by Wm.
Burton 4 April 1791. Joseph Downs, J.P. Recorded. December 17. 1791.

Deed Book D: 85
November 12, 1791. Samuel Saxon, Esquire, Sheriff of 96 District, South
Carolina in consideration of the sum of £23, 9 shilling 6 pence do well to
Lewis Saxon one negro woman named Eade about 40 years old, 2 horses,
one saddle and bridle, 8 heads of cattle, 7 head of hoggs, one feather bed
and furniture. Etc.. By a writ of tested by Wm. Mason, clerk of the court of
common pleas in Charleston at the Instruction of Isaac Delyon vs. Charles
Saxon et al. Wit. Lydall Allen, John martin. Jonathan Downs, J.P. Recorded
January 16, 1792.

Deed Book D: 99
No Date: Bill of Sale. We John and Saran Griffen of Laurens County, South
Carolina to John Williams, Junr. for £100 Sterling; sundry slaves, two negro
boys, named Filas and Cato, one mulatto boy named Nat. 26 October 1789
Signed John Griffen, Sarah Griffen. Wit. Richard Griffen, William Watson.
Proved 25 January 1792 by William Watson before Thomas Wadsworth,
J.L.C. Recorded February 2, 1792.

Deed Book D: 99
October 26, 1789. Bill of Sale. I Joseph Griffen of Laurens County, South
Carolina to John Williams, Junr. for the sum of £100 Sterling sundry
Negroes slaves , Viz., one Negroes woman slave named Suckey and three
children, Milley, Lewis and Sue to have and to hold... 26 October 1789
signed Joseph Griffen, Wit. James Tindsley, Richard Grooms. Proved by
Richard Groom 25 January 1792 before Thomas Wadsworth JLC. Recorded
February 2, 1792.

Deed Book D: 100
October 26, 1789. Bill of Sale. I James Attwood Williams of Laurens
County, South Carolina to John Williams, Junr. in consideration of £ 90
Sterling; sundry slaves, Viz., one old Negro woman named Sarah and a
male child named John, one Negro woman named Flora... 26 October 1789.
James A. Williams, Wit. John Owen, Richard Groom. Proved by Richard
Groom 25 January 1792 before Thomas Wadsworth, JLC. Recorded
February 2, 1792.

Deed Book D: 101
October 26, 1789. Bill of Sale. We James and Washington Williams of
Laurens County, South Carolina to John Williams, Junr. For £ 350 Sterling
sundry slaves, Viz., one Negro man named Frank, one Negro girl named
Juda, one old Negro woman named Linda and three male children, Viz.,
Mingo, Simon and Billy, a Negro woman named Dina with 2 female
children Patty and Daphney, and one Negro woman named Liddy with a
young male child named Ned.. Signed 26 October 1789. James Williams
Junr. Washington Williams. Wit. James Goodman, Jonathan Mote. Proved
by Benjamin Goodman 25 January 1792 before Thomas Wasdsworth,
J.L.C. Recorded February 2, 1792.

Deed Book D: 155
April 17, 1792. Bill of Sale. James Flin, of Laurens County, South Carolina
in consideration of the sum of £120 Sterling have sold unto John Doyal , a
negro woman named Sela, about 35 or 36 years of age, country born. Also
one negro girl named Tabbey about 10 or 11 years of age, also one other
negro girl child named Willey about 7 years of age and one other negro
child named Dicey about 2 years old all three the children of said Sela.
James (mark) Flin, Wit. Robert Adair, James Adair. Proved by Robert
Adair 11 May 1792 before Roger Brown, J.P. Recorded May 15, 1792.

Deed Book D: 158
February 4, 1792. Bill of Sale. I Adam Hickman of Orangeburgh District,
South Carolina, to John F. Wolff of the State aforesaid and District of 96 in
consideration of £ 22 Sterling; a certain negro girl named Eve. Signed 4
February 1792 Adam Hickman, Wit. Jonathan Downs, Vincent Davis.
Proved by Jonathan Downs 14 May 1792 before Joseph Downs, J.P.
Recorded May 16, 1792.

Deed Book D: 261
February 16, 1792. Bill of Sale. I Benjamin Arnold of the State of Georgia
in consideration of £ 120 money to me in hand paid hath bargained and sold
and delivered in plain and open market to Anderson Arnold of the Laurens
County State of South Carolina one Negroes boy slave named Natt, of a
yellow complexti9on about 13 or 14 years of age...Signed 16 February 1792
Benjamin Arnold. Wit. John Arnold, Mary McCune. Proved by John Arnold
2 March 1792 before Joseph Downs, J.P. Recorded August 28, 1792.

Deed Book D: 331
January 2, 1793. Bill of Sale. James Finney, of Laurens County, South
Carolina in consideration of the sum of £30 Sterling, to Hugh Crumbley,
one Negro fellow named Peter about 40 years of age.. Wit. James Rodgers,

John Martin, Jeremiah Ward. Proved by Jeremiah Ward 7 January 1793 before George Anderson, J.P. Recorded February 11, 1793.

Deed Book D: 334
December 22, 1792. Bill of Sale. I Zebulon Mathis of Laurens County, South Carolina to John Miller, planter, of the aforesaid place for £ 70 Sterling; one Negroes boy about 17 years old named Deamond and one Negroes girl 12 years of age named Harriott; other ways called Poos and one bay mare 10 years old about 13 ½ hands high...Signed 22 December 1792 Zebulun Mathis, Wit. .Israel Teague, Samuel Mathis. Proved by Israel Teague 8 February 1793 before Wm. Hunter, J.P. Recorded February 27, 1793.

Deed Book D: 335
December 22, 1792. Bill of Sale. I Nicholas Vaughan, planter, of Laurens County, South Carolina to Wadsworth and Turpin, Merchants of the aforesaid place; in consideration of £250 Sterling; 10 Negroes, Viz., a fellow called Andrew about 36 years of age, a fellow called John about 17 years of age, a fellow called Jingo about 17 years of age, a wench called Jinney with 3 children, Viz., Hannah, Peter and Absalom, a wench named Jender with one child called Sarah and one wench called Rachel and also 2 horse, one bay horse.. Set his hand 1 September 1792. Wit. James Young, Wm. Young. Proved by James Young 17 November 1792 before Wm. Hunter, J.P. Recorded February 27, 1793.

Deed Book D: 347
January 14, 1793. Bill of Sale. I Daniel McKie, Junr. of Newberry County, South Carolina to Wm. McTeer, planter, of Laurens County, state aforesaid, for the sum of £ 65 Sterling; a Negro man named Caroline about 30 years of age. Set his hand Daniel McKie. Wit. David Spiers, Nathaniel Vance. Proved by David Speers 15 February 1793. William Hunter, J.P. Recorded March 1, 1793.

Deed Book D: 356-357
July 23, 1792. Bill of Sale. I Daniel Williams, Sr. of Laurens County, South Carolina to John Williams, son of Daniel and John Williams Junr., both, of the State of South Carolina and District on 96 in consideration of £1500 Virginia Currency; 27 Negroes slaves Viz. Phill, a man of about 40 years old, Jack a man of about 35 years old, Will a man of about 35 years old, Kezer a man of about 22 years old, Chooses a boy of about 18 years old, Harry a boy of about 18 years old, Jacob a boy of about 18 years old, Judah a woman about 20, Isabell, a woman of about 22 years old, Ruth a girl of about 14 years old, Easter, a girl of about 14 years old, Rose a woman of

about 35 year old, Agga a woman about 35 years old, Aaron a boy of about 9 years old, John a boy about 6 years old, Dave a boy about 6 years old, Frankey a woman about 45 years old, Sukey a girl about 12 years old, Sarah a girl about 9 years old, Edom a small boy about 3 years old, Little Phill a small boy about 3 years old, Soloman a small male child about 9 months old, George a small male child about 1 year old, James a small boy of about 4 years old, Litt a girl of about 11 years old and Winney a small girl about 2 years old and Chovis a male child about 10 months old..Set his hand 23 July 1792 Daniel Williams. Wit. Howell Moss (X), Daniel Williams Junr. Jurat. Proved in the November Court 1792 by oath of Daniel Williams, Mr. A. Henderson C.C. Granville, County, North Carolina. Recorded April 12, 1793.

Deed Book D: 362-363
February 20, 1793. Bond. James McNees of Laurens County, South Carolina of the one part and Thomas Wadsworth and William Turpin otherwise called Wadsworth & Turpin, merchants of South Carolina, whereas I the same James McNees by bond of obligation bearing date 20 February 1793 in the sum of £ 100 Sterling have bargained and sold in open market deliver into the said Wadsworth and Turpin a certain negro fellow named George about 20 years of age..James McNees, Wit. Lewis Saxon, Joseph Mahon. Proved by Lewis Saxon 22 February 1793 before Joseph Downs, J.P. Recorded April 12, 1793.

Deed Book D: 393
March 24, 1793. Bond. Indenture between Patrick O'Bryant of one part and John Adair and Alexander Fairbarn, of Laurens County, South Carolina. That the said Patrick Bryant in consideration of the sum of £124 Sterling owe to and stand justly indebted to the said John Adair and Alexander Fairbarn in two different debts 1) security bond of £ 74 Sterling payable in 3 years being my security for the heirs of John Jones, deceased, as being administrator of the estate of John Jones, deceased. 2) bond of £ 50 Sterling due to Alexander Fairbarn on a bond payable in 2 years from date. . I have granted, bargained and sold unto the said John Adair and Alexander Farebarn one negro wench named Pole being 40 years old, likewise one negro boy 5 years old named Tom, one brown mare 12 years old about 14 hands high branded T.H. One brown horse about 13 hands high, 14 years old branded S. R... cattle, farm equipment, etc..Patrick (OO), OBryant. Wit. Charles Neighbours, Judith Saxon. Proved by Charles Saxon 26 March 1793 before Charles Saxon, J.P. Recorded April 18, 1793.

DEED BOOK E: 1793 - 1795

Deed book E: 57
February 21, 1793. Bill of Sale. I Memucan Walker, of Orangeburgh
District and State of South Carolina for the sum of £ 50 Sterling paid by
Patrick Cunningham of Laurens County in 96 District and State aforesaid do
sell and deliver unto the said Patrick Cunningham one Negroes boy about
16 years old named Absolum..Set my seal dated at Carleston {sic} on 21
February 1793 Memucan Walker. Wit. John Cunningham, Samuel Brown.
Proved by Mr. Samuel Brown in Charleston District 22 February 1793
before Stephen Ravenel J.P. Recorded October 14, 1793.

Deed Book E: 59
May 13, 1793. Bill of Sale. I Maluchiah Powell,, of the State of South
Carolina hath sold a Negro man called Jim about 22 years of age unto David
Madden of the same state for £12 Sterling £10 paid in hand the balance to
be paid in Charleston for which I bind myself my heirs.. dated 13 May 1793
Malichiah Powell. Wit. John Baugh, Junr., Mabra Madden. Proved in
Laurens County by John Baugh, Junr. before Joseph Downs, J.P. 17 July
1793. John Baugh, Junr.

Deed Book E: 62
April 18, 1793. To all to whom these presents shall come between Ann
Craddock of the one part and Thomas Wadsworth and William Turpin,
otherwise called Wadsworth & Turpin, Merchants of the state aforesaid.
Whereas the said Ann Craddock by her bond or obligation bearing date 18
April 1793 in the penal sum of £ 49, 19 shillings Sterling with a
consideration the under written for the payment of the same of £24. 14
shillings 6 Pense with lawful interest to be paid annually unto said
Wadsworth & Turpin 1 January 1793... Have granted and sold in plain open
deliver unto the Wadsworth & Turpin two fellows, Viz., one called Reubin
about 19 years old, the other called David about 17 years old yellow
complexion. . . Signed 18 April 1793 Ann Carddock. Wit. Aberam
Lawrence, James Young. Sworn by James Young 1 October 4, 1793 before
John Hunter, signed James Young. Recorded November 2, 1793.

Deed Book E: 65
April 14, 1792. I Shadrach Martin, planter to Thomas Wadsworth and
William Turpin, merchants, for the sum of £80 Sterling, do convey unto
said Wadsworth & Turpin one Negro fellow called Isaac about 50 years old,
one by mare three white feet star in her forehead branded thus S.S. . Signed
14 April 1792 Shadrack Martin. Wit. William Young, James Young. Proved

12

by James Young 10 Nov. 1793 before Lewis Saxon, J.P. Signed James Young. Recorded November 10, 1793.

Deed Book D: 101
April 8, 1793. Mortgage. Whereas Saxon and Willson and Co. stand indebted to Robert Ross of Laurens County, South Carolina in the sum of £ 145 Sterling 5 shillings to be paid on or before the 1st day of March 1795 with interested . . mortgage unto the said Robert Ross one negro man named Peter, one negro man named Bob, one negro woman named Aggy and her child a girl names Milly. S. Saxon, Wit. Joshua Downs, Nathaniel McCoy. Proved by Joshua Downs on 26 August 1793 before Wm. Hunter, J.P. Recorded February 22, 1794.

Deed Book E: 122
October 5, 1793. Bill of Sale. I John Penington in consideration of the sum of £40 Sterling sell to James McClintock a Negro boy named Jack..... John Penington. Wit. John McClintock, Junr., Jacob Penington. Proved by John McClintock 17 Feb. 1794 before Angus Campbell, J.P. Recorded February 17, 1794.

Deed Book E: 163
January 1, 1794. Bond. Between Thomas Elliott, Senr , of one part and Lewis Saxon, of the other part for debt of £ 60 Sterling, bond , and have sold at open market deliver unto the said Lewis Saxon one negro woman named Pegg between 30 and 40 years old....Thomas Elliott (seal). Wit. John Abercrombie, Lydall Allen. Proved by Lydall Allen 22 January 1794 before Charles Saxon, J.P. Recorded February 24, 1794.

Deed Book E: 245
May 20, 1794. Bond. I Wm. McTeer of Laurens County, South Carolina hath by his bond, obligation bearing date 4 January 1794 for the sum of £ 70 . 5 shillings; and for the better securing the payment of said bonds, binds himself his Exec. In the penal sum of £ 145, 10 shillings Sterling to pay John Simpson of the same place.. A Negroes man named Caroline about (blank) years old...29 May 1794 William McTeer. Wit. Andw. Smith, Junr., John Willson, Nathaniel Vance. Proved by John Willson 1 July 1794 before {J}.R. Brown, JNC. Signed John Willson. Recorded July 4, 1794.

Deed Book E: 299
October 22, 1794. Deed of Gift: I Robert Sims, of the State of South Carolina, 96 District in the County of Laurens in consideration of the Love and Good-will and affection I have and do bear towards my loving friend Drury Boyce in the same District and County, planter. I have given and

granted unto the said Drury Boyce all my singular goods and chattels, one
Negroes wench named Atha and 4 head of cattle and 2 feather beds and
furniture and a silver watch...22 October 1794 Robt. Sims. Wit. Fleman (X)
Hatcher, Nancy Hatcher (X) . Sworn by Fleman Hatcher 24 October 1794
before Jonathan Downs, J.P. Recorded November 6, 1794.

Deed Book E: 308
July 4, 1794. Bill of Sale. I David Smith and Ann my wife for the
consideration of £30 Sterling in hand paid by Hanna Musgrove. Have
bargained, sold and delivered to said Hannan Musgrove during the term of
my said Ann's natural life the following Negroes, Viz., Tom, a fellow,
Philles a wench, Lott a girl, Joe and Tom two boys. ... Set unto 4 July 1794.
David Smith, Ann Smith. Wit. Edward Hooker, Anty Foster, Junr. Proved
by Edward Hooker 13 December 1794 before Roger Brown one of the
Justices of said County. Recorded December 14, 1794.

Deed Book E: 309
July 4, 1794. Bill of Sale. I David Smith and Ann my wife for the
consideration of £10 Sterling paid by Landen Waters. Have bargained, sold
and delivered unto said Landen Waters a Negroes girl named Keze with her
future increase during the term of my said wife Ann's natural life. 4 July
1794. David Smith, Ann Smith Wit. Wedend Hooker, Anthony Foster, Junr.
Proved by Edward Hooker 13 December 1794 before Roger Brown ,
Justice. Recorded December 14, 1794.

Deed Book E: 370
February 12, 1795. Bill of Sale. I Patrick O'Bryant, planter, of Laurens
County, South Carolina in consideration of the sum of £60 Sterling paid by
Joseph Adair of the County and State aforesaid sell one Negroes Wench
named Poll ages about 40 years old, one Negroes boy named Jacob, One
grey horse, one black mare, and one bay cold mare, three cows, one black,
one spotted, one red and 3 calves..... 12 February 1795. Signed Patrick (O)
OBryant. Wit. John Adair, James Adair. Proved by John Adair 14 Feb. 1795
before Roger Brown, Justice of said County. Recorded February 18, 1795.

DEED BOOK F: 1795 - 1800

Deed book F: 12
1794. Bill of Sale. Between James Sullivant of the one part and Thomas
Wadsworth & William Turpin of the State aforesaid, Merchants, Whereas
the said James Sullivant by his bond or obligation dated {blank} in the year

1794 in the sum of £1960, 8 shillings 10 pence unto the said Wadsworth & Turpin, on 10 November 1799. Hath sold unto said Wadsworth & Turpin 12 negro slaves named as follows, Viz., Jane, Ned, Lewis, Lid, Peter, Andrew, Lucy, Bartley, Tom, Primus and Isaac, all County born......9 April 1794. James (mark) Sullivan. Wit. Eze. Fr. Roland, James Young. Proved by James Young 5 August 1795 before John Hunter. Recorded October 9, 1795.

Deed Book F: 23 check
May 30, 1795. Bill of Sale. I Danl. Williams Sr. of the State and District aforesaid in consideration of the sum of £ 434 Sterling paid by Elizabeth Williams and Ursla Williams have sold and deliver unto the said Elizabeth Williams and Ursla Williams 15 negro slaves, namely Jack a man about 52 year of age, Jacob a man about 21 years old, Rose a woman about 42 years old, Latt a woman about 14 years of age, Saxon a boy about 11 years of age, John a boy about year of age, James a boy about 6 years old, Winney a girl about 5 years of age, Virgin a female child about 3 months old, Easter a woman about 17 years of age, Ben a boy about 1 year old, Sukky a woman about 15 years old, Aggy a woman about 45 years old, Phill a boy about 6 years old, Isham a boy about 1 year old... Signed Danl. Williams, Sr. Wit. Wm. Neely, William Golding. Before J. R. Brown, J.L.C. Proved by Wm. Neely 2 June 1795 before Thomas Wadsworth. Recorded July 21, 1795.

Deed Book F: 24
May 30, 1795. Bill of Sale. I Daniel Williams Sr. of the District of 96, State of South Carolina to Daniel Williams, Junr. In consideration of the sum of £280 Sterling; six Negro slaves; namely, Peter a man about 55 years of age, Isabella a woman about 21 years old, Edom a boy about 8 years of age, Solomon a boy about 3 years of age and Collin a man child about 2 months of age, and William about 40 years of age - also one bay gelding, one brown bay man, two roan geldings, one book case... dated 30 May 1795. Danl. Williams, Sr. Wit. William Neely, William Golding. Note: Interlined before assigned in these words (and William about 40 years of age). Proved by William Neely before Thomas Wadsworth 2 June 1795. Recorded July 21, 1795.

Deed Book F: 24
May 30, 1795. Bill of Sale. I Daniel Williams, Sr. of the District of 96, State of South Carolina to Elizabeth Williams and Ursla Williams, in considera-tion of the sum £ 434 Sterling, 15 negro slaves, named Jack a man of about 52 years of age, Jacob a man about 21 years old, Ron a woman about 42? years old, Latt a woman about 14 years old, Aaron a boy about 7 years old, John a boy of about __ years old, James a boy about 6 years old, Winney a

15

girl about 5 years of age, Virgin a female child about 3 months old, Easter a woman about 17 years of age, Ben a boy about 1 year old, Sukky a woman of 15 years of age, Aggy a woman about 45 years old, Phill a boy about 6 years old, Joham a boy about 1 years old, which said negroes with all their offspring to the said Elizabeth Williams and Ursla Williams.. Danl. Williams, Sr. Wit. William Neely, William Golding. Proved by William Neely 3 June 1795 before Thomas Wadsworth JLC. Recorded July 21, 1795.

Deed Book F: 24
Daniel Williams, Senr, of 96 District, South Carolina, to Danl. Williams, Junr, in consideration of the sum of £289, 10 shillings Sterling, have sold unto said Daniel Williams, Junr. Six negro slaves, namely, Peter a man about 55 years of age, Isabella a woman about 21 years old, Edom a boy about 8 years old, Solomon a boy about 3 years old, and Collin a man child about 3 months of age and William about 40 years of also, also one bay gelding, one brown bay mare, two roan gelding, one bookcase.. Daniel Williams, Sr. Interlined before assigned in these works (and William about 40 years of age). Wil. William Neely, William Golding. Proved by William Neely, 2 June 1795 before Thomas Wadsworth, JLC.

Deed Book F: 28
January 9, 1795. Bond. William Arnold, Junr., planter, of Laurens County, South Carolina, to Wadsworth and Turpin, merchants for £ 80 Sterling; bond on one negro woman called Hannah and her child called Tom, 2 years old, one black man 3 years old next spring, one sorrel cold, 3 cows, cattle, livestock, crops, farm equipment, etc.... William (mark) Arnold, Junr. Wit. Wit. James Young. James Boyce. Proved by James Young 5 August 1795 before John Hunter, J.P. Recorded September 22, 1795.

Deed Book F: 49
August 31, 1795. Bill of Sale. I George Berry, of Laurens County, South Carolina to James McClintock in consideration of £ 5 Sterling; a Negro fellow named Man - Set my hand 1 August 1795 - George Berry. Wit. John McClintock, Junr., Starling Tucker. Proved by John McClintock before John Hunter 12 October 1795. Recorded October 12, 1795.

Deed Book F: 53
March 28, 1795. Bill of Sale. Indenture made 28 March 1795 between Danl. Williams Sr., planter, of 96 Dist, Laurens County, South Carolina, to Saml. Henderson and James Waldrop of said County. Whereas the said Danl. Williams is and justly indebted unto the sd. Saml. Henderson and James Waldrop in the sun of £400 Sterling has sold one Negro fellow names Harry

and one named Moses and one Negro wench names Jude and her children, George and Levi and one Negro girl names Sarah... Signed Daniel Williams Sr. Wit. William Caldwell, Jno. Simpson. Proved by John Simpson 18 July 1795 before William Hunter, J.P. Recorded July 23, 1795.

Deed Book F: 92
February 29, 1796. Mortgage. William Harris to Thomas Murphy in consideration of the sum of £30 Sterling have made over by way of Mortgage a certain negro girl named Reana.. ... William Harris. Wit. S. Saxon, Henry Langston. Proved by Henry Langston 11 April 1796 before John Cochran, DC. Recorded April 11, 1796.

Deed Book F: 99
May 9, 1796. Bill of Sale. Solomon Langston, of Laurens County, South Carolina to Henry Langston, of the same place, in consideration of the sum of £100, have sold unto said Henry Langston a certain negro boy named Adam, age 16 years next April... Solomon Langston. Wit. Bennet Langston, Solomon Langston. Proved by Bennet Langston 10 April 1796 before Roger Brown., J.P. Recorded April 12, 1796.

Deed Book F: 99
September 1, 1795. Bond. Indenture between Ezekiel S. Roland, of Laurens County, South Carolina on one part and John F. Wolff, Merchant, of the same place. Ezekiel S. Roland by bond or obligation dated 1 September 1794, in the amount of £40 Sterling have sold unto said John F. Wolff a negro girl names Lucy, 6 head of cattle, 13 head of hogs, 2 new feather beds, and furniture...Ezek. Roland. Wit. Edward Morgan, Isom Histelow. Proved by Edward Morgan 16 February 1796 before Joseph Downs, J.P. Recorded February 29, 1796.

Deed Book F: 108
February 22, 1795. Bill of Sale. Lewis Duvall and Thomas Nobles, both of Laurens County, South Carolina to Daniel Wright, Esq. In consideration of the sum of £14 Sterling, have sold one negro boy named Abraham about 3 years old... Lewis Duvall, Thomas (T) Nobles. Wit. John Brockman, Joseph Lyon, Francis Ross. N.B. If I Daniel Wright should conceive at any time, that the above negro could be obtained from one according to Law, that is should be at my pleasure to give the said negro without entering into a course of Law and the above bound Lewis Duvall and Thomas Nobles shall pay in all the damages that I Danl. Wright may sustain by said negro.. Proved by John Brockman before Hudson Berry, J.P. Recorded May 9,1796.

Deed Book F: 116
July 11, 1796. Bill of Sale. Indenture between William Hunter, Esq. Of the County of Laurens, and Joseph Galligly and Thomas Roberts, both of said County. In consideration of the sum of £ 86 Sterling delivery by Moses McCreay and Samuel Dillard, Admrs. To the Estate of Matthew McCreary dec'd in the purchase of a Negro fellow, sold to the said Wm. Hunter and for which the purchase of said Negro the said Joseph Galligly and Thos. Roberts stands security for the sd. Wm. Hunter. .... one Negro fellow named Sam and one Negro woman named Aney.... Signed William Hunter. Wit. Jno. Cargill, Peter Kelly, George David (x). Proved by John Cargill 13 July 1796 before John Hunter. Recorded July 15, 1796.

Deed Book F: 124
April 12, 1796. Bill of Sale. I John Rodgers, of the County of Laurens, South Carolina to Saml. Cuningham, for the sum of £ 30 Sterling; one Negro girl named Happ. Set my hand 12 April 1796 John Rodgers. Wit. McNess? Rodgers, John Waldrop. Proved by McNess Rodgers 19 July 1796 before Joseph Downs, J.P. Recorded July 19, 1796.

Deed Book F: 133
December 29, 1795. Mortgage.. John B. Bennet, of Newberry District, South Carolina to Lord Dulen, of Laurens County, South Carolina in consideration of the sum of £51 Sterling; have bound myself and delivery unto the said Dulen one negro boy ... Jno. B. Bennet. Wit. John Bourland. Proved by John Bolland (sic) 18 August 1796 before George Whitmore, J.P. Recorded August 18, 1796.

Deed Book F: 139
October 3, 1796. Bill of Sale. I Pleasant Sullivant, of the State of South Carolina and Greenville County unto Stephen Mullings of the same State and Laurens County sell one Negroes Boy named Hall about 7 or 8 years old for the sum of 160 Silver Dollars. Set my hand 4 April 1796. Pleasant Sullivant. Wit. Owen Sullivant, Hewlet Sullivant. Proved by Hewlet Sullavant on 3 Oct. 1796 before Thomas Camp, J.P. Recorded October 20, 1796.

Deed Book F: 154
May 27, 1796. Bill of Sale. I Elijah Tucker of the State of Virginia and Halifax County sell to Sarah Wright, of the State of South Carolina and County of Laurens one Negro man named Sam about 25 years old about 6 feet high a blacksmith for the sum of £70 Sterling. Set his hand 16 May 1796. Elijah (X) Tucker. Wit. William Abannon, James Clements, Stel. Wood. Proved by James Clements on 4 August 1796 before and George

18

Anderson. Note: I assign the within Bill of Sale to Andrew Rodgers for value Recd. 4 Aug. 1796 Sarah Wright. Recorded December 3, 1796.

Deed Book F: 155
5 December 1796. Bill of Sale. I John Simmons, of the State of South Carolina, County of Laurens to John Hunter of the state and County aforesaid, for the sum of £84, 10 shillings Sterling; 2 Negroes; one girl about 9 years old named Jane, one boy names Will, about 6 years old. John Simmons. Wit. Reuben Pyles, Chas. Smith. Proved by Charles Smith 5 December 1796 before Reuben Pyles, J.P. Recorded December 5, 1796.

Deed Book F: 184
December 15, 1796. Bill of Sale. Joseph Adair and Thomas Hughey, both of Laurens County, South Carolina, planters, to Bryant Leek, of the same place in consideration of the sum of $152, sell one negro boy named Jacob to said Bryant Leek. Joseph Adair, Thomas Hughey. Wit. Robert Adair. William Saxon. Proved by William Saxon 4 January 1797 before Roger Brown, J.P. Recorded February 21, 1797.

Deed Book F: 184
August 27, 1796. Deed of Gift. James Jones, of Laurens County, South Carolina, planter, in consideration of the love good will and affection which I have and do bare towards my sone Jesse Jones, give unto said Jesse Jones, a negro man called George about 22 years of age and also a negro girl called Clark about 9 years old, a negro boy called Toney about 2 years old.. James (x) Jones. Wit. Joseph Jones, Martha (x) Whitmore. Proved by Joseph Jones 27 August 1796 before Joseph Whitmore, J.P. Recorded February 21, 1797.

Deed Book F: 192
November 26, 1796. Bill of Sale. Robert Pasley of Laurens County, South Carolina, to James McCaa for the sum of £35 Sterling; to give and sell unto James McCaa one out landish negro woman about 30 years old named Charlotte with her female child about 17 years old named Jeane. Robert Pasley. Wit. Charles Allen, Joseph Cox. Proved by Charles Allen the 13 April 1797 before Charles Smith , J.P. Recorded April 13, 1797.

Deed Book F: 201
April 30, 1796. Bill of Sale. I Jorden Jones, of the County of Meckenburg, State of North Carolina to John McClinto, of the State of South Carolina and County of Laurens for the sum of $260; a likely sensible well grown County born Negro boy named (blank). Set my hand and seal in the affirmation of Wyche Goodwin, Esqr. Of George? for the consideration. 30

April 1796. Jorden (D) Jones, Wyche Goodwin. Wit. George Berry. Proved by George Berry 3 August 1796 before James Saxon, J.P. Recorded May 8, 1797.

Deed Book F: 217
June 14, 1797. Bond. I Silvanus Walker of the County of Laurens , by my bond or obligation baring date 14 June 1797 to John Cuningham of the City of Charleston stand bound in the sum of $5000... Three Negroes names Toby, Harry and Jane with the issue of the female and also all my stock... Dated 14 June 1797 Silv. Walker. Wit. John Cuningham, George Watts. Proved by John Cuningham 18 July 1797 before Zach. Bailey, J.P. Recorded July 18, 1797.

Deed Book F: 283
November 15, 1797. Deed of Gift: I John O'Neal, of the State of South Carolina, Laurens County, for Love and Affection which I have and do bare towards my loving daughter Margret Scott, of the aforesaid County, wife of Thomas Scott, have given and grant and freely give said Margret Scott a Negro Girl named Lucy. Set my hand 15 November 1797. John O (mark) Neale. Wit. James Golding, Charles Murphey. Proved by Charles Murphey on 7 January 1798 before Angus Campbell, J.P.

Deed Book F: 318
January 17, 1798. Bill of Sale. Horatio Walker, of Laurens County, South Carolina do sell unto Thomas and William Burnside for the sum of £ 100 Sterling; a negro man named Ned. Hor. Walker. Wit. A. Rodgers, Junr. Wm. A. Rodgers. Proved by Wm. A. Rodgers 14 May 1798 before John Davis, J.P.

Deed Book F: 323
January 13, 1798. Bill of Sale. Wm. Spurgin, in consideration of the sum of $367 sell unto said James McClintock, one negro wench named Bet to have and to hold the said negro wench with future issue. William Spurgin. Wit. Starling Tucker, Samuel Fleming. Proved by Samuel Fleming 16 May 1798 before James Saxon, J.P.

Deed Book F: 347
July 12, 1790. Deed of Gift: I Martha Lazenby, widow of Laurens County and 96 District, State of South Carolina give to my daughter, Sarah Duckett, wife of Jacob Duckett of the aforesaid place a certain Negro girl about 4 years old called Jane Set my hand 12 July 1790 Martha Lazenby. Wit. Joseph Jeanes, John Prather Odell, Elizabeth Davis. Proved by John Prather Odell 5 May 1791 before James Montgomery, J.P. Recorded____.

Deed Book F: 362
April 12, 1798. Bill of Sale. Andrew Rodgers of Laurens County, South
Carolina have sold unto John Francis Wolff for $400; one negro boy named
Paul. A. Rodgers. L.S. Wit. Reuben Pyles, Mansil Crisp. Proved by Reuben
Pyles 12 April 1798 before Joseph Downs, J.P.

Deed Book F: 363
March 30, 1796. Received of John F. Wolff from John Thompson, $400
which is full payment for a negro delivered named Jacob about 26 years old.
John Thompson. Wit. Elihu Creswell, Frances Ross. Proved by Frances
Ross 19 July 1798 before Joseph Downs, J.P.

Deed Book F: 379
August 9, 1798. Bill of Sale. Received of Mr. David Caldwell $265, from
James Irwin for one negro girl named Beth (or Beck). Jos. Irwin, Wit.
Robert Creswell. Proved by Robert Creswell 15 October 1798 before Joseph
Downs, J.P.

Deed Book F: 380
November 24, 1798. Deed of Gift. Thomas Cox, of Laurens County, South
Carolina. Know ye that I the said Thomas Cox, for divers good causes and
valuable consideration to me here unto moving have given and granted unto
my well beloved son Thornton Cox of the same place one negro woman
named Rachel, one negro boy named Joe about 7 years of age, one negro
girl named Silvy about 2, one negro woman named Milley, and her child,
one negro man named Pancly about 27, one negro girl named Tanny about
12 years old. Also one negro boy named Charles about 14 years old. Also
all my household furniture and stock and all other my substance whatsoever
in whom handy custody possession or keeping the same or can or may be
found. To have and to old all said property whatsoever _ said Thomas Cox
unto the said Thornton Cox. Thomas Cox. Wit. John Martin, Ezel. Roland.
Proved by Ezel. Roland 24 October 1798 before Charles Smith, J.P.

Deed Book F: 385
August 17, 1798. Deed of Gift. James Jones, of Laurens County, South
Carolina in consideration of the Love, Good will and affection which I have
and do bear towards my sone Miles Jones, of the same place, give one a
negro boy called Tom, about 1 years old. James Jones. Wit. Jesse Jones,
Joseph Jones. Proved by Jesse Jones 16 August 1798 before George
Whitmore, J.P.

21

Deed Book F: 385
August 17, 1798. Deed of Gift. James Jones, of Laurens County, South
Carolina in consideration of the Love, Good will and affection which I have
and do bear towards my sone Benjamin Jones, of the same place, give one a
negro boy called Squire about 3 years old. James Jones. Wit. Jesse Jones,
Joseph Jones. Proved by Jesse Jones 16 August 1798 before George
Whitmore, J.P.

Deed Book F: 401
October 10, 1797. Bill of Sale. We William Spurgin and John Spurgin,, of
the State of South Carolina, County of Laurens, in consideration of the sum
of 135 Silver Dollars paid by James McClintock, planter, of the aforesaid
place, one Negro girl named Silvy about 12 years old. Set his hand 10
October 1797 William Spurgin, John Spurgin. Wit. Starling Tucker, John
McClintock. Proved by John McClintock 12 January 1799 before Starling
Tucker, J.P.

Deed Book F: 402
11 February 1799. John Davenport, of Laurens County, South Carolina sell
to Ezekiel Stephen Roland a certain negro boy named Joe which is in his
possession, for £25 Sterling. John Davenport. Wit. George Madden, Charles
Smith. Proved by George Madden 11 February 1799 before Charles Saxon,
J.P.

Deed Book F: 407
January 1, 1799. Bill of Sale. I Samuel Powell of the County of Laurens,
South Carolina sell to Daniel Osborn, Sr. in consideration of $300; one
Negro girl named Silvey. Set my hand 15 January 1799. Samuel (X) Powell.
Wit. Silv. Walker, Junr., Wm. Glenn, Sarah Walker. Proved by Silv.
Walker, Junr. 18 Feb. 1799 before Chas. Smith, J.P.

Deed Book F: 409
October 18, 1798. Bill of Sale. We Silvanus and Horatio Walker of Laurens
County sell to Samuel Powell of the County and state aforesaid; for the sum
of $128.57; one Negro man named Ceaser, 25 years old...Set his hand 15
October 1798. Silvs. Walker, Hor. Walker. Wit. Memn. Walker, John
Davis. Proved by George Watts 18 February 1799 before Zechr. Bailey, J.P.

Deed Book F: 413
December 31, 1792. Bill of Sale. We Langston Drew, Joshua Robert and
wife Sarah to John Simpson, of the aforesaid County of Laurens in
consideration of the sum of 60 £ Sterling; the following Negroes. Beck and
her son Solomon together with their future increase. Set our hands 31

December 1792 Langston Drew, Joshua Roberts. Wit. Andrew Smyth, David Speers. Proved by David Speers 18 May 1795 before Wm. Hunter, J.P._____.

Deed Book F: 431
September 1, 1798. Bill of Sale. Thomas Gary, of Laurens County, South Carolina in consideration of the sum of $00?? have sold to James Adair for, of the same place, two negroes, one woman named Cynthia and the other a negro girl named Jemina. Thomas Gary, L.S. Wit. J.P. Williams, David Mason. Proved by David Mason 19 February 1799 before Roger Brown, J.P.

Deed Book F: 431
February 21, 1799. William Bryson, of Laurens County, South Carolina, in consideration of the sum of $350, sell unto William Mitchell, of the same place a certain negro woman named Beck about 35 years of age. William Bryson. Wit. Thomas Dendy, Robert Bryson. Proved by Thomas Dendy 23 February 1799 before Jonathan Downs, J.P.

Deed Book F: 433
August 17, 1798. Deed of Gift: I James Jones of Laurens County, South Carolina in consideration of the love, goodwill and affection which I have and do bear towards my son Dred Jones of the aforesaid place, give a certain Negro boy called Toney about 5 years old. Set my hand 16 August 1798 James Jones. Wit. Jessee Jones, Joseph Jones. Proved by Jessee Jones 17 August 1798 before George Whitmore, J.P.

Deed Book F: 433
August 17, 1798. Deed of Gift: I James Jones of Laurens County, South Carolina in consideration of the love, goodwill and affection which I have and do bear toward my son Joseph Jones of Newberry County and State aforesaid. To give freely a certain Negro girl called Bett about 7 years old. James Jones. Wit. Jesse Jones, Joseph Jones. Proved by Jesse Jones 17 August 1798 before George Whitmore, J.P.

Deed Book F: 442
December 3, 1798. Bill of Sale. Sarah Clary and Cornelius Cargill now of Washington District, Greenville County, South Carolina, on the 7th of January 1790 did sell unto Patrick Cunningham of the District of 96 and of Laurens County a negro wench named Hannah and her child named Lewis for £70 Sterling and received the full amount, now in consideration of $50 present by John and William Cuningham Executors of said Patrick Cuningham, deceased the receipt we have acknowledge and sold unto John

and William Cuningham, Executors, the said negro wench's other four children having been born since she became the property of Patrick Cuningham consisting of 2 boys and 2 girls named Jeofry and Sam, Margarit and Ritter. Cornelius Cargill, Sarah (C) Clary. . Wit. Ann Cunningham, Elijah Burgess. Lewis Graves, J.P. Proved by Elijah Burgess 2 May 1799.

Deed Book F: 475
September 16, 1799. Silvanus Walker, of Laurens County, South Carolina to Samuel Fleman, of the same place, for $350; one negro named Gideon. Silvs. Walker. Wit. Robert Hunter, John Hunter. Proved by Robert Hunter 15 October 1799 before Joseph Downs, J.P._____.

Deed Book F: 477
November 22, 1799. Bill of Sale. E. L. Roland, of Laurens County, South Carolina sell unto J. F. Wolff, of the same place a certain negro girl 12 or 13 years old named Caicy, it being a girl which James Sullivan Senr raised.. (no amount stated). Ezeklr. Roland. Wit. Thos. Lewers, A. Morrison. Proved by Thos. Lewers on 22 November 1799 before Chas. Smith, J.P.

Deed Book F: 478
August 5, 1799. Bill of Sale. I Joseph Gallegly of Laurens County, South Carolina, planter, to John Simpson, in consideration of £ 200 SC money, sell one Negro fellow named Sampson, one Negro woman named Darkes, one Negro boy named Mose, one Negro boy named David and two horses 15 head of cattle, 5 feather beds and furniture, one wagon... Dated at Belfast on 22 July 1799 Jo. Gallegly. Wit. John Gallegey..Proved by Cohn Gallegly 3 October 1799 before Chas. Griffin, J.P.

Deed Book F: 488
November 22, 1799. Bill of Sale. I Jesse Allen of Laurens County, South Carolina to Lydall Allen, of the state and County aforesaid; in consideration of $270; a certain Negro boy slave named Gorton. Set his hand 22 November 1799. Jesse Allen. Wit. J.F. Wolff, Saml. Cooper. Proved by J.F. Wolff 22 November 1799 before Joseph Downs, J.P._____.

Deed Book F: 488
August 21, 1798. Bill of Sale. I Joseph Martin of Laurens County, South Carolina to Cornelius Donohoe, in consideration os $320; a Negro woman slave named Ryna. Set my hand 21 August 1798 Joseph Martin. Wit. Henry Williamson, Hugh Abernathy. Proved by Hugh Abernathy 28 September 1799 before Zechr. Bailey, J.P.

DEED BOOK G: 1798 - 1803

Deed Book G: 11
February 5, 1799. Emancipation. William Selby, of Accomack County,
Virginia do hereby forever manumit and set free from me and my heirs,
executors and administrators Negro man, Robin. William Selby. June 4,
1799 there was delivered unto me the subscriber the foregoing deed of
manumission in order to be enrolled among the records of Worcester
County which said Deed of Manussission is according recorded among the
same records in Liber T folic 134 & 135. State of Maryland Worcester
County. John C. Handy, M.

Deed Book G: 36
May 10, 1799. Bill of Sale. I Silvanus Walker Junr. of Laurens County,
South Carolina to Elizabeth Swift, of Newbury, and state aforesaid, in
consideration of $384; two Negroes, Viz., one Negro woman named Mary
and one Negro girl named Sully between 4 and 5 years old and the woman
about 20. Silvanus Walker. Wet. Horatio Walker, Salley N. Walker. Proved
by Horatio Walker 22 May 1800 before R. Creswell, CC.

Deed Book G: 94
April 22, 1800. Mortgage: Bartlett Brooks of Laurens District, South
Carolina to Timothy Goodman of the same place, in consideration of $475;
2 certain Negroes namely a Negro wench called Mary aged about 31 years,
a Negro boy called Sam aged about 6 years which were under a mortgage to
Wadsworth & Turpin and now to be released from said mortgage, which
said Negroes with their future increase to the said Timothy Goodman. Set
my hand 22 April 1800 Bartlett (x) Brooks. Wit. R. Brown, B. Glenn.
Recorded Oct. 21, 1800.
I James Young acting agent for William Turpin, the surviving copartner of
Wadsworth & Turpin in consideration of Timothy Goodman having this day
given his obligation for $475 payable to Wadsworth and Turpin to release
the within mentioned 2 Negroes (namely Mary a wench about 31 years old
and Sam a boy about 2 years old) from the said mortgage...22 April 1800.
For Wadsworth & Turpin James Young. Wit. R. Brown, B Glenn. Proved
by Blackgrove Glenn 14 May 1800 before Wm. Burnside, J.P.

Deed Book G: 95
April 28, 1800. Bill of Sale. I Bartlett Brooks of Laurens District, South
Carolina to Timothy Goodman of the same place, in consideration of $375;
two certain negroes namely a boy called Lymas about 4 years old and a girl
called Rachel about 5 years old, which said Negroes with all their increase
to the said Timothy his heirs and assigns. Set my hand 28 April 1800.

25

Bartlett (X) Brooks. Wit. Drury Satterwhite. Proved by Drury Satterwhite 24 April 1800 before J.R. Brown. Recorded Oct. 21, 1800.

Deed Book G: 115
January 9, 1800. Bill of Sale. John Gray and Thomas Steele, of Laurens County, South Carolina, of one part and William Turpin and Benjamin Cudworth, Executers of Thomas Wadsworth Esquire, decd. of the other part. Whereas the said John Gray and Thomas Steele by their articles of agreement with Thomas Wadsworth for the rent of his Tanyard and the stock put in by said Wadsworth , Viz., $600 stock and $230 per year as by their agreement dated August 27, 1798 for the payment of $830 with lawful interest unto the said William Turpin and Benjamin Cudworth executors of the said Thomas Wadsworth Esquire deceased assigns on or before the 1 December next being had to the said agreement...have bargain and sold and by these presents do bargain sell and in plain open market deliver unto the said William Turpin or Benjamin Cudworth Exr. To the above said decd. Two certain Negro fellows, Viz., one called Dave about 22 years old, the other called Jim about the same age, to have and to hold the said two Negroes fellows unto the said William Turpin or Benjamin Cudsworth Exrs....Set his hand 9 January 1800. John Gray, Thomas Steele. Wit. Jas. Bowie, Jas. Young. Proved by James Young 1 Dec. 1800 before R. Creswell. Recorded December 1, 1800.

Deed Book G: 135
January 2, 1801. Bill of Sale. Received James McClintock the sum of $500 being the full price of negro wench named Silvia and her child which property I warrant and defend by these presents. John Spurgin Wit. John Hutchinson, Robert Fleming. Probed by Robert Fleming 2 January 1801 before Robert Hutchison, J.P. Recorded January 20, 1801.

Deed Book G: 148
January 10, 1801. Bill of Sale. Receipt received of James Glenn for $300 on file for a Negro boy named Isham about 13 years of age, January 27, 1801. David Spears. Wit. David Glen. Proved by David Glen 10 January 1801 before Starling Tucker, J.P. Recorded January 27, 1801.

Deed Book G: 159
November 17, 1787. Deed of Gift: I John Falconer of Laurens District, South Carolina , lying in perfect health and of sound mind and memory, do of my own free will and accord give unto Silvanus Walker, Sr of the aforesaid place five Negroes, Viz., Priscilla aged 32 years, George aged 19 years, Judith ages 6 years, Ephraim aged 3 years and Milly aged 6 months old and their increase, likewise all my stock of horses, cattle and hogs

together with all my household furniture unto him the said Silavanus Walker... Set his hand 17 October 1787 John (mark) Falconer. George Anderson, Justice for the County and State aforesaid did acknowledge the within deed of Gift.. 26 January 1787 Geo. Anderson, J.P. Recorded February 25, 1801.

Deed Book G: 186
January 8, 1799. Bill of Sale. I Galanus Winn to William Dendy, in consideration of the sum of $300 sold and delivered to the said William Dendy one Negro girl named Tanney. Galanus Winn. Wit. Wm. (X) Ramsey. Proved by William Ramsey 28 February 1807 before W. Burnside, J.P. Recorded March 1, 1801.

Deed Book G: 228
August 8, 1798. Bill of Sale. I Joseph Erwin to Abner Teague in consideration of the sum of $1000 have sold to the said Abner Teague five Negroes, Viz., Morris and Poll his wife and three children Flora, Joe and Will... Joseph Erwin. Wit. David Speers, John Chandler. Proved by John Chandler __ June 1800 before Wm. Mitchell, J.Q. Recorded June 1, 1801.

Book G: 229
December 27, 1799. Bill of Sale. I Tyree Glen of Greenville County, South Carolina to Abner Teague of Laurens County, South Carolina, in consideration of $500 do sell and deliver unto said Abner Teague one Negro slave named Benjamin....Tryee Glen. Wit. Henry T. Walker, Jas. Cuningham. Proved by Henry T. Walker 1 June 1801 before Chas. Allen, J.Q. Recorded June 1, 1801.

Deed Book G: 253
March 19, 1801. Bill of Sale. I Horatio Walker to Robert Creswell, of Laurens District, South Carolina in consideration of $250; sold and delivered unto Robert Creswell one Negroes wench named Dinah... Set my hand 19 March 1801. Horatio Walker. Wit. James Sills. Proved by James Sills 27 July 1801 before J.A. Elmore JQ. Recorded July 29, 1801.

Deed Book G: 253
March 14, 1801. Bill of Sale. I John McLaughlen of Laurens District, South Carolina to Robert Creswell, of the aforesaid place in consideration of $420 sold and delivered unto Robert Creswell a Negro fellow named Abb, formerly the property of the Estate of William Harris, deceased. Set my hand 14 March 1801 John McLaughlen. Wit. J. Sills, John Garlington. Proved by James Sills 27 July 1801 before J.A. Elmore, JQ. Recorded July 29, 1801.

Deed Book G: 297
April 16, 1801. Bill of Sale. David Madden of Laurens District, South
Carolina to Benjamin Byrd, of the same place, in consideration of $340; sell
unto Benjamin Byrd a Negro boy named Moses now in the possession of
said Byrd.. Set my hand 16 April 1801. David Madden. Wit. Charles Word.
Wit. By Charles Work 3 October 1801 before Robert Hutchinson, J.P.
Recorded October 5, 1801.

Deed Book G: 301
February 19, 1799. Bill of Sale. I James McCaa of Greenville County,
South Carolina to Jeane Kellet in consideration of the sum of £80 Sterling,
sell and deliver unto Jane Kellet one Negro which named Charlott about 35
years of age with her female child named Jane... Set my hand 9 February
1799 James McCaa. Wit. Hezekiah Dyer. Proved by Hezekiah Dyer in
Laurens District, South Carolina 20 October 1801 before James
Abercrombie, J.P. Recorded October 20, 1801.

Deed Book G: 302
October 1, 1801. Bill of Sale. I Larkin Cason and John Mosely of Edgefield
County, South Carolina to William Teague of Laurens County in
consideration of $500 do sell unto said William Teague one Negro woman
named Lucy and her child Austen...Set my hand this 1 October 1801 Larkin
Cason, John Moseley. Wit. Gabriel Jones, Joseph Cason. Proved by Joseph
Cason 19 October 1801before W. Burnside, J.P.   Recorded October 21,
1801.

Deed Book G: 330
July 22, 1799. Bill of Sale. Received of Moses Madden 400 Silver Dollars
for one Negro man named Ned which Negro servant to be well sound and
healthy to the best of my knowledge. Set my hand 22 July 1799 J. Robinett
Wit. David Madden, Jesse Robinett. Proved by David Madden 6 November
1801 before Robert Creswell Recorded November 10, 1801.

Deed Book G: 353
April 3, 1801. Bill of Sale. I Bartlett Brooks of Laurens District, South
Carolina to Charles Gwinn of Edgefield District in consideration of
$132.67; do sell and deliver unto the said Charles Quinn one certain
Negroes woman called Jude about 50 years old. ..Set my hand 3 April 1801.
Bartlett Brooks. Wit. James Young, James Boyce. Proved by James Young
4 April 1801 before William Neel J.Q. January 22, 1802.

Deed Book G: 369
May 21, 1801. Bill of Sale. I John Arnold, planter, of Laurens District, South Carolina to Col. John F. Wolff, merchant of the same place in consideration of $550; sell unto Col. J.F. Wolff one Negroes man named Jack, this country born about 18 years old and 6 feet high. Set my hand 1 May 1801. John Arnold. Wit. John Pringle, Michael Waldrop. Proved by Job Pringle 15 September 1801 before Joseph Downs, J.P. Recorded February 20, 1802.

Deed Book G: 386
January 25, 1794. Deed of Gift: I James Giddens of Laurens County South Carolina, planter, in consideration of the love and goodwill and affection which I have and do bear towards my loving son James Giddins of the same County and District do give and present freely give unto said James Giddens one Negro woman names Silva now being in the possession of William Giddins in the State of George of which before signing of these presents I have delivered him the said Jas. Gidden.... Set my hand this 25 January 1794 James Gidding. Wit. Alexander Taylor, John Power. Proved by John Powers 15 March 1802 before Starling Tucker J.P. Recorded March 16, 1802.

Deed Book G: 399
August 31, 1801. We Richard Griffin, Sr., of the District of Laurens, James Caldwell and Thomas Farrow of the District of Newberry Send Greeting. Whereas it appeared that Daniel Williams, deceased, of Greenville County in North Carolina on or about 15 of {?} 1759 willed to his daughter Maryra Goodman three Negroes namely Major, Jenny and Patt with all their increase. During the natural life of the said Mary and at her death the said Negroes with their increase to be equally divided amongst the lawfully issue of the said Mary and whereas the said Negroes have increased to the number of 16 and where as the said Mary being now willing to give up the said negroes to her children and to raise from them in leu thereof the sum of $125 during her natural life for her support and maintenance and whereas the said children and heirs that is to say Joseph Goodman, Samuel Goodman, Charles Goodman, Timothy Goodman, Claiborne Goodman and Bartlett Brooks for himself and Chesley his wife being all willing and desirously to receive the said Negroes and to pay the said Maria in the yearly sum of $175 during her natural life and whereas the said pantie by their joint bond given to the said Mary dated 27 July 1800 have mutually chosen us the same Richard Griffin Sr., James Caldwell and Thomas Farrow to appraise, divide and Lott of the said Negroes aforesaid among them the aforesaid Joseph Samuel Charles Timothy Cliburn and Bartlett Brooks for himself and Castle his wife...said Richard Griffin Sr., James

Caldwell and Thomas Farrow did meet on the said 27 January 1800 at the house of the said Maryas and have divided the said Negroes in the manner following that is to say Lott number 1 was comprised of a Negro fellow called Frank and a Negroes girl called Suke and appraised to $600. Lott 2 was composed of a Negro boy called Tom and a Negro girl called Cisly and appraised to $600; Lott 3 was composed of three Negroes namely Bob, Matts, and Jane and appraised to $800; Lott 4 comprised of 3 Negroes namely Esther, John and Cressey and appraised to $800; Lot 5 was composed of 3 Negroes Sarah, Nell and Cate and appraised to $850; Lot 6 was composed of 3 Negroes namely Tanny, Joe and Anarky and appraised to $800...Joseph Goodman chosen Lot Number 1, Barttlett Brooks chosen Lott Number 2; Timothy Goodman chosen Lott number 3, Charles Goodman chosen Lot number 4, Clabourne Goodman chosen lott number 5; Samuel Goodman chosen Lott number 6... Lott number 1 consisting of 2 Negro namely Frantes? and Secke to Joseph Goodman; Lot 2 consisting of 2 Negroes namely Tom and Cisly to Barttlett Brooks; Lott number 3 consisting of 3 Negroes namely ?, Matt and Jane and to Timothy Goodman Lot 5 consisting of 3 Negroes namely John and Creasey; Lott 5 consisting of 3 Negroes namely Sarah, Mill and Cate to Clabourne Goodman; Lot Number 6 consisting of 3 Negroes namely Fanny, Joe and Annasky? To Saml. Goodman.. Dated 31 August 1801. Richard Griffin, James Caldwell, Thomas Farrow. Wit. JR Brown, Asa Griffin. Wit. Proved by J.R. Brown 15 March 1802 before Angus Campbell, J.P. Recorded March 27, 1802.

Deed Book G: 414
March 12, 1802. Bill of Sale. Joseph Blackerby Sr. of Laurens District, South Carolina to Giles Cason of the same place, in consideration of $2500 have sold and delivered unto said Giles Cason - three Negroes, Viz., Harry, Wenna and Lucy.. Set my hand Joseph Blackerby, Sr. Wit. Wm. Osborne, Joseph Blackerby, Junr. Proved by Joseph Blackerbey, Junr. 12 March 1802 before Wm. Mitchell, J.P. Recorded April 5, 1802.

Deed Book G: 429
September 28, 1799. Bill of Sale. William Bird, of Laurens County, South Carolina sell unto Samuel Leeke, of the same place, for $171, a negro boy named Dennard 7 years old. William Bird. (Seal). Wit. A. Morrison, John Luke. Proved by John Luke 17 November 1801 before George Gordon, J.P. Recorded April 27, 1802.

Deed Book G: 447
January 5, 1801. Bill of Sale. Joseph Blackerby of Laurens District, South Carolina to Justinian Maddox of the same place, in consideration of $250 have sold and delivered two Negroes, Viz., Jude and Charles and also one

forth part of the stock namely cattle, horses, hogs, and sheeP..Set my hand 5 January 1802. Joseph Blackerbey, Sr. Wit. Wm. Cosborne, Joseph Blackerbey, Junr., Giles Cason. Proved by Joseph Blackerbey, Junr. 12 March 1802 before Wm. Mitchell, J.Q. Recorded June 22, 1802.

Deed Book G: 448
January 5, 1801. Bill of Sale. Joseph Blackerbey Sr. of the District of Laurens, South Carolina to Joseph Blackerbey, Junr. of the aforesaid place in consideration of $2500 have sold and granted unto said Joseph Blackerbey, Junr., Viz., five Negroes namely Peter, George, Moll, Gabe, Dill, Amers and also the tract of land whereon I now live containing 250 acres ... Set my hand 5 January 1802 Joseph Blackerbey, Sr. Wit. Wm. Osborne, Justinian Maddox, Giles Cason. Proved by Justinian Maddox 10 May 1802 before Wm. Mitchell, J.Q. Recorded June 22, 1802.

Deed Book G: 450
January 2, 1802. Bill of Sale. I Daniel Wadkins of Laurens District, South Carolina to Aaron Starnes in consideration of $200 sell unto Aaron Starnes a Negroes girl by the name of Alice, 7 years of age. ..Set my hand 2 January 1802 Daniel Watkins. Wit. William Burnside, Clabourn Goodman. Proved by Clabourn Goodman 20 January 1802 before Wm. Burnside. Recorded June 23, 1802.

Deed Book G: 452
March 25, 1803. Bill of Sale. I John Milam of the District of Laurens, State of South Carolina to Elisha Mitchell of the same place in consideration of $500; sell unto said Elisha Mitchell a certain Negroes wench called Nancy and child called Hes. Set my hand this 25 March 1802 John Milan. Wit. Wm. Glen, Charles Harris. Proved by Charles Harris 1 July 1802 before Wm. Mitchell J.Q. Recorded July 13, 1802.

Deed Book G: 460
July 6, 1801. Ailsey Abbott, of Laurens District, South Carolina to Anderson Arnold, of the same place, for $500 one negro man named Titus about 38 years of age, this country born. Elsey Abbott. Wit. J.F. Wolff, Nancy Wright. Proved by Col. J.F. Wolff 5 August 1801 before Daniel Wright, JQ. Recorded July 29, 1802.

Deed Book G: 472
June 7, 1802. Deed of Gift: I John Satterwhite, Sr. Of Newberry District, South Carolina to John and James Mitchell, sons of my wife Mary, a Negroes Girl named Cate, a chestnut Sorrel mare and both a feather bed and furniture which as to remain in the possession of my wife during her natural

life, except the colt...Set my hand 7 June 1802. Wit. Isaac Mitchell, Jas.
Atwood. Proved by James Atwood 23 August 1802 before Wm. Burnside,
JQ. Recorded September 13, 1802.

Deed Book G: 473
May 31, 1802. Bond. To all to whom these presents shall come Greetings -
Between Elihu Creswell of the one part and George Watts, both of Laurens
District, South Carolina, by his obligation to wit - one bond dated 1 Feb.
1799 and payable on the demand of the real sum of £47, 3 shillings and 2
pence; one other bond bearing date 31 May 1802 payable on demand for the
sum of £ 22, 14 shillings and 3 pence with interest from the first day of
January 1798, one other bond bearing date 31 May 1802 in the sum of £15,
6 shillings and 11 pence with interest. ...have delivered unto the said Elihu
Creswell two Negroes, one Negroes girl named Leah about 5 years old,
one Negro boy named Stephen about 2 years old, also the mother of these
small Negroes a Negro woman named Hannah about 20 years old.. Set my
hand 31 May 1802 Geo. Watts in the before of J. Garlington. Probed by
John Garlington 12 September 1802 before Charles Saxon, J.P.. Recorded
September 13, 1802.

Deed Book G: 500
June 1, 1799. Bill of Sale. We Horatio Walker and Henry Tandy Walker,
planters, of Laurens County South Carolina to Lewis Davis Yancey, planter,
of the same place, in consideration of £ 61, 16 shillings and 8 pence Sterling
sell and deliver unto the said Lewis Davis Yancey a Negro wench named
Grace together with her increase...Set my hand 13 June 1799 Hor. Walker,
Henry T. Walker. Wit. John Powell, Samuel N. Powell, John Smith. Proved
by John Powell 18 October 1802 before Z. Bailey, J.P. Recorded October
18, 1802.

Deed Book G: 502
November 11, 1801. Bill of Sale. I Benjamin Smith of the Laurens District,
South Carolina to Robert Allison, of the same place, a certain Negro man
slave named Cesar about 30 or 35 years of age. Also his wife named Leah
about 30 years of age. Set my hand 16 November 1800 B. Smith. Wit. N.
Franks, N. Day. Probed by N. Franks 21 October 1802 before James
Abercrombie, J.P. Recorded October 20, 1802.

Deed Book G: 505
March ? 180?? Bill of Sale. Charles Deen, of (torn) District, south Carolina
for and in consideration — love, goodwill and affection which I have to my
loving son John Deen of said district, do freely give unto John Deed (torn)

13 years of age, named Lit(torn)ton. Wit. Job? Deen., Elizabeth (mark) Humphrey. Page torn.

Deed Book G: 514
November 18, 1802. Bill of Sale. I Thomas Flewallen of Laurens District, South Carolina to Reuben Flannagan and wife Ann Thomas Flannagan, his wife for the sum of $100; sell one Negro man named Frank. Thomas Flewallen. Wit. David Smith, Joseph Martindale. Proved by Joseph Martindale 24 November 1802 before Geo. Whitmore, J.P. Recorded November 29, 1802.

Deed Book G: 532
November 18, 1802. Bill of Sale. I Thomas Flewelling of Laurens District, South Carolina to Elizabeth Flewelling in consideration of $100; sell unto said Elizabeth Flewelling one Negro man named James. Thomas Flawelling. Wit. James Gibson, William Dillard (x). Proved by William Dillard 12 Dec. 1802 before James Dillard, J.P. Recorded December 14, 1802.

Deed Book G: 532
November 18, 1802. Bill of Sale. I Thomas Flewalling of Laurens District, South Carolina to William Dillard and Susannah, his wife; in consideration of the sum of $100; sell unto said William Dillard and Susanna one Negro woman named Vina.. Thomas Flewelling. Wit. James Gibson, Joseph Martindate (mark). Proved by James Gibson 29 November 1802 before Geo. Whitmore, J.P. Recorded December 14, 1802.

Deed Book G: 545
November 20, 1802. Bill of Sale. I Joseph Motes of Laurens District, South Carolina to William Fleming in consideration of $120 sell undo said William Fleming the following Negro wench named Violet .. Joseph (mark) Motes. Wit. John Simpson. Proved by John Simpson 7 February 1803 before Robt. Hutchison, J.P. Recorded February 15, 1803.

Deed Book G: 546
November 20, 1802. Bill of Sale. I John Motes of Laurens District, South Carolina to John Brison of the same place, in consideration of $500 sell the following Negro fellow named Charles unto John Brison. John Motes. Wit. John Simpson. Proved by John Simpson 1 February 1803 before Robert Hutchunson, J.P. February 15, 1803.

33

Deed Book G: 584
June 14, 1796. Bill of Sale. I William Tennant, Sheriff of 96 District, South Carolina by virtue of a Writ of Fieri Facies which issued from the Courts of common Pleas at the said Charles Sims against the estate of D. Musgrove, deceased to all and singular the sheriffs of the said State did levy and seize upon a certain Negro girl names Biz and after notice of the intended sale of the said Negroes did on the First Monday in May last openly and publicly expose her to sale to the highest bidder at Bainbridge in the District aforesaid and the said Negroes being so exposed was s truck off to Alex. Morison for the sum of 61 £ at that being the highest and last bid for the same. I William Tennant for and in consideration of the said sum of 61 £ sell unto Alexander Morrison the said Negro girl. Set my hand 14 June 1796 Wm. Tennent. Wit. Alexr. McDowall, Salvs. Walker, Junr. Proved by Silvanus Walker, Junr. 23 March 1802 before Robert Hutchinson, J.P.

Deed Book G: 590
March 9, 1803. Bill of Sale. I Jacob Whitworth of Laurens District, South Carolina to Capt. John Watts in consideration of the sum of $186.64 have delivery unto Capt. John Watts three certain Negro children; one by the name of Miller, one by the name of Adam the other by the name of Benjamin. ..Set his hand 9 March 1803. Wit. Richard Watts, Samuel W. Whitworth, William (mark) Smith. Proved by Richard Watts 22 March 1803 before J.R. Brown, QM. Recorded March 26, 1803.

Deed Book G: 621
October 5, 1802. Deed of Gift: I Elizabeth Bryson of Laurens District, South Carolina for the love and good will I bear unto my brother John Hutchison assign two Negroes; namely a winch called Phillis and child called Milley and their increase and also all my personal property and what cash I may have or be possessed of at my decease.. Set my hand 5 October 1802 Elizabeth Bryson (mark). Wit. George Berry, Levi Compton. Proved by George Berry 4 April 1803 before William Rountree, J.P. Recorded April 4, 1803.

Deed Book G: 633
January 13, 1803. Daniel Wright, Executer to the estate of Daniel Abbot deceased; in consideration of the sum of $300 sold at publick sale agreeable to law one Negro boy about 8 years named Zachary unto said William Thomason of the state and district aforesaid. Set my hand 13 January 1803 Daniel Wright. Wit. (?) Young, Anderson Arnold. Proved by Anderson Arnold 4 June 1803 before Joseph Downs, J.P. Recorded June 4, 1803.

Deed Book G: 633
January 13, 1803. Daniel Wright, Executor of Estate of Daniel Abbott, deceased, in consideration of the sum of $520 sold at publick sale agreeable to law three Negroes; one woman named Pencur about 50 years of age and two Negro children a boy about 5 years of age named Alfred and a girl named Lauronda about 2 years of age unto said to Anderson Arnold. Set my hand 13 January 1803 Daniel Wright. Wit. (?) Young, William Thomeson. Proved by William Thomeson 4 June 1803 before Joseph Downs, J.P. Recorded June 4, 1803.

Deed Book G: 671
September 8, 1803. Mortgage. Gracey Curnal, Curtis Curnal and Polly Curnal, of the one part to John Watts, of the other part. Where as the said Gracey Curnal, Curtis Curnal and Polley Curnal by this note of hand dated 11 March 1803 herewith stand bound to the said John Watts in the sum of $2285, mortgage, six negroes to wit, Sam, Gabriel, Elias, Enoch, Ewing and Nancy with their increase . Gracy (her mark) Curnal (seal), Curtis Curnal (seal), Polly (her mark) Curnal. Wit. W. Pollard, Wilson (mark) Sanders, John (mark) Smith. Angus Campbell, J.P. Recorded October 19, 1803.

Deed Book G: 678
November 16, 1791. Bill of Sale. I Thomas Brandon of Union County, South Carolina to Sarah Gist in consideration of the sum of £35, sold and delivered unto Sarah Gist a Negroes girl named Aff. Set my hand 16 November 1790 Thos. Brandon. Wit. James Woodson. 22 November 1791 - I assign over all my right and title of the within mentioned Negro girl Aff to Doctor George Ross for his use and behoof. Sarah Gist. Wit. Jas. Woodson. Proved by James Woodson 25 October 1803 that he saw the within named Thomas Branden sign the Bill of ale and also saw the within Negro Girl Aff delivered by the said Thomas Branden to Sarah Gist, and was present when the within Bill of Sale was assigned over to Doctor George Ross by the said Sarah Gist before Andw. Tarrant, QM. Recorded October 21, 1803.

Deed Book G: 680
September 24, 1803. Bill of Sale. John Cason of Laurens District, South Carolina to William Foster of North Carolina in consideration of the sum of $250; sell a certain Negro man named Nubon about 27 years old unto said William Foster. John Cason. Wit. J. Garlington, John Chiles. Proved by J. Garlington 31 October 1803 before Chas. Allen, JQ. Recorded October 21, 1803.

Deed Book G: 680
June 7, 1803. Emancipation. Jacob Niswanger of Laurens District, South Carolina to Charles Watkins; in consideration of the sum of $2000 sell unto the said Charles Watkins - The condition of the above obligation is such that if the above bound Jacob Niswanger does will and truly at the expiration of ten years and seven months manicipate and forever set free a certain Negro man named Dinnis that he bought of William Walkins then the above obligation to be void or otherwise to be in full free and virtue. Signed Jacob Niswanger. Wit. G. Brook, John Watkins. Proved by John Watkins 31 October 1803 before Josiah Blackwell, J.P. Proved November 1, 1803.

DEED BOOK H: 1803-1808

Deed Book H: 1
May 1, 1802. Mortgage. John Arnold of the one part and Arthur Taylor of the other, both of Laurens District, South Carolina; in consideration of the sum of $1000 to sell unto said Arthur Taylor all that plantation of 51 acres on Reedy River .... also two Negroes slaves, Viz., Prince, a fellow and Lucy his wife... Signed John Arnold. Wit. Mary (O her mark) Pugh, John Cockran. Wit. By John Cockran 3 October 1803 before Saml. Cunningham, J.P. Recorded December 20, 1803.

Deed Book H: 2
December 17, 1803. Agreement. The legatees of John Cason, Senr. deceased have mutually agreed to divide the said estate after the decease of said Cason agreeable to his wish and desire there being no will that is known, and the legatees all of full age have divided the property of said John Cason deceased estate amongst themselves in the following manner; that Giles Cason to have as how share of said estate the land where he now lived about 50 acres and ½ of a certain tract on Bush River, it being equally divided between Giles and John, and John is likewise to have the land when Elizabeth Cason, their mother, now lives after her death, David Greer to have a house and bed that he have in possession or had and Chooses said Greer is to have a Negroes Boy named Wigdon after the death of his mother in law Elizabeth Cason, Milly Cason to have one mare and med and one Negroes Wench named Sarah after her mothers death, Rachel Cason or Rachel Chamblin to have £50 Sterling, one Negroes girl Jude and bed and some other articles..... Set our hands 17 December 1803 Giles Cason, David Greer, John Cason, Mary Cason, Daniel Chamberlin. Wit. William Teague,

Joseph Bluckerby. Proved by William Teague 21 December 1803 before R.H. Saxon. Recorded December 20, 1803.

Deed Book H: 27
March 3, 1804. Bill of Sale. Thomas Cason of Laurens District, South Carolina to Mary and Sarah Cason of the District aforesaid; one Negro man named Frank, two horses, three cattle and hogs and household furniture and all the tools belonging to the plantation for the sum of $700. Set my hand March 8, 1804 Thomas Cason. Wit. Jos. Miller, Job Deen. Proved by Jos. Miller 23 March 1804 before Robert Hutcheson, J.P. Recorded March 24, 1804.

Deed Book H: 49
August 10, 1804. Power of Attorney - I Charity Clarke of New Kent County, Virginia have ordained constituted and appointed Benjamin H. Saxon of Laurens County, South Carolina my true and lawful Attorney for me and in my name to ask, demand, sue for and receive a certain Negro woman named Cloe and her children all and severally which said Negro woman Cloe was devised to me by my deceased father Hezekiah Harding will and afterward sold Edward Clarke who intermarried with my mother Mary Harding and since found in the possession of Moses Madden, L. Berry Sullivant and for now a delivery of the said woman Cloe and her children or any one or more of them to inter which or take other steps which as the law shall require for the recovery of the same... Set my hand 10 August 1804 Charity (x) Clarke. Wit. Richard Thompson, William Thompson. Virginia City of Richmond. Be it known that upon the 11 August 1804 Charity Clarke personally appeared before me Robert Mitchell Major of the City of Richmond in the State aforesaid .. Robert Mitchell, Mayor. Recorded September 5, 1804.

Deed Book H: 58
February 18, 1804. Bill of Sale. George Dale, of Laurens District, South Carolina, to Thomas Lewers, of the same place, for $400, one negro woman named Mary Ann about 28 years of age. Geo. Dale. (Seal) Wit. Andrew Todd, James Caldwell. Proved by James Caldwell 25 October 1804 before Joseph Downs, J.P. Recorded October 27, 1804.

Deed Book H: 69
January 17, 1803. Deed of Gift. I Bryant Leak of Laurens District, South Carolina to grant unto my two sons, Viz., William Leak I give a Negro boy named Reuben and to Burel Leak a Negro boy named Jacob . Bryant (X) Leak. Wit. James Young, Samuel Leek (mark). Proved by James Young 6 January 1803 before Wm. Mitchell, J.Q. Recorded February 7, 1804.

Deed Book H: 75
February 16, 1805. Mortgage. Thomas Davenport to Pleasant Wharton for debt of $1500, mortgage on negroes, cattle, furniture, etc. Wit. Fredk. Bentz, L. Madden, Charles Allen, J.P. Recorded March 23, 1805.

Deed Book H: 79
August 8, 1796. I William Tennent, Sheriff of 96 District, South Carolina by virtue of a writ of Fieri Fuceas which I issued from the court of common please at the such of John Cunningham against the estate of Edmund Craddock deceased directed to all and singular the sheriff of the said did buy and seize upon two Negroes fellow of a yellowish complection, one known by the name of Rubin About 21 years old, the other is called David about 20 years old and after notice of the ordered sale of the said Negroes did on the First Monday in July last, openly and publickly them to sale to the highest bidder at Cambridge in the district aforesaid and the said Negroes being so deposed was struck off to Thomas Wadsworth and William Turpin for the sum of £ 52 that price bing the highest and last bidder for the same..... Set my hand 8 Aug. 1796 Wm. Tennent, Sheriff 96 Dist.
Hitheron Oct. 15, 1798 I assign to James Saxon Esq. All our rights little interest or claim to the within named fellow Rubin and David. Signed Thomas Wadsworth for Wadsworth & Turpin. Proved by James Young 20 March 1805 before Geo. Whitmore, J.P. Recorded March 25, 1805.

Deed Book H: 81
February 12, 1805. Bill of Sale. I Nathaniel Rook (in text) of Laurens District, South Carolina in consideration of the sum of $350 have sold to John Black, of said District and State a Negroes woman named Peggy and her child China with all her future increase unto said John Black. Set my hand this 12 February 1805 Nathaniel (R) Rook. Wit. By Wm. Black, James Moore. Proved by Wm. Black on March 2, 1805 before W. Burnside, J.P. Recorded March 26, 1805.

Deed Book H: 97
June 6, 1805. Deed of Gift: I Sarah Featherston of Laurens District, South Carolina have our of Pure Love and Affection which I have and do bear to my to my grandson Richard Land, son and heir of Sumpter Land and Obedience Land of the State of Kentucky and also to my son William Featherstone and Luch Featherston my daughter, given and granted to the aforesaid Richd. Land, William Featherston and Lucy Featherston one Negroes man named Brister for 20 £, one Note of hand on Richard Featherston, one cow and calf, which is now in my possession. In manner following, Viz., That the whole of the said property by this my deed. I put in

the possession of Thomas Land by these presents as trustee or guardian to the aforesaid three children and hereby direct him the said Thomas Land to sell the said Negroes man Brister and the other property aforesaid and make an equal division of the same amongst the three children aforesaid, Viz., when my said daughter Lucy arrives to the age of 18 years and further give to my dais daughter Lucy one feather bed and furniture at my decease which I keep in my own possession, and hereby authorize and instruct the said trustee Thomas Land to dispose of the aforesaid property as he shall think proper for the profit and advantage of the aforesaid children... Set my hand 6 June 1805. Sarah Featherston. Wit. E.S. Roland, John Land. Wit. Proved by John Land 7 June 1805 before B.H. Saxon, J.Q. Recorded June 8, 1805.

Deed Book H: 97
June 6, 1805. Bill of Sale. I Sarah Featherston of Laurens District, South Carolina in consideration of the sum of $736 paid by Thomas Land doth grant unto said Thomas Land a certain Negro man named Brister being a Negro man which I have at this time loaned to John McCrary, Esq., Sheriff of Chester District, state aforesaid. Set my hand 6 June 1805 Sarah (X) Featherston. Wit. E.S. Roland, John Land. Proved by John Land June 8, 1805 before R.H. Saxon, J.Q. Recorded June 8, 1805.

Deed Book H: 101
July 24, 1805. Bill of Sale. I James Wallace of York District, South Carolina to Thomas Lewer of Laurens District, South Carolina in consideration of the sum of $450 sold unto the said Thomas Lewers a Negro man named Snow aged about 28 years which I do warrant sound, healthy and honest and not runaway. Set my hand 24 July 1805 James Wallace. Wit. (?) Brannon, A. Gray. Proved by Alexander Gray 14 August 1805 before Joseph Downs, J.P. Recorded March 14, 1805.

Deed Book H: 114
November 18, 1805. Bill of Sale. I Alexander Henry of Laurens District, South Carolina to Elihu Creswell in consideration of the sum of $350 have sold unto the said Elihu Creswell a Negro girl named Hester about 10 years of age, which said Negro girl Hister I do hereby warrant to be sound and healthy in body and mind.. Set my hand 18 November 1805. Alexr. Henry. Wit. David Speers, John Garlington. Proved by John Garlington 28 December 1805 before Robert Creswell. Recorded December 28, 1805.

Deed Book H: 116
November 22, 1805. Bill of Sale. I Alexander Morison of Laurens District, SC to John Taylor, of the District aforesaid; in consideration of the sum of $350 do sell and deliver unto the said John Taylor one Negro boy named

Tom near 13 years old...Set my hand 2 November 1805 A. Morison. Wit. James Hunter, Williams Taylor. Proved by James Hunter 6 January 1806 before Robert Hutchinson, J.P. Recorded January 7, 1806.

Deed Book H: 119
April 22, 1802. Deed of Gift: I George Gordon of Laurens District, South Carolina in consideration of the good will Love and Affection which I bear to my to daughter Charlotte Gordon, two Negro girls, Rachel and Violet with all their future issue and increase forever. Set my hand 22 April 1802 George Gordon. Wit. Benj. Tillison, John Hunter. Proved by Benjamin Tillison 15 October 1805 before J. Puckett, J.P. Recorded January 8, 1806.

Deed Book H: 120
April 22, 1802. Deed of Gift. I George Gordon of Laurens District, South Carolina in consideration of the good will and affection which I bear unto my Daughter Catherine Gordon I have given granted and conveyed unto said Catherine Gordon two Negroes named Sophia and Henry with all their future issue and increase forever. Set my hand 22 April 1802 George Gordon. Wit. Benjamin Tillison, Jno. Hunter. Proved by Benjamin Tillison 15 October 1805 before J. Puckett, J.P. Recorded January 8, 1806.

Deed Book 120
April 22, 1802. Deed of Gift. I George Gordon of Laurens District, South Carolina in consideration of the good will and affection which I bear unto my Daughter Jean Gordon I have given granted and conveyed unto said Catherine Gordon two Negroes named Hector and Lid with all their future issue and increase forever. Set my hand 22 April 1802 George Gordon. Wit. Benjamin Tillison, Jno. Hunter. Proved by Benjamin Tillison 15 October 1805 before J. Puckett, J.P. Recorded January 8, 1806.

Deed Book H: 120
November 12, 1805. Deed of Gift. To all whom it may concerned be it remembered that I Amelia Brockman widow of John Brockman, deceased by the power vested in my by the last will of the said deceased John Brockman do by these presents give, bequeath unto Amelia Owens my lawful granddaughter one Negro girl named Vina which said girl I have purchased since the death of my said husband Job Brockman said girl age about 9 or 10 years old. Set my hand 12 November 1805 Amelia Brockman (X). Wit. Richd. Young. Danl. Wright. Proved by Daniel Wright 7 January 1806 before Robt. Creswell. JQ. Recorded January 9, 1806.

Deed Book H: 120
May 17, 1805. Oath. Personally appeared Mr. James Caldwell and gave
oath that he was present at the house of Meria Goodman on 15 December
1799 or 1800 and saith that he was requested by Barttlett Brooks to bear
witness to a gift of a small Negro girl by the name of Sisley to her little
daughter Betsey Goodman Brooks which said Brooks did by taking said
Negro girl by the hand and put it into the hand of his daughter as aforesaid
which he this deponent considered as a gift. Sworn 17 May 1805 James
Caldwell - Wm. Burnside, J.P. Recorded January 9, 1806.

Deed Book H: 121
?? Check microfilm. Personally appeared Mr. Richard Griffin and gave oath
that he was present at the house of Maria Goodman on 15 December 1799
or 1800 and saith that he was requested by Barttlett Brooks to bear witness
to a gift of a small Negro girl by the name of Sisley to her little daughter
Betsey Goodman Brooks which said Brooks did by taking said Negro girl
by the hand and put it into the hand of his daughter as aforesaid which he
this deponent considered as a gift. Sworn 17 May 1805 by Richard Griffin
before Wm. Burnside, J.P. Recorded

Deed Book H: 121
January 6, 1806. Bill of Sale. Made the 1 January 1806 between Robert
Word, Sheriff of Laurens District of the one part and James Young. Of the
same place of the other, whereas Francis Lester of the state and district
aforesaid was seized and possessed of a Negro girl about 4 years of age
named Ruth and whereas a writ of Fieri Facia issued from the court of
common pleas held for the District of Laurens aforesaid under the hand of
Elihu Creswell Esq. Clerk of said court dated 18 Marcy 1865 directed that
the goods and chattles houses, lands and tenements of the said Francis
Lester they should cause to be the sum of $124.06 which Daniel Williams
lately of the court of common please held for the District aforesaid received
against the said Francis Lester for debt as also the sum of $34.10 for his
costs and charges - did cause to be sized and taken the Negro girl and said
Negro girl to sale by public outcry at the court house of the said District
aforesaid and on the 7 Oct. last for satisfaction of the debt coasts and
charges aforesaid openly publicly and fairly did sell the said Negro girl unto
said James Young for the sum of $130 he being the highest price and last
bidder. Set my hand P. Work. S.L.District. Wit. B. Nabours. James Boyd.
Proved by Benjamin Nabours 6 January 1806 before Starling Tucker, J.Q.
Recorded January 9, 1806.

Deed Book H: 121

December 18, 1805. Oath. Personally appeared Zachariah Bailey before me and made oath that he was in company with Bartlett Brooks and said Brooks was going to give him a Mortgage of his Negroes and his wife was naming over the Negroes names and his wife mentioned a Negro girl by some name I cant recollect her name but Mr. Brooks said he did not claim her, she belonged to his little daughter and did not put her in the mortgage, Z. Bailey. Sworn 15 December 1805. John Rowland, J.P. Recorded January 9, 1805.

Deed Book H: 121

Personally appeared Paul Findley before one of the Justices of said District and made oath that he herd Bartlett Brooks often say that he had given a little Negro girl to his daughter Elizabeth and did not claim her as his property. Sworn 18 Dec. 1805 Paul Findly before Z. Bailey, J.P.

Deed Book H: 124

August 12, 1798. Bill of Sale. I LittleBerry Harris of Newberry County, South Carolina to Samuel Goodman of Laurens County, South Carolina in consideration of $200 have sold to Samuel Goodman one certain Negro boy about 12 years old named Bob commonly called (Butt) a country bourn and strong stout well made - .. Set my hand 12 August 1798 Little B. Harris. Wit. R. Brown, David Gillam. Proved by David Gillam before Angus Campbell, J.P. Recorded February 11, 1806.

Deed Book H: 126

February 8, 1806. Emancipation. I do hereby certify unto all whom it may concern that for and in consideration of the sum of $500 to me in hand paid by Sam a Negro man Slave and William Arnold his security I have bargained sold Emancipated and freed, and by these presents do bargain sell Emancipate and free the said Negro, and do hereby warrant and forever defend the said Negro in his freedom against my self and my heirs and assigns and against all persons whomsoever claiming him the said Negro man Sam, as their property and the said Negro is hereby declared free without any let, hindrance, molestation or interruption of any person or persons whomsoever either in this state or in the United States. Given under my hand and seal this 8 February 1806. Arthur Taylor. Wit. Jeremiah Hollingsworth, Thomas Kelly. Proved by Thomas Kelly 8 February 1806 before Jonthan. Downs. JQ. Recorded February 12, 1806.

Laurens District, South Carolina: Agreeable to an act of assembly of the state aforesaid bearing date 20 December 1800 I Jonathan Downs one of the Justices of the Quorum being informed by Arthur Taylor that he had intended to Emancipate and set free a certain Negro man names Sam pursuant thereto I issued summons to five free holders who attended accordingly the said slave being present and after asking the said Taylor the necessary Questions on oath prescribed by law do give the following certificate, Viz., we do hereby certify upon the Examination of oath of Arthur Taylor the owner of a certain Slave named Sam 36 or 7 years old, five feet ten inches high, stout and well made a Blacksmith by trade Satisfactory proof has been given to us that he said slave is not of bad character and is capable of gaining a livelihood by honest means, Certified by us this 8 February 1806. Jonthn. Downs, J.Q., William Arnold, J.P., Abm. Box, James McClannahan, Thomas Kelly, Jeremiah Hollingsworth

Deed Book H: 128
January 3, 1806. Bill of Sale. I John Davenport of Laurens District, South Carolina for and in consideration of the sum of $250 have sold to Richard Davenport, my son two Negro girls. One by the name of Dinah ages 5 years, the other by the name of Meriah about 4 years old .. John (X) Davenport. Wit. Jonat. Johnson, Elizabeth Johnson. Proved by John Johnson 11 February 1806 before Zachariah Bailey, J.P. Recorded February 13, 1806.

Deed Book H: 129
August 2, 1805. Deed of Gift: I Barbary Burk of Laurens District, South Carolina for and in consideration of love and good will and affection which I have and do bear unto my loving son Jesse Briggs of said district have granted and present s do freely grant unto said Jesse Briggs one Negro boy named Ned about 2 years old.. Barbara (X) Burk. Wit. Solomon Bobo, John Cargill. Proved by Solomon Bobo 19 November 1806 before Robert Hutcheson, J.P. Recorded February 14, 1806.

Deed Book H: 131
February 4, 1806. Deed of Gift. William Tweedy, of Laurens District, South Carolina in consideration of my future support and maintenance and also the good will, Love and Affection which I bear unto my son in law Charles Simmons I have given and conveyed unto said Charles Simmons, all my real and personal estate, Viz., one negro woman named Hanna, 4 head of cattle, one bed and furniture, all my household and kitchen furniture and also all my notes, bonds and accounts due me. William (mark) Tweedy (seal). Wit. John Garlington. Jno. Black. Proved by John Black 3 March 1806 before Starling Tucker J.P. Recorded March 4, 1806.

Deed Book H: 132
February 28, 1806. Deed of Gift: I Amelia Brockman of Laurens District, South Carolina for and in consideration of the sum of $100 sold to Amelia

43

Owens of District aforesaid one Negro girl named Edy two years old...... Set
my hand 28 February 1806. Amelia (X) Brockman. Wit. Archd. Young.
Danl. Wright. Proved by Daniel Wright 3 March 1806 before Elihu
Creswell. Recorded March 4, 1806.

Deed Book H: 133
February 28, 1806. Deed of Gift: I Amelia Brockman of Laurens District,
South Carolina for many good causes hereunto made do give bequest and
forever defend unto my grandson John Owens and grand daughter Betsey
Bolinger and Amelia Owens one Negro woman named Bet about 20 years
old with her increase to be equally divided between the said John Owens
and Betsey Balinger and Amelia Owens after my death by sale or otherwise
as they may agree the said Negro Bet being property that I have purchased
since the death of my husband John Brockman. Set my hand 28 February
1806 Amelia Brockman (X) Wit. Archd. Young. Danl. Wright. Proved by
Daniel Wright 3 March 1806 before Elihu Cresell. Recorded March 4, 1806.

Deed Book H: 134
March 16, 1806. Mortgage: I Thornton Cox of Laurens District, South
Carolina as mortgage unto Joseph Cox of the same place assign a Negro boy
about 13 years of age named Joe which Negro boy stands mortgaged or
pledged as security for $108, which mortgaged boy Joe as aforesaid or the
$116 as aforesaid at the aforesaid mentioned time I do bind myself my
heirs, executors, to deliver up subject to be sold as other mortgaged property
by Law sold or to pay the $116 aforesaid. Set my hand 16 March 1806
Thornton Cox. Wit. Benjn. Strange, Danl. Craddock, Bartlett Milan. Proved
by Benjn. Strange 18 March 1806 before John Boyd. J.P. Recorded March
17, 1806.

Deed Book H: 135
September 23, 1805. Bill of Sale. I Stephen Mullings of Laurens District,
South Carolina sell unto James Mills one Negro Boy named Hall for the
sum of £ 30, 12 Shillings and 3 pence. Set my hand 27 February 1805.
Stephen Mullings. Wit. Rob. Fleming Junr. The condition of the above
obligation is stuck of the said Stephen Mullings do well and truly pay the
sum above mention on or before 25 December next therein the above to be
void and of no effect otherwise to remain in full force and virtue in law as
witness my hand 27 Feb. 1806 Stephen Mullings. Wit. Rob Fleming, Junr.
Proved by Robert Fleming Junr. 24 March 1806 before John Boyd. J.P.
Recorded March 24, 1806.

Deed Book H: 136
March 22, 1806. Mortgage: Indenture made between Ambrose Hudgens of
Laurens District South Carolina of the one part and Thomas Lewers of the
same district and state aforesaid, whereas the said Ambrose Hudgens by his
note did promise to pay the said Thomas Lewers $134.04 in full from the
date aforesaid 10 February 1808 as mentioned in the said reference... have
delivered into said Thomas Lewers one Negro woman named Bidda and her
child named Jenny... Set my hand Ambrose Hudgens. Wit. Deborah McGill,
Alexdr. R. Gray, John (W his mark) Taylor. Proved by Alexander Gray 7
April 1806 before Chas. Allen, J.Q. Recorded April 15, 1806.

Deed Book H: 139
December 15, 1805. Bill of Sale. John McHargh and Susannah McHargh,
administrator and administratrix of Wm. McHarg, deceased sold to James
Thommasson for $210; a certain negro boy named Ben, 5 years of age.
John McHarg (seal), Susannah McHarg (seal). Wit. Anderson Arnold, John
Bolt. Proved by Anderson Arnold 15 April 1806 before Robert Hutchinson,
J.P. Recorded April 17, 1806.

Deed Book H: 148
February 17, 1806. Deed of Gift. Edwin Garlington, of Halifax County,
Virginia to my daughter Nancy Garlington of Laurens District, South
Carolina, in consideration of the sum of $1. Give unto said daughters Nancy
Garlington a negro girl named Jean about 12 or 13 years old, the right and
title of the said negro Jean and all her future increase. Edwin Garlington.
Wit. J. Garlington, E. Curwell. Proved by J. Garlington 13 June 1806 before
R. Creswell, JQ.

Deed Book H: 150
July 19, 1806. Deed of Gift: I Sarah Wright, widow, of Laurens District,
South Carolina, having a daughter by the name of Sarah, who several years
ago did intermarry with one Stephen Wood of said District and as the said
Wood has removed unto the District of Greenville and there has left his said
wife, Sarah Wood, without any support, Now be it known on that for the
good will and affection I have for my said daughter Sarah Wood, and in as
much as possible to return her the said Sarah, in her present distress, I have
by these presents give and bequeath unto my truly friend David Anderson
Esquire, of the said District, in whose fidelity I much confide in and for the
use of my said daughter Sarah Wood, and her heirs, one Negro boy the
name of Martin about 3 years old for to have and hold the said Negro boy
for the use and behoof of the said Sarah Wood.. . I. Set my hand 19 July
1806 Sarah Wright. Wit. Burwell Moseley, Littleton Moseley. John
Rowland, J.P. Recorded July 21, 1806.

Deed Book H: 156
December 17, 1803. Bill of Sale. I John Arnold of Laurens District, South
Carolina in consideration of the sum of $700 paid by Charity Arnold, sell
unto said Charity Arnold three Negroes named Luce, Tom and Mill... Set
my hand 17 December 1803 John Arnold. Wit. Henry Ridgeway, William
Gunnell (X). Proved by William Gunnell 30 August 1806 before William
Arnold, J.P. Recorded September 1, 1806.

Deed Book H: 187
March 5, 1806. Bill of Sale. John Rowland, administrator of James Boyce,
deceased to James Young for $300, my right and title in a negro man Tom
which said James Young and James Boyce bought of Hannah Cureton, T. T.
Cureton and Edward Thweat, executor and executrix of John Cureton, Senr,
deceased. Wit. James H. Dendy, Wm. Walker, Z. Bailey, J.P. Recorded
January 7, 1807.

Deed Book H: 189
February 23, 1806. Bill of Sale. I Mecajah Hendrick of Laurens District,
South Carolina in consideration of $400 paid by David Anderson of the
same place, sell unto said David Anderson one Negro girl about 13 years
old by the name of Ann... Set by hand 23 February 1806 Macajah Hendrick
(X). Wit. W. Burnside, T.(Thomas) Babb. Proved by William Burnside 10
January 1807 before James McMahan, J.P. Recorded January 12, 1807.

Deed Book H: 214
February 24, 1807. Deed of Gift: I Ebenezer Moss (Morss) of Spartanburgh
District, South Carolina send Greetings. Know ye that I the said Ebenezar
Morss for and in consideration of the love good will and affection which I
have and do bear towards by grandson Jefferson Gallaton Morss, son of my
son James Morss of Laurens District, South Carolina have given and
granted unto the said Jefferson G. Morff a certain Negro Boy about 4 years
old named Tom... Set my hand 24 February 1807 Ebenezar (mark) Morss.
Wit. Samuel Bell. Proved by Samuel Bell 10 March 1807 before Starling
Tucker, J.Q. Recorded April 7, 1807.

Deed Book H: 219.
April 10, 1807. Special Agreement: Know all men by these presents that in
the 10 April 1807. I Absalom Bobo and Anny Bobo do enter this day into a
special agreement with William Powell and Nancey Powell his wife and by
these presents do bargain contract and formerly agree with the said William
Powell and Nancy his wife, that by their faithful performance on their part
in their obligation that we Absolum Bobo, and Amy Bobo, as our part give
up and contract all my land, that we are now in possession of likewise the

46

improvements thereon, also all my Negroes, that is to say Catren, Jacob, Jean, Hannah, Jiller, Milley, Delilah, Willes, Peter, Nutty, Anny, Masten, Letty, Harry, Canders, Micklry, Dennis, likewise four feather beds and furniture, also all the residence of my household, kitchen furniture, and plantation tools, all my stock of horses, cattle, sheep, hogs, pottery,... That the said William Powell and Nancey his wife contract to furnish them a good and comfortable support and maintenance for them both as long as they both shall live, of decent diet, lodging and apparel... Set our hands Absolum (X) Bobo, Anney (mark) Bobo, William Powell, Nancey (mark) Powell. Wit. Larkin Gains, Betsey (X) Gains. Proved by Larkin Gains 10 April 1807 before James Powell, J.P. Recorded April 21, 1807.

Deed Book H: 230
November 1, 1804. Mortgage. John Head, of Edgefield District, South Carolina do send greetings, whereas I the said John Head by my bond am firmly bound unto Samuel Farr, Esquire, of Spartanburg District, in the sum of $1657.75 a mortgage on five negro slaves. , Viz.,. Bachusa a negro man about 30 years of age, Sall a negro woman about the same age and her three youngest children, Tille a negro girl about 5 years of age, Phillis a negro girl about 3 years old, and Waties a negro boy about one year old to have and to hold the said five negroes, with their future increased unto the said Samuel Farrow...John Head. Wit. Chaney Farrow, Thomas Miles, Junr. Proved by Thomas Miles Jurn. 4 April 1805 before John Puckett, J.P. Robert Word, sheriff of Laurens District, sold said negroes at Laurens Court House on the first Monday in May 1807 to highest bidder Samuel Farrow for $1000. Recorded June 4, 1807.

Deed Book H: 252
October 31, 1807. Deed of Gift. Wm. Barksdale, planter to son Higgerson Barksdale Deed of Gift: I William Barksdale, of Laurens District, South Carolina, Planter, in consideration of the love good will and affection which I have and do bear towards my loving son John Barksdale of the same place I do freely give and grant unto the said Higgerson Barkesdale two Negroes to Wit. Blum and Betty, one bay mare called Phoenix, two cows and calves, one feather bed and furniture, two cows and calves and one third part of my household and kitchen furniture, one third part of plantation utensils, also one third part of my stock of Hogs and sheep.. Set my hand 31 October 1807 William Barksdale. Wit. John Clark, Ann Saxon. Proved by John Clark 31 October 1807 before James Saxon, J.Q. Recorded November 2, 1807.

Deed Book H: 253
October 31, 1807. Deed of Gift: I William Barksdale, of Laurens District, South Carolina, Planter, in consideration of the love good will and affection which I have and do bear towards my loving son Higgerson Barksdale of the same place I do freely give and grant unto the said Higgerson Barkesdale two Negroes to Wit. Ailson and Sarah, one bay filly called Piggon, two feather beds and furniture, two cows and calves and one third part of my household and kitchen furniture, one third part of plantation utensils, also one third part of my stock of Hogs and sheeP.. Set my hand 31 October 1807 William Barksdale. Wit. John Clark, Ann Saxon. Proved by John Clark 31 October 1807 before James Saxon, J.Q. Recorded November 2, 1807.

Deed Book H: 253
October 31, 1807. Bill of Sale. Received of Samuel Barkesdale $400 in full for two Negroes namely Tom and Clarissa which Negroes I do warrant and defend unto the said Samuel Barkesdale his heirs and assigns from the lawful claim of my self my heirs or assigns or from any person.. Set my hand 31 October 1807. William Barksdale. Wit. John Clark, Ann Saxon. Proved by John Clark 31 October 1807 before James Saxon, J.Q. Recorded November 2, 1807.

Deed Book H: 257
October 23, 1807. Deed of Gift: I Grace Kernel do send Greeting, Know ye that I the said Grace Kernel of Laurens District, South Carolina in consideration of the love good will and affection which I do bear toward my son Curtis Kernel of the same place, have given and granted unto the said Curtis Kernal one Negro boy named Elias aged 11 or 12 years last August, also the sum of $300 be the same more or less, now in the hands of Samuel Caldwell together with all and singular. My goods and Chattles belonging to me or in which I have my lawful claim of which before this signing of these presents I have delivered to him the said Curtis Kernel... Set my hand 23 October 1807 Grace (X) Kernel. Wit Horatio Walker, Damilion Deal. Proved by Demilion {Darnelion} Deal 2 November 1807 before Angus Campbell, J.P. Recorded November 24, 1807.

Deed Book H: 259
March 3, 1807. Bill of Sale. James Sullivant, of Laurens District, South Carolina in consideration of the sum of $370, sell to James Young, merchant, of the same place, a certain negro boy called Cacob (sic) about 12 years old. James Sullivant. Wit. James (mark) White. Proved by James White (mark) 21 November 1807 before Z. Bailey, J.P. Recorded December 8, 1807.

Deed Book H: 262-263
February 10, 1807. Bond. I the said Richard Hodges by this note and one
bond or obligation bearing the said two notes baring date 1 January 1807 the
said bond the 6 February 1807 became held and firmly bound into David
Anderson and James Young. In the penal sum of $972.28 by bond... I have
sold unto David Anderson and James Young, 100 acres of land I now live
on, one Negro woman named Jude, five horses, ten bolts together with all
my household and kitchen furniture...Set my hand 10 February 1807
Richard Hodges. Wit. Saml. Anderson, Silvanus Walker, Junr. Proved by
Silvanus Walker 12 December 1807 before John Roland, J.P. Recorded
January 5, 1808.

Deed Book H: 266
January 16, 1808. In Trust. I George Lawing of Laurens District, South
Carolina, whereas I am indebted to the several persons whose names are
mentioned in a ------- hereon inevised? in the sums therein mentioned and
whereas I am now and sent and half to bail for the said debts and demands
and being unable to make bail to the said accuser I the said George Lawing
for the payment and satisfaction of the said debts and demands in the said
sales deal mentioned and also in consideration of the sum of $5 to me in
hand paid by William Dunlap, John Boyd and Robert Crewell. I do grant
and unto the said William Dunlap, John Boyd and Robert Creswell in trust,
the following to Wit. Five Negroes Phillis and her two children, Alexander
and Aggy, one gray steed, two black horses, all manner of goods wares and
merchandise... Set my hand 16 January 1808 George Lawing. Wit. Geo.
Jones, Jas. H. Lervry. Proved by George Jones 22 January 1808 before
John Garlington. [list of Notes in list] Recorded January 22, 1808.

Deed Book H: 269
July 25, 1803. Robert Coker, Junr., of Laurens District, South Carolina sell
unto Jesse Garrett for $320, a negro or mulatto gerral (sic) named Hannah.
Robert Coker, Junr. Wit. Jno. Pringle, John McHery. Proved by John
Mchery 11 January 1808 before Jonathn. Downs, J.P. Recorded February 3,
1808.

DEED BOOK J: 1808-1812

Deed Book J: 7
April 25, 1808. Bill of Sale. Ambrose Hudgens sold to Thomas Lewers for
one negro wench and four children, Viz., Biddy the wench, Henry, Jennny
and the youngest not named... Ambrose Hudgens (seal). Wit. J. Brannon.

Proved by James Brannon April 16, 1808. J. Garlington CC. Recorded April 26, 1808.

Deed Book J: 47
November 16, 1808. Bill of Sale. I David Caldwell of Laurens District, South Carolina in consideration of the sum of $600 to me paid by Samuel Vaughan, of the same place sell unto the said Samuel Vaughan four Negroes named as follows, Viz., Cloe, Selvey, Sarah and Edmond..... Set my hand 10 November 1808. David Caldwell, Moses Madden. Wit. John Wallis, Junr., William Fowler, Mathew Hunter. Proved by William Fowler and John Wallis, 16 November 1808 before Stephen Garrett. Recorded December 12, 1808.

Deed Book J: 65
March 22, 1809. Bond: Indenture made 22 March 1809 between William Fuller of Laurens District, South Carolina of one part and John Abernathy of the other part . Witnesseth that whereas the said William Fuller and Jacob Miller my their note of hand dated 15 August 1806 and promise to pay to John Burns on order $110 on or before 25 December then next - also one other not of hand duly executed by the said William Fuller and Jacob Miller dated 15 August 1806 to pay to the aforesaid John Burns on order $117.70 on or before 25 December 1808. .. The said William Fuller hath granted and sold unto the said John Abernathy a certain Negro woman named Milley about 17 or 18 years of age.... Wm. Fuller. Wit. Thomas Porter, John Garlington. Proved by Thomas Porter 29 March 1809 before John Garlington, JQ. Recorded March 31, 1809.

Deed Book J: 85
April 22, 1809. Deed of Gift: Know ye all men that for the Love and Affection which I do bear unto my grandson Randal Sullivan of Laurens District, South Carolina, have given, granted and delivered unto the aforesaid Randel Sullivan one Negro Boy named Edmund 6 years old, one other Negro boy named Hannibel aged 4 years old, one waggon and gears and four horses, also at my wifes decease I give the whole of my movable property unto the said Randel Sullivan consisting of all my stock of cattle, hogs, horses, household furniture and all other personal property that I may die possessed of and my tract of land which I now live on containing 250 acres, and at my wifes decease he is to see the said land at public sale and to pay to my son Larkin Sullivan one third part of the purchase money, one third part of the said purchase money he is to pay to my grandson Tilley - Francis Sullivan - the other third part of the purchase money I have to him the aforesaid Randel Sullivan, also the said Randel Sullivan is to pay to my grandson Robert Burton $128.50 and a horse saddle and bridle.. Set my

50

hand 2 April 1809 James (mark) Sullivan. Wit. Saml. C. Stedman, Daniel Osborne, John Cochran. Proved by Saml. Stedman 5 June 1809 before Robert Hutcherson, J.P. Recorded June 6, 1809.

Deed Book J: 92
April 22, 1809. Deed of Gift: To all presents shall come Greeting. Know ye all men by these presents, that for the Love and Affection which I do bear unto my loving Son Larkin Sullivan I give and delivered unto the said Larkin Sullivan the following named Negroes at my and my wifes decease, Viz., Lewis, Tom, Bart, Fender, Lydd and Amy, at my and my wifes decease. Set my hand 2 April 1809. James (mark) Sullivan. Wit. Saml. C. Stedman, Daniel Osborn, John Cochran. Proved by Samuel C. Stedman on 29 July 1809 before John Garlington Q.M. Recorded July 29, 1809.

Deed Book J: 93
April 23, 1809. Deed of Gift: To all presents shall come Greeting - Know ye all men by these presents that for the Love and Affection which I do bear unto my grand son Tully Frances Sullivan - I do give grant and deliver unto him one Negro boy named Isaac, also one Negro girl named Lucey at my and my wifes decease - Set my hand 2 April 1809. James (mark) Sullivan. Wit. Saml. C. Stedman, Daniel Osborn, John Cochran. Proved by Samuel C. Stedman on 7 August 1809 before Z. Bailey, J.P. Recorded August 9, 1809.

Deed Book J: 93
April 23, 1809. Deed of Gift: To all presents shall come Greeting - Know ye all men by these presents that for the Love and Affection which I do bear unto my granddaughters - Edney and Lucinda Sullivan - I have given granted and delivered unto them one Negro girl named Easter and her increase to be equally divided between then the said Edney and Lucinda at time that Lucinda comes of age. Set my hand 22 April 1809 James (mark) Sullivan. Wit. Saml. C. Stedman, Daniel Osborn, John Cochran. Proved by Saml. C. Stedman 7 August 1809 before James Dunklin, J.P. Recorded August 7, 1809.

Deed Book J: 93
April 23, 1809. Deed of Gift: To all presents shall come Greeting - Know ye all men by these presents that for the Love and Affection which I do bear unto my grandchildren the offspring of my daughter Sally I do give grant and deliver unto the aforesaid children one Negro girl named Meley to be equally divided her and her increase when the youngest of these said children comes of age - and the said Negro girl Miley I have in the care of Randal Sullivan until the youngest child of the said Sally comes of age. Set my hand 2 April 1809 James (mark) Sullivan. Saml. C. Stedman, Daniel

Osborn, John Cochran. Proved by Saml. C. Stedman 7 August 1809 before
Z. Bailey, J.P. Recorded August 7, 1809.

Deed Book J: 93
March 8, 1809. Mortgage. Thomas Franks of Laurens District, South
Carolina to Jeremiah Collins of the same has sold to Jeremiah Collins for
$235, one negro girl called by the name of Fanney aged 9 or 10. With the
profits there on. Thomas (X) Franks. Wit. Lewis Graves, Henry Box.
Proved by Lewis Graves August 7, 1809 before Z. Bailey, J.P. Recorded
August 7, 1809 John Garlington, Registrar.

Deed Book J: 104
August 7, 1809. Deed of Gift: To all presents shall come Greeting - Know
ye all men by these presents that for the Love and Affection which I do bear
unto my daughter Margaret Gibson, wife of John Gibson of Laurens
District, South Carolina and also for other good causes and considerations
hereunto I give and grant unto the said Margaret Gibson one Negro girl
names Lucey about 9 or 10 years old who is now in the possession of the
said Margaret Gibson, by virtue of verbal contract made some years past,
that the said Negro girl Luch shall be the sole and alone property of the said
Margaret Gibson, during her natural life, and shall at her decease be the
property of her children, lawfully be gotton and the said Lucy and her
offspring are hereby declared to be incapable of being transferred to any
other person or persons, but that she the said Lucy with all and everyone of
her offspring shall be the property of her the said Margaret Gibson and of
her children grand children forever... Set my hand 7 August 1809 Ezekiel
Mathews (X). Wit. J.T. Wolff, John Coker, Samuel Matthews.
Memorandum, that on the day and year last within written delivery was
given and made by the within named Ezekiel Mathews unto the said
Margaret Gibson of the said Negroes girl Lucy.. Proved by John Coker4
September 1809 before Samuel Cunningham, J.P. Recorded September 4,
1809.

Deed Book J: 122
October 11, 1809. Deed of Gift. James Ewen of Laurens District, for and in
consideration of the love and good will which I do bear unto my two
daughters Betsey Ewen and Judy F. Ewen have given unto the aforesaid
Betsey Ewin and Judy F. Ewin all that plantation where on I now live
containing 187 and one half acres; also one negro girl named Polly and all
her increase. Also one sorrel horse, six head of cattle, one feather bed, 17
head of hogs, all plantation tools and household furniture.. I freely give all
this property above mentioned to Bartlett Milam or his hands to rise and
maintain the said Betsey Ewin and Judy F. Ewin as he things proper, after

these children are raised and schooled whatever property remains unto the said B. Milam hands shall be equally divided between the said Betsy Ewin and Judy F. Ewin, whenever the come of age or marry... I now deliver this property to the said Bartlett Milam to raise and school these children B. Ewin, Judy F. Ewin .. James Ewin. (Seal). Wit. Ferrill Milam, Thomas Milam, Benjamin Milan. Proved by Ferrill Milam December 23, 1809 before John Garlington, Recorded December 23, 1809.

Deed Book J: 136
February 5, 1810. Deed of Gift: Know all men by these presents that I James McDavid of Laurens District, South Carolina in consideration of the Love and Affection I bear unto my son Jonathan McDavid of the same place have granted and given unto my said son Jonathan the following Negroes, Viz., one Negro man named Jack about 29 years old, one Negro woman named Esther about 30 years old, one Negro girl named Tamier, 5 or 6 years old, one Negro boy named Sam 8 or 9 years old and a Negro boy named Abraham 11 or 12 years old. .. Set my hand 5 February 18010. James McDavid. Wit. W.F. Downs, D. Saxon. Proved by William F. Downs 5 February 1810 before Jonthn. Downs, J.Q. Recorded March 9, 1810.

Deed Book J: 136-137
March 13, 1810. Bill of Sale. I Alexander Morrison of Laurens District, South Carolina in consideration of the sum of $700 paid by Archibald. McLachlan of Charleston, merchant, have bargained sold and delivered unto the said Archibald McLacklan a Negro woman named Beck with her two children, the eldest a girl named Lexina and the youngest a boy named Albert... Set my hand 13 March 1810. A. Morison. Wit. Jno. McKillar. Proved by John McKillar 14 March 1810- before John A. Elmore, JQ. Recorded March 27, 1810.

Deed Book J: 137
February 7, 1809. Bill of Sale. I Jeremiah Manly in consideration of the sum of $73.75 for which I have given my note to Robert Matthews both of Laurens District payable the 1 March 1810 have sold and do bargain or mortgage unto Robert Matthews one Negro woman named Pheby about 17 or 18 years of age, one Negro boy named Price between 2 and 3 years of age, one sorrel mare 4 or 5 years old blind in one eye, one brown colt between 1 and 2 years old, one chest, one table, 2 beds and furniture...Set my hand 2 February 1809 Jeremiah (mark) Manly. Wit. Robert Lowry, Polly Lowry. Proved by Robert Lowry 31 March 1810 before Samuel Cunningham, J.P. Recorded April 2, 1810.

Deed Book J: 141
July 3, 1809. Bill of Sale. Received of John Boyce $150 for a certain negro
boy named Toney about 35 years of age. . That I William Summers, Jr on or
before December 25, 1810 do pay to the said John Boyce his heirs the above
mention sum of $150 on the delivery of said negro to said William
Summers, Jr. William Summers, Jr. Proved by D.T. Milling 17 April 1810
before D. Boyce, J.P. Recorded April 17, 1810.

Deed Book J: 147
February 26, 1810. Bill of Sale. I James Duncan of Newberry District,
South Carolina in consideration of $70 paid at or before the unsealing and
delivery of these presents by John Jeans of Laurens Districk do hereby
acknowledge and am fully satisfied and have granted and sold unto the said
John Jeans one Negro woman named Beck also one Negro child daughter of
said Beck, named Rachel to have and to hold the said bargained Beck and
Rachel with their increase unto the said John Jeans, his heirs and assigns...
Set my hand 26 February 1810 James Duncan. Wit. John Pearson, Frederic
(mark) Jones. Proved by John Pearson 14 April 1810 before D. Boyce, J.P.
Recorded April 18, 1810.

Deed Book J: 155
December 4, 1809. Mortgage. I Isaac Roberts of Laurens District, South
Carolina in consideration of the sum of $578.27 have mortgaged and made
over unto the said John Pugh one Negro woman named Rose and her child
named Susannah, one feather bed and furniture, one check and all the estate
that is coming to me of the Estate of Jacob Roberts deceased... Set my hand
4 December 1809 Isaac Roberts. Wit. William Gilbert. D. Mitchersson.
Proved by William Gilbert 16 May 1018 before Thomas Parks, J.P.
Recorded June 4, 1810.

Deed Book J: 157
March 10, 1810. Mortgage. Marmaduke Pinson of Laurens District, South
Carolina for the sum of $217 paid by William Johnson, of same, have
mortgaged one negro girl named Viney. Marmaduke Pinson (seal) Wit.
Mary Cochran, John Cochran. Proved by John Cochran 7 January 1811. J.
Garlington, Registrar.

Deed Book J: 168
September 5, 1809. Bill of Sale. John McHarg of the County of Laurence to
Peter Hammonds, of the same place, for $900, one negro fellow a slave the
name of Gorg about 20 years of age and also one negro girl name of Sary
about 14 years of age it being the same negro fellow that I bought of Peter

Hammonds and the negro girl that I bought of William McHarg. Wit. William Hammond., Peter Hammond. Proved by Peter Hammonds 3 September 1810 before. Garlington Registrar. Recorded September 3, 1810.

Deed Book J: 171
April 21, 1810. Mortgage. Moses Madden of Laurens District, South Carolina to David Caldwell of the same place, for $2000 bond or mortgage on 370 acres belonging to said David Caldwell, John Ritchey, John Findley, Geo. Funk. And do sell and deliver unto said David Caldwell a certain negro woman named Winny, about 18 years (See suit vs. David Caldwell and wife for Trover.) Wit. R. Creswell, George Davis. Proved by George J. Garlington, Clk. Recorded September 12, 1810.

Deed Book J: 177
December 4, 1809. Bill of Sale. I Benjamin Jones of Newberry District, South Carolina in consideration of the sum of $250 paid by Thomas Hendrix of Laurens District, state aforesaid, hath sold and by these present delivered unto the said Thomas Hendrix a Negro boy named Abraham about 5 years old to have and to hold - ... Set my hand 4 December 1809 Benjamin Jones. Wit. James Waters, Dred (X) Jones. Proved by James Waters 15 October 1810 before D. Boyce, J.P. Recorded October 15, 1810.

Deed Book J: 180
June 2, 1810. Deed of Gift. Know all men by these presents that I Richard Shackleford of Laurens District, South Carolina for and in consideration of the love good will and affection which I have and do bear toward my daughter in law Mary Shackleford, (the present wife of my son George Shackleford) of the state and district aforesaid, to the children lawfully begotten by them that is living at the time of the said Mary Shacklefords death have given and by these presents do freely give unto the said children aforesaid one Negro girl slave about 15 years of age named Esther and her increase to have and to hold the said slave before mentioned unto the said children aforesaid their heirs and assigns forever -.. After the death of said Mary Shackleford the said Negro together with their increase (if any there be) to be equally divided between the surviving children of the said George and Mary Shackleford. Set my hand 2 June 1810 Richd. Shackleford. Wit. Jas.{James Atwood} Atd. Williams, Jas. Dyson. Proved by James Dyson 23 October 1810 before Charles Griffin, J.P. Recorded November 14, 1810.

Deed Book J: 182
October 13, 1810. Bill of Sale. I James Word of Laurens District, South Carolina in consideration of the sum of $500 paid by Thomas Lewers have sold unto the said Thomas Lewers one Negro boy named Edmund about 17

years of age and do hereby warrant him sound sober and honest... Set my hand 13 October - James Word. Wit. William Irby. Proved by William Irby 22 December 1810 before John Garlington, Clerk Laurens Dist. Recorded December 22, 1810.

Deed Book J: 204
February 12, 1810. Bill of Sale. I James Medley of Laurens County, south Carolina in consideration of the sum of $250; sell unto said James Young, merchant, of same place, a certain Negro called Sarah, new, about 8 years old, which is willed to me the said Medley by James Young, deceased, my father in law in his last will and testament.... Set my hand Set 12 February 1810 James Medley. Wit. B. Nabers, Saml. Barksdale. Proved by Samuel Barkesdale 4 March 1811 before Wm. Arnold, J.Q. Recorded March 5, 1811.

Deed Book J: 205
September 22, 1809. Bill of Sale. I John Dobbins of Rockingham, North Carolina in consideration of the sum of $670; sell unto the said James Young, merchant, Laurens District, South Carolina two Negro woman, one of the name of Sharlott about 18 years old the other named Milley about 23 years of age both dark complection.. Set my hand 22 September 1809. John M. Dobbins. Wit. James H. Dendy, Thomas White. Proved by James H. Dendy 22 October 1810 before Z. Bailey, J.P. Recorded March 5, 1811.

Deed Book J: 208
November 17, 1810. Mortgage. I George Madden of Laurens District, South Carolina have for and in consideration of an obligation or note of hand given by said Madden and John Watson security to Martin and Wm. Graves administrators of the Estate of Lewis Graves, deceased for $520 which note was given for two Negroes named Rachel and her child Phillip from the property of the said L. Graves, deceased, which Negroes above named I do mortgage and by these presents deliver to John Watson of the same place, for his use and behoof for his giving me in the said note above mentioned or mortgage... dated 17 November 1810 George Madden. Wit. Joseph Jones, Patsy (mark) Jones. Proved by Joseph Jones 17 November 1810 before Larkin Gaines, J.P. Recorded April 2, 1811.

Deed Book J: 212
January 8, 1811. I Jeremiah Manley, of Laurens District, South Carolina in consideration of the sum of $125 have sold unto to John P. Cunningham of the same place a certain Negro woman named Phebe and her child Mary, the wench about 18 or 19 years old, and the child something more that one year. .. Set my hand 8 January 1811 Jeremiah (mark) Manley. Wit. John

Cochran, Robert Matthews. Proved by John Cockran that he was present and did see Jeremiah Manley sign and deliver the within mortgage . 1 April 1811 before Robert McNess, J.P. Recorded April 13, 1811.

Deed Book J: 218
December 12, 1810. Bill of Sale. Whereas before my intermarriage with Judith Swan for and in consideration of a marriage contract between the said Judith and myself. I became bound unto William Ligon, Trustee of the said Judith in the penal sum of $3000; execute good and different rights in law and Equity to the property herein after mentioned to the said William Ligon, trustee. I do hereby sell and dispose of unto the said William Ligon, trustee all my right, title or claim to the following property; namely one Negro man named Scurm and Negro woman named Polly with Lusen her child, and girl Mariah, together with their future increase, one boy Tom and one feather bed and furniture in trust for Judith Swan, formerly but now Judith Allen, my wife to be disposed of at her will and pleasure. Set my hand 20 December 1810 Saml. Allen. Wit. John Bickley. Proved by John Bickley 10 June 1811 before John Garlington, Clk. Laurens Dist. Recorded June 10, 1811.

Deed Book J: 219-220
November 26, 1810. Bill of Sale. Peter Hammond of Laurens District, South Carolina to John McHarg for $900, one negro man named George and one negro woman called Sarah. Peter Hammond. Wit. John Milner, William Garrett. Proved by John Milner 20 April 1811 before Joseph Downs, J.P. Recorded June 10, 1811. John Garlington, Register.

Deed Book J: 221
March 8, 1811. Bill of Sale. I John Puckett, Esquire, of Laurens District, South Carolina in consideration of the sum of $257 paid by Alexr. Wilkinson of the same place, have sold unto the said Alexr. Wilkinson one Negro girl named Jane, supposed to be about 13 years old, which Negro has been in the possession of the said Alexr. Wilkinson about 12 months,... Set my hand 8 March 1811 John Puckett Wit. Joe. McCrarey, Thomas McCrary, Junr. Proved by Thomas McCrary Junr. 10 June 1811 before Robert Long. Recorded June 17, 1811.

Deed Book J: 224
June 19, 1811. Separation Suit. Whereas Judith Williams, wife of Josiah Williams of Laurens District, South Carolina hath by her next friend John A. Elmore, filed a bill against the said Josiah Williams in the Court of Equity for Washington District praying for a separate maintenance and that but three daughters Louisa, Ann and Martha be give up to her, to be raised

and educated under her care, and whereas upon the bearing thereof it was ordered that alimony be allowed to the said Judith, that the said three daughters be given up to her and a sum allowed for their support., maintenance and education, and the said Josiah Williams being willing to give up the said children and little certain property .. Know all men by these present that I Josiah Williams in consideration of the promises above mentioned and of the sum of $1830 to me paid hereby have sold unto John A. Elmore of the same place the following property. Tom a fellow about 35 years of age, Doll a Negro woman about 30 years old, Bet a girl about 14, Munna a girl about 9 years old, two feather beds, bedsteads and furniture, ... unto the said John A. Elmore and his heirs is for the use and benefit of the said Judith Williams and her three daughters Louisa, Ann and Martha, and after the death of the said Judith to be equally divided between the said Louisa, Ann and Martha or the survivors -...Set my hand 19 June 1811 Josiah Williams, Wit. Patrick Noble, R. Creswell Proved by Robert Creswell 8 July 1811 before John Garlington, Clk. Laurens Dist. Recorded July 8, 1811.

Deed Book J: 227
August 8, 1811. I James Dial of Laurens District, South Carolina do hereby deliver unto the said Hastings Dial and his lines all my right, title, interest and claim, which I have under and by virtue of the last will and testament of my father Hastings Dial, deceased to the following Negroes, to wit. Pat, Mary, Mary Ann, Lavinia, Anderson, Anne, Caesar, Fanny and Prince; also all my household and kitchen furniture, plantation and working tools stock of cattle, hogs and sheep; also my first cut crop of corn, oats, cotton, fodder...all and singular the property above mentioned unto the said Hastings Dial and his lines in trust to and for the following uses, interest and purposes, to wit, for the sole and separate use, lawful and behalf of my wife Elizabeth Dial, for and during the time of her natural life and after her death for the use and ---------all the children, I now have or hereafter may have by my said wife Elizabeth, to be equally divided Share and share alike, and their respective shares to be delivered to them as they respectively arise to the age of 21 years or are married, and I do hereby have myself, my heirs, executors and administrators to warrant and forever unto the said Hastings Dial.... Set my hand 8 August 1811. James Dial. Wit. R. Creswell and C. Saxon. Proved by Charles Saxon 8 August 1811 before John Garlington, Clk. Laurens Dist. Recorded August 8, 1811.

Deed Book J: 228
August 8, 1811. Bill of Sale. I George Wolff of Laurens District, South Carolina, in consideration of the sum of $700 paid by James Word have sold and delivered unto said James Word two Negroes, to Viz., Lewis and

Sam ... Set my hand 15 August 1811. George Wolf. Wit. R. Cresell, Wm. Irby. Proved by William Irby on 16 August 1811 before John Garlington, Clk. Laurens Dist.

Deed Book J: 229
August 15, 1811. Bill of Sale. George Wolff, of Laurens District, South Carolina, in consideration of the sum of $700 have sold to Samuel Nabors, of the same place, two negroes Harry and Jack. George Wolf (Seal) Wit. R. Creswell, James Word. Proved by Robert Creswell August 16, 1811 before J. Garlington, Clerk Laurens Dist. Recorded August 16, 1811. John Garlington, Register.

Deed Book J: 233
June 1, 1811. Bill of Sale. I Lewis Saxon of Laurens District, South Carolina in consideration of the sum of $350 paid by William F. Downs of the same place, have sold unto the said William F. Downs, a certain Negro woman named Alice about 24 years of age with her future increase in trust to and for the following use and purpose to Wit., for the use of Charles Simmons, Lewis Simmons, Pamela Simmons, John Simmons and Polley Simmons, the children of John Simmons by his late wife Judah Simmons deceased until the youngest child Polley Simmons comes of age, then the said Negro woman Alice with her future increase to be divided equally between the said Charles Simmons, Lewis Simmons, Pamela Simmons, John Simmons and Polly Simmons or the survivors of them share and share alike. Set my hand 1 June 1811. L. Saxon. Wit. J. Laughridge, John Simmons. Proved by James Laughridge 2 October 1811 before John Garlington, Ckl. Laurens Dist. Recorded October 2, 1811.

Deed Book J: 237
October 25, 1811. Deed of Gift. James Robert and Salley Roberts, of Laurens District, South Carolina for the Natural Love and Affection which I have for the said James Atwood have granted and released unto said James Atwood all our plantation containing 100 acres and all the slaves and other articles of property. Jas. (Mark) Roberts, Sally (Mark) Roberts. Wit. Jacob Williams, Ann Shirley. Bob, Seld, Hannar, Sarah, Amsted, William, Rachal and Cheve and Harness 3 head of horses, 11 head of cattle, one mans saddle and womans, 34 head of hogs, crops: corn, cotton, wheat, and oats, tobacco. ...... Jas. (Mark) Roberts, Salley (mark) Roberts. Proved by Ann Shirley October 25, 1811. Wit. Jacob Williams, Ann Shirley before Gabriel Jowell, J.P. Recorded Oct. 25, 1811.

Deed Book J: 238
October 21, 1811. Deed of Gift: I James McCary of Laurens District, South Carolina in consideration of the Natural Love and Affection which I have and bear unto my beloved daughters Caty and Nancy McCary and also for other divers good causes and considerations I do here by grant and present unto the said Caty and Nancy McCary one Negro woman named Any and her two children named Maria and Samuel to have and to hold ... Set my hand 21 October 1811 James McCary. Wit. A. Crenshaw, James Laughridge. Proved by James Loughridge 26 October 1811 before John Garlington, Q.M. Recorded October 25, 1811.

Deed Book J: 247
October 19, 1811. Bill of Sale. Whereas certain disputes have for some time past existed between Jesse Reese and his wife Nancy and whereas the said Jesse Reese hath agreed as well for the present a future happiness of himself and family to settle the property herein after mentioned in trust for the sole and separate use and benefit such children as the said Jesse now has or hereafter may have by his said wife Nancy. Now know all men by these presents that I Jesse Reese of Laurens District, South Carolina, in consideration of the primuses above mentioned and also for an in consideration of the sum of $2000 paid by Jonathan York of the County of Bedford, State of Tennessee have sold and released into said Jonathan York one tract of land whereon my said wife Nancy Reese now lives containing 247 acres, and every species of personal property to me belonging or in my wife appertaining excepting one gray horse saddle and bridle and one feather bed and furniture which I now have in my possession consisting of the following pieces of property, Viz., one Negro boy named Jack, one black mare, five heads of cattle eighteen heads of hogs, fourteen heads of geese and other pottery, two feather beds and furniture. . . . . Set my hand 19 October 1911 Jesse Reese. Wit. Archd. Young. William Pugh. Proved by William Pugh 1 January 1872 before John Garlington, Q.M. Recorded January 1, 1812.

Deed Book J: 250
October 20, 1811. Marriage Settlement Bond: I Moses Tennent of Laurens District, South Carolina in consideration of a certain Bond given by me on the 4 March 1809 for the sum of $2000 to John D. Heath of the City of Charleston, South Carolina conditioned for the settling and securing of estate and property to that amount in South Carolina upon my wife Frances H. Tennant in consideration of her agreeing to sell her marriage portion which as a plantation tract of land owned by her of the value aforesaid in Kent County, on the Eastern Shore of Maryland which said plantation has since been sold accordingly, in further consideration of the Natural Love

and Affection which I have and bear to my said wife and for the settling and securing her marriage portion aforesaid in conformity with the condition on the said bond and in conformity with the dictates of natural Justice and Equity And also for the valuable consideration of $1000 to me in hand paid by the said John D. Heath as a further augmentation of the marriage portion or fortune of the said Frances H. Tennant, which last mortised sum I do hereby acknowledge to have received and do hereby acquit and release unto said John D. Heath these several tracts of land owned by me in Laurens District, and which were purchased by me, as to the first plantation on which I now reside of George Adair, and the other on which my saw mill is erected of Mary Campbell, James Campbell, Casey Campbell, Elijah Campbell, Michael Garman, Mary Garman, Henry Campbell and the other kin and heiresses of the said estate and also the following Negro slaves to Wit. One Negro man named Jacob, one Negro woman named Hagen, one Negro girl named Harriet, one Negro boy named Thomas, one Negro girl named Matilda together with the future issue and increase of the female slaves, and also the following stock and household furniture....having ben purchased from the funds resulting from the sale of the marriage partition or estate and property of the said Frances H. Tennant in Kent County in the State of Maryland ..... Set my hand 13 October 1811 Moses Tennett. Wit. John Withers, John Withers, Junr. Proved by John Withers, Junr. 14 January 1812 before Chas. Allen, Q.M. Recorded January 16, 1812.

Deed Book J: 253
June 9, 1810. Marriage Agreement. Be it known to all whom it may concern that I John Creecy have intermarried with Elizabeth Sims, widow of Zachariah Sims, deceased, and as there has been a settlement with the said legatees of the said deceased, by the administrator of the said deceased - as I would wish to assist the said children with the consent of my wife Elizabeth I do hereby give unto the said children of the said deceased, and my wife the following Negroes annexed to their several names (to Wit) to John Sims the Negro girl names Sintha, to Thomas Sims the Negro boy names Aaron, to Jessie Pugh and his wife Lyda the Negro girl named Roda and to James Wit and Sarah his wife the Negro boy named Harry, and James Sims one Negro girl names Betsey to have and to hold the said Negroes to them and to their heirs and as my wife sometime before our marriage did make certain deeds of gifts or other instruments of righting to some of the said children certain Negroes, as the said conveyance did not give unto all the said children an equal part of my wifes estate and to do equal justice between said children respecting said Negroes that did belong to my wife. I do hereby convey the said Negroes to the persons above named as annexed to them now and we the said children of the said deceased being of lawful age do hereby agree that all rights enters into by our mother Elizabeth Sims

61

between her and us before her present marriage to be rescinded and null and void to all interest and purposes. Set our hand 9 June 1810. Jesse (X) Pugh, John Creecy, James Wait, James Sims, John Sims, Thos. Sims. Wit. Dd. Anderson, John Wait. Proved by David Anderson (blank) 1812 before William Fulton, J.P. Recorded February 5, 1812.

Deed Book J: 253
December 12, 1811. Mortgage. Indenture made 12 December 1811 between Moses Tennant of Laurens District, South Carolina of the one part and David Speers of the same place of the other part, whereas the said Moses Tennant by his note of hand dated 28 September 1811 did promise to pay to the said David Speers or bearer $126.33 with interest from the date there of one or before 15 April.. Witnesseth that for and in consideration of the sum of $5 for the better securing the payment of the said sum of $126.33 to the said David Speers according the true intent and promising of the said note, the said Moses Tennant hath sold and delivered unto the said David Speers a certain Negro boy named Thomas about 6 years old ... Set my hand 12 December 1811.Moses Tennant. Wit. R. Creswell. Proved by Robert Creswell 3 February 1812 before Wm. Arnold, J.Q. Recorded February 5, 1812.

Deed Book J: 260
November 11, 1811. Deed of Gift: I John Miller of Laurens District, South Carolina in consideration of the Natural Love and Affection which I have and bear to my beloved son and daughter John Cason and his wife Sarah and also for divers other causes and consideration to me the said John Miller hereunto moving have given granted and confirmed, unto the said John and Sarah Cason one Negro woman named Chloe and her female child about 4 or 5 weeks old to have and to hold...Set my hand 17 March 1812. John (mark) Miller. Wit. David Greer, Anderson Miller, William Miller. Proved by Anderson Miller 18 March 1812 before Wm. Neill, J.P. Recorded April 6, 1812.

Deed Book J: 260
No date. Bill of Sale. Laurens District, South Carolina. Received April 13, 1822 of Titus Bunnel, Junr. Of the State of Connecticut and County of Litchfield $100 the same being in full value for a certain Mulatto female child about 18 months old named (_) ------_the same I have bargained and sold unto the same Titus Bunnel with all her future increase and issue and for the full consideration of the above sum of $100... Set my hand Asa Bunnel. Wit. Robt. (R) Spence, Thomas Waldrop. Proved by Thomas Waldrop on (no date) before David Speers, J.P. Recorded April 13, 1812.

Deed Book J: 268

January 3, 1812. Mortgage. Indenture made 23 January 1812 - Whereas
John Madden of Laurens District, South Carolina hath this day given three
notes of hand to Randal Sullivan for $290 - one of $94 payable 1 March
1813, one for $100 payable 25 December 1813, and one for $100 payable
25 December in 1814 a for better securing the said John Madden from
payment of only part thereof and for and in consideration of the sum of $5
to me in hand pad before sealing have bargained sold and agreed to
mortgage the following property, Viz., one Negro girl about 14 or 15 years
of age named Amy, also a tract of land containing 250 acres whereon
James Sullivan in his lifetime lived and now whereon I now live bounded
by lands belonging to John Boyd, John Madden, Noah Sullivan, Junior,
Charles Madden, Burtons and Stromans..... Set my hand L. Sullivan . Wit.
Thomas Porter, R. Sullivan. Proved by Thomas Porter 22 June 1812 before
John Garlington, Q.M. Recorded June 22, 1812.

Deed Book J: 272

July 17, 1812. Mortgage. To all whom these presents shall come William
Bowen of Laurens District and Horatio Griffin of Greenville District in
South Carolina send Greeting. Whereas we the William Bowen and Horatio
Griffin by our bond are held and firmly bound unto John and Charles Bulow
in the sum of $17,762.92 with a condition the sunder written the payment of
the sum of $8,881.06 unto the said John and Charles Bulow and condition
thereunder written doth more fully and at large appear. Now, Know ye that
we the said William Bowen, and Horatio Griffin for the better securing the
payment of the said sum assign together with lawful interest have bargained
and sold by these presents unto the said John and Charles Bulow - Roddy
about 26 years of age with her three children Jerry, Frank and Monday;
Harry about 18 years old, Jude about 30 years of age with her mulatto child
Nancy; Abb a boy 18 years of age with her boy child Job, Minty about 18
years of age, Big Jim about 26 years of age, Little Sam about 18 years of
age, Big Jack about 35 years of age, Dianna his wife almost 36 years of age,
Will 35 years of age, Febey about 35 years of age with her girl child
Charley, Caroline 26 years of age and Florra 35 years of age...... Set my
hand Wm. Bowen, Senr. Horatio Griffin. Wit. William Bowen, Junr.
Edmond Griffin. Proved by Edmund Griffin 20 July 1812 before Geor. W.
Earle, C.C. & J.Q. Recorded July 25, 1812.

DEED BOOK K: 1812 - 1821

Deed Book K: 3-4
November 12, 1812. Deed of Gift: Josiah East of Laurens District, South
Carolina in consideration of the love and good will that I have and bear to
my son Langsdon East and Elizabeth, his wife have given and bequeathed
unto my son Langdon East four Negroes, namely Jude, Peggy, William and
Fanny forever.... Set my hand 19 August 1812 Josiah East. Wit. Joseph
Willson, A. Glenn. Proved by Joseph Willson 1 January 1813 before Wm.
Niell, J.P. Recorded January 6, 1813.

Deed Book K: 10
October 15, 1812. Bill of Sale. I Gallanus Winn of Laurens District, South
Carolina in consideration of $100 paid by Andrew Winn, do bargain and
sell unto the said Andrew Winn one Negro girl named Vianna about 5
months old the property of the said Vianna I warrant and forever defend
unto the said Andrew Winn. Set my hand 15 October 1812 Gallanus Winn.
Wit. Daniel Winn. Proved by Daniel Winn 5 April 1813 before Wm.
Dendy, J.P. Recorded April 6, 1813.

Deed Book K: 10
October 15, 1812. Bill of Sale. Gallanus Winn of Laurens District, South
Carolina in consideration of $150 have granted and sold unto Rebecca Winn
one Negro girl named Narcissi ... Set my hand 15 October 1812 Gallanus
Winn. Wit. Daniel Winn. Proved by Daniel Winn 5 April 1813 before Wm.
Dendy, J.P. Recorded April 6, 1813.

Deed Book K: 36
August 13, 1813. Deed of Gift: I Ezekiel Griffith of Laurens District, South
Carolina in consideration of the love and good will and affection which I
have towards my grand son Hiram Jones of Greenville District I do freely
give and grant unto said Hiram Jones one Negro boy named Benisten which
boy before signed of these presents I have delivered him the said Hiram
Jones... Set my hand 13 August 1813 Ezekiel (X) Griffith. Wit. Joseph
Brown, Therisa Jones. Proved by Joseph Brown 26 August 1813 before
Thomas Parks, J.P. Recorded December 6, 1813.

Deed Book K: 38
August 11, 1813. Bill of Sale. I Thomas Simmons of Williamson County,
Tennessee in consideration of the sum of $200 paid by Moses Leak have
sold unto said Moses Leak one Negro boy named Lea about five years
old...Set my hand 11 August 1813 Thomas Simmons. Wit. Wm. Anthony,

Wm. Leak. Proved by William Leak 13 November 1813 before Wm.
Dutten, J.P. Recorded December 27, 1813.

Deed Book K: 40
July 23, 1813. Deed of Gift: I Judith Allen, Laurens District, South Carolina
in consideration of the Natural Love and Affection which I have and bear to
my son in law Obadiah Mishouse and also for divers other good causes and
considerations I have granted and do give to Obadiah Mishouse a Negro girl
named Susan to have and to hold.. Set my hand 23 July 1813 Judith Allen.
Wit. Saml. Allen, John P. Swanson. Proved by Samuel Allen 2 January
1814 before James Strain, J.P. Recorded January 3, 1814.

Deed Book K: 42
January 11, 1814. Deed of Gift: I Leonard Miller for the love good will and
affection which I have and do bear unto Mary Hughes, of the same place,
and in consideration of the sum of $1. To me paid by the said Mary Hughes
have sold, conveyed the following property, Viz., all that plantation of land
of 200 acres in the District aforesaid, on the waters of Durbins Creek... also
one Negro girl named Cordelia about 8 years old, four horse creatures, Viz.,
one bay horse about 7 years old and mare sorrel about 10 years old one filly
about 3 years old and one bay horse about 3 years old, household furniture,
plantation tools, etc..... Set my hand 11 January 1814 Leonard (mark)
Miller. Wit. A. Durkee, Thomas Porter. Proved by Thomas Porter 12
January 1814 before John Garlington, Q.M. Recorded January 12, 1814.

Deed Book K: 44
December 24, 1813. Bill of Sale. Indenture made 24 December 1813
between Capt. Josiah Williams of the one part and Josiah Williams, Jr of
the other part, that the said Capt.. Josiah Williams doth deliver one tract of
land containing 380 acres in said District on Dunkins waters of Enoree and
all other property, Viz., one Negro man by the name of Dick, one small
Negro boy by the name of Richard, four feather beds and furniture, all my
stock of cattle, hogs, sheep, geese, chickens and household furniture,
plantation utensils, one waggon, three horses, etc. unto the said Josiah
Williams, Junr. for the sum of $1250. .. Set my hand Josiah Williams. Wit.
John Williams, Daniel Williams. Proved by John Williams 1 February 1814
before Robt. Long, J.P. Recorded February 7, 1814.

Deed Book K: 57
April 25, 1814. Emancipation. Laurens District, South Carolina. We hereby
certify upon the examination and oath of Mary Arnold the owner of a
certain slave named Matt about 5 feet 8" high of a yellow completion , stout
made, about 36 years of age satisfactory proof have been given to us this

65

the said slave is of a good character and capable of gaining a livelihood by honest means. Certified by us this 25 April 1814. Jonathan Downs, J.P., Jesse Childress, J.P., Jessey Garrett, Robert Coker. {Freeholder - Abraham Botte, Ezekl. Mathews, J.P.

Know ye I Mary Arnold of the state and District aforesaid in consideration of the sum of $500 to me paid by my fellow named Matt do emancipate and set free the said Negro man to all intents and purposes... Set my hand 23 April 1814. Mary Arnold. Proved by Ezekiel Mathews, 27 April 1814 before Jonathn. Downs, J.Q. Recorded April 27, 1814.

Deed Book K: 57
January 21, 1814. Deed of Trust. I George Bowen of Laurens District, South Carolina in consideration of the sum of $50 paid by Hardy Conant of the same place so sell and deliver unto said Hardy Conant one Negro girl slaved named Oban? Unto said Hardy Conant and to the intent that the said Hardy Conant shall at all time permit my wife Tabertha Bowen to have process and the use the said Negro girl for and during her natural life and to apply the profits of these to maintenance of my said wife and my who children and at the death of my said wife the said Hardy Conant shall convey the said slave and her increase in equal parts to my said children both of them shall be then living, or to the survivors and.... Wit my hand 21 January 1814 Geo. Bowen. Wit. Wm. Dendy. Proved by William Dendy 2 May 1814 before John Garlington, Q.M. Recorded May 2, 1814.

Deed Book K: 60
December 3, 1812. Administration of Estate. Mrs. Young as you one about administering on William Young estate and I do not know whither you understand the way he held the woman Doll I never invested myself of the unite to her until since the death of my daughter then from the great regard I had for him I agreed to let him keep her and her increase during his lifetime and if she ever had children they might have them and if she had none that at her death they were to return to me from your friend .... Joel Lipscomb. November 30, 1812. Wit. Mrs. Betsey Young. Jos. Neely.

I do hereby give and relinquish all my right title and claim of the within mentioned Negro woman Doll all per present and further increase to my two children, Viz., Agnes Lipscomb Young and William Jones Young to them and their heirs... 3 December 1812 Elizabeth Young. Wit. Jos. Neely. Proved by Joseph Neely 7 Feb. 1814 before S. Cuningham, J.P. Recorded May 2, 1814.

Deed Book K: 61
February 7, 1814. Bill of Sale. Hardy Conant, of Laurens District, South
Carolina to Stephen Garrett, Esq. For the sum of $300a negro woman
named Nancy, dark complexion, 11years old. Hardy (C) Conant (seal). Wit.
Turner Richardson, Stephen Harris. Proved by Turner Richardson May 4,
1814 before John Garlington, J.P. Recorded May 14, 1814. John Garlington,
Registrar.

Deed Book K: 67
March 14, 1814. Deed of Gift. Whereas John Miller in his lifetime and
before his intermarriage with Sarah Cason his last wife to wit sometime in
the month of October 1807 did by a deed of gift duly executed in the
presence of William Niell Esquire and John Hunter give and convey to his
children William Teague and Elizabeth his wife, John Cason and Sarah his
wife, Zebulon Matthews and Jane his wife, Abraham Johnson and Ann his
wife, Joseph Cason and Rebecca his wife, George Miller, James Miller,
Joshua Smith and Polly his wife, John Miller, Anderson Miller, and William
Millers there heirs and assigns the tract of land the first tract whereon the
said John Miller then lived containing 600 acres on Bush River in Laurens
District adjoining Joshua Teague, Elizabeth Teague, Thos. Cason, William
Cason, William Niell and lands said to belong to Kirk, the other tract of
land situated on Bush River in Newbury containing 120 commonly called
Chandlers Mill Place adjoining John Level, Charles Crew, Charles Leopart
and West Gary. Also the following Negroes to Wit. Moses, Poter, Easter,
Cloe, Anni, Nelly, Rachel, Charles and David to be equally divided between
his said children share and share alike and since the execution of the said
deed one of the above Negroes to Wit. Cloe has had two children, one
named Polly and the other name not recollected being in the possession of
John Cason and another of the above named Negroes to Wit. Annis has had
one child named Nancy and whereas the said John Miller before his
intermarriage with the said Sarah showed to her the said deed that she might
know in what manner he had disposed of his property and whereas the said
Sarah with a free knowledge of the said deed afterwards intermarried with
the said John Miller on or about the 2 February - case departed this life
intestate leaving the said Sarah his widow and Elizabeth the wife of W.
Teague land, the wife of John Cason, Jane the wife of Zebulon Mathews,
Ann the wife of Abraham Johnson, Rebecca wife of Joseph Cason, George
Miller, James Miller, Polley the wife of Joshua Smith, John Miller,
Anderson Miller and William Miller whereby the said Sarah the widow of
the said John Miller would have been entitled to one third percent of the
said tracts of land and Negroes, herein before mentioned have not the said
John Miller prior to his intermarriage with the said Sarah given the said

lands and Negroes to his said children by the deed aforesaid. And whereas since the death of the said John Miller's administration on his goods and chattels rights and credits hath been granted to his son George Miller and whereas the said children of the said John Miller hath become dissatisfied in consequence of the destruction of the said deed of gift under a belief that the said Sarah intends to contract with them for her distributive share of the real and personal estate mentioned in the said deed and whereas said Sarah is willing to remove these dissatisfactions and reinstate these sights under the said deed by relinquishment to them all the right title claim or demand which she as the widow of the said John Miller might or could have in law or Equity to the said lands and Negroes mentioned in the said deed.

I Sarah Miller of Laurens District, South Carolina, widow and relict of the said John Miller, deceased for an in consideration of the promises herein before stated have conveyed and released unto the said William Teague and Elizabeth his wife, John Cason and Sarah his wife, Zebulon Mathews and Jane his wife, Abraham Johnson and Ann his wife, Joseph Cason and Rebecca his wife, George Miller, James Miller, Joshua Smith and Polly his wife, John Miller, Anderson Miller and William Miller all my right title claim ro demand which I as the widow of the said John Miller might or could have to the tracts of land and Negroes herein before stated to have been conveyed and given by the said John Miller before his intermarriage with me by the deed of Gift aforesaid... Set my hand 15 March 1814 Sarah (X) Miller. Wit. John Monro, John Hewet. Proved by John Hewit on 30 July 1814 before Wm. Neill, J.P. Recorded August 1, 1814.

Deed Book K: 69
March 8, 1814. Bond. Indenture between Samuel Todd and Larkin Sullivan, both of Laurens District, South Carolina. A bond on 242 acres on Beaverdam Creek and Little River; bounded on Charles Madden, Benj. Sullivan, Stroman, John Boyd, Widow Madden, where said Larkin Sullivan now lives. Also one negro man named Lews aged about 50 years and one negro woman Lyd aged about 45 years, one gray name aged 12 years, one bay mare aged 5 years... etc. L. Sullivan (seal). Wit. Tho. Porter, William Manly. Proved by Thomas Porter 8 August 1814 before Starling Tucker, JQ. Recorded August 30, 1814. John Garlington, Registrar.

Book K: 72
October 14, 1814. Deed of Gift. Whereas William Roberts of Halifax County, Virginia did by a deed dated 13 April 1775 give to Maryan Shackelford and her husband Richard Shackelford the use, labour and profits of a certain Negro girl slave named Lucy with her issue during each of the natural lives to the only proper use of the said Maryann Shackelford and Richard Shackelford her husband and after there decease did give the

68

said slave together with her increase if any to be divided amongst the children of the said Maryann Shackelford the issue of her body by her husband Richard Shackelford in the form and manner they should think proper. Know ye that we Richard Shackelford and Maryann Shackelford in pursuance of the power vested in us by the said deed to divide the said Negro slave and her increase among our children in such form and manner as we thought proper did lend unto our beloved daughter Elizabeth on her marriage with Abner Pyles a small Negro girl named Jane now know ye this that as our beloved daughter Elizabeth Pyles has departed this life, we Richard and Maryann Shackelford in confirmation of our original intention do freely and clearly give unto our grand daughter Matilda Pyles and after her decease to the issue of her body the said Negro slave Jane together with all her issue one small boy excepted by the name of Jim whom we freely give unto our grandson Newton Pyles but in case either should die without issue we give the said Negroes with there increase to be equally divided amongst the children of Elizabeth Pyles deceased all of which property we do give to Matilda and Newton Pyles in the manner mentioned ... Set my hand 1814 Richard Shackelford, Maryann (X) Shackelford. Wit. George Shackelford . Recorded October 14, 1814.

Deed Book K: 76
October 4, 1814. Mortgage. Indenture 4 October 1814 between Priscilla Clopton of Laurens District, South Carolina of the one part and Isaac Johnson and Ainsowrth Middleton of the same place of the other part. Whereas the said Priscilla Clopton administrix on her husband David Clopton, deceased estate sometime in December last and the said Jesse Johnson and Airsworth Middleton were her securities to David Anderson ordinary of Laurens District for the sum the sum of $1017. Now this Indenture that the said Presilla Clopton in consideration of the security ship as above stated and for the better securing the said Jesse Johnson and Ainsworth Middleton doth mortgage the following property .. To wit: one Negro man named Frank, one Negro woman named Mary, one Negro boy named Jerry about 12 or 14 years old, one Negro girl named Charity about 12 years old with their future issue -also one third part of an undivided tract of land on the waters of Indian Creek in said District containing 207 acres it being the place where the said Priscilla Clopton now lives. ... Set my hand Pricellah (X) Clopton. Wit. Robert Johnson, Oswell Bevis. Proved by Oswell Bevis 3 December 1814 before W. Niell, J.P. Recorded December 29, 1814.

Deed Book K: 111
January 20, 1815. Mortgage. Whereas Hiram Sims of Laurens District, South Carolina by his note of hand indebted to Charles Saxon and William

F. Downs administrators of Lewis Saxon deceased in the sum of $510
payable 12 months after date referenced... Now know ye that the said Hiram
Sims for the better securing the payment of the said sum of $510 to the said
Charles Saxon and William F. Downs administrators as aforesaid recorded
to the time intent and meaning of the said note of hand have granted and
sold unto the said Charles Saxon and William F. Downs. Administrators,
two parcels of land...... and take into possession the said tracts of land and
the said Negro boy Stephen and the same to sell and dispose of returning the
overage if any to the said Hiram Sims... Sit his hand 1815 Hiram Sims. Wit.
B. Nabers, Jonathn.. Downs, Junr. Proved by Benjamin Nabers 8 December
1815 before Robert McNeese, J.P. Recorded December __, 1815.

Deed Book K: 116
September 9, 1815.Deed of Gift: I William Irby of the District of Laurens,
South Carolina, planter, for and in consideration of the love good will and
affection which I have and do bear towards my loving daughter Frances Irby
of the same place have given and granted unto the said Frances Irby one
Negro boy named Tony which before the signing I have also delivered her
the said Frances Irby an inventory signed with my own hand ... Set my hand
9 September 1815 Wm. Irby. Wit. Rody Kennedy, Hennietta Irby. Proved
by Rody Kennedy 2 February 1816 before John Garlington, QM. Recorded
February 2, 1816.

Deed Book K: 116
August 12, 1815. Deed of Gift: I William Irby of the District of
Laurensville, South Carolina, planter, for and in consideration of the love
good will and affection which I have and do bear towards my loving
daughter Polly Irby of the same place have given and granted unto the said
Polly Irby one Negro girl named Pat which before the signing I have also
delivered her the said Frances Irby an inventory signed with my own hand
... Set my hand 12 September 1815 Wm. Irby. Wit. J.H. Irby, Heta. Irby.
Proved by James H. Irby 3 February 1816 before John Garlington, Clk of
Laurens Dist. QM. Recorded February 3, 1816.

Deed Book K: 116
August 24, 1815. Deed of Gift. I William Irby of the District of Laurens,
South Carolina, planter, for and in consideration of the love good will and
affection which I have and do bear towards my loving daughter Nancy Irby
of the same place have given and granted the following goods and chattels,
Viz., one Negro boy know and called by the name of Ben and I have also
delivered her the said Frances Irby an inventory signed with my own hand
... Set my hand 24 August 1815 Wm. Irby. Wit. J.H. Irby, Polly Irby.

Proved by James H. Irby 3 February 1816 before John Garlington, QM. Recorded February 3, 1816.

Deed Book K: 117
October 1, 1815. Deed of Gift: I William Irby of the District of Laurens, South Carolina, planter, for and in consideration of the love good will and affection which I have and do bear towards my loving daughter Sarah Irby of the same place have given and granted unto the said Sarah Irby one Negro girl named Eady now in my possession and all her future increase I have also delivered her the said Sarah Irby an inventory signed with my own hand... Set my hand 6 February 1816. Wit. Frances Irby, Polly Irby. Proved by Frances Irby 6 February 1816 before John Garlington, QM. Recorded February 6, 1815.

Deed Book K: 117
December 24, 1815. Deed of Gift: I Benjamin Burch Cheshire of Laurens District, South Carolina in consideration of the Natural Love and Affection which I bear to my son Hezekiah Cheshire as for the further consideration fo $1. To me in hand paid have given and granted to the said Hezekiah Cheshire my son a Negro boy named Pleasant, also a girl named Maria to have and to hold forever... Set my hand 24 December 1815 Benja. B. Cheshire (BBC). Wit. Wm. Black, Jno. Black. Proved by William Black 23 December 1815 before Elijah Watson, J.P. Recorded February 6, 1816.

Deed Book K: 136
July 20, 1816. Emancipation. I Mary Williams of Laurens District, South Carolina in consideration of the sum of $800 do hereby acknowledge this day emancipated and set free to all interest and purposes, my two Negroes, Viz., Humphry about 35 years of age, 5 feet 6 in. High, black complexion and Hetty his wife about 36 hears old, 5 feet six in. High, black complexion. I do hereby forever relinquish all claim whatever to the services of the said Humphry and Hettey; as slaves. And I do hereby request all good citizens of this State and the United States, to treat, them as free Negroes. Set my hand this 20 July 1816. Signed Mary Williams. Wit. B. Nabers, Gabriel Jowel. Proved by Benjamin Nabours 22 July 1816 before Chas. Allen, QM.

We hereby certify, that upon the examination on oath of Mary Williams, the owner of two slaves, named Humphry and Hetty about 36 years old, 5 feet 6 In. High of black complexion. Satisfactory proof has been given to us, that the said slaves are not of bad character and quite capable of gaining a livelihood by honest means. Given under our hands this 26 July 1816. B. Nabers, Isaac Dial, Gabriel Jowell, John Madden [free holders] Recorded August 5, 1816.

Deed Book K: 138
August 20, 1816. Emancipation. Laurens District, South Carolina: In obedience to a summons issued by Jonathan Downs, J.P. agreeable to an Act of the General Assembly in such case made and provided, we whose names are hereunto subscribed do hereby certify that upon the examination and oath of Mary Arnold (widow) the owner of a certain Negro man slave named Titus, 5 ft. 10" high about 60 years of age. Satisfactory proof has been given us that the said Negro man Slave Titus is of good character, capable of gaining a living by honest means. Certified 20 August 1816 by Freeholders Rob. Coke, Calvill A. Cromer, William Gary, Jesse Garrett, T.F. Wolff before Jonthn. Downs, J.Q.

Know all men by these presents that I Mary Arnold of the State and District aforesaid, in consideration of the sum of 400 paid in hand do hereby acknowledge and manumitted and set free a certain Negro man slave named Titus 5' 6" high about 60 years of age, and hereby warrant and forever defend the said Negro in his freedom against myself and my heirs, and against every other person lawfully claiming the said Negro. And I do hereby relinquish all my right and title to im the said Negro or his services henceforth... Set my hand 20 August 1816. Mary Arnold. Wit. C. Saxon, Wm. C. Gary, John Dourah. Proved by Charles Saxon 20 August 1816 before Jonthan. Downs, JQ.
Recorded August 21, 1816.

Deed Book K: 139
April 6, 1816. Bill of Sale. I Marmaduke Pinson of one part for and in consideration of the sum of $100; paid by Abijah Pinson of the other part whereof I do hereby acknowledge have bargained sold and delivered in plain and open market deliver unto the said Abijah Pinson a certain female Negro salve named Moline, to have and to hold the said slave and her future offspring, and increase unto the said Abijah Pinson .... Set my hand 6 April 1816 Marmaduke Pinson. Wit. David Madden, Js. Pinson. Proved by David Madden, Junr 2 September 1816 before Chas. Allen, Q.M. Recorded September 3, 1816.

Deed Book K: 139
March 5, 1816. Bill of Sale. Know all men by these presents that I William Hollidy, Senior in consideration of the sum of $300; to me paid by Thomas Norris Senior has bargains sold and do sell unto the said Thomas Norris a Negro woman by the name of Sarah which said Negro woman I warrant said property I also warrant and defend her from my sold and my heirs... Set my hand 5 March 1816 William Holiday. Wit. Robert Hollidy, Matthew

Hollidy. Proved by Matthew Hollidy 2 September 1816 before S. Cunningham, J.P. Recorded September 3, 1816.

Deed Book K: 139
September 9, 1816. Deed of Gift: I Nancy Couch of Laurens District, South Carolina in consideration of the Natural Love and Affection which I have to my daughter Roady Couch as well as for the consideration of $1; to me in hand paid have given and granted unto my said daughter Roady Couch , her heirs and assigns forever a certain female Negro child named Phillis about 15 years old... Set by hand 10 September 1816 Nancy (X) Couch. Wit. Archd. Young. Jno. N. Young. Proved by John N. Young 10 September 1816 before John Garlington, QM. Recorded September 10, 1816.

Deed Book K: 140
December 2, 1815. Mortgage. Allen Kelley to Robert Creswell, mortgage on one?? acres lot adjacent Swancy Road, Crenshaw and Jones horse lot. Also on a mulatto slave Peggy purchased from Nancy Liles. Wit. John Cunningham, Caty Cunningham. Proved by John Cunningham 9 September 1816. Before J. Hitch, J.P. Recorded September 10, 1816, John Garlington Register.

Deed Book K: 148
October 28, 1816. Bill of Sale. Laurens District, South Carolina February 8, 1810. Know all man by these presents that I David Davenport do bargain and sell unto Richard Davenport two Negro girls, one named Rose, the other Seal which was wiled {sic} to him my his father John Davenport in consideration of the sum of $400... Set my hand David Davenport. Wit. Jno.(mark) Varill, David Whiteford. Proved by John Verrell 28 October 1816 before Wm. Dendy, J.P. Recorded November 5, 1816.

Deed Book K: 162
January 15, 1817. Emancipation: Laurens District, South Carolina, We do hereby certify upon the examination on oath of Henry Harding the owner of a certain slave named Andrew supposed to be about 67 years of age satisfactory has been given to us that the said slave is not of bad character and is capable of gaining a likelihood by honest means. Given under out hand 15 January 1817. Wm. Niell, J.P., John Monry, Josh. {Joseph} Blackerby, George Miller, Thomas Goggans, Abraham (X) Johnson.

To all to whom these presents come Greeting Know ye that I Henry Haring of the district above mentioned, did for divers good causes and considerations thereunto me have this day set free and forever Emancipated my Negro man Andrew supposed to be about 67 years old, which Negro was left to me by my father William Harding, and which hath been adjudged by a justice and free holders agreeable to the Act of Assembly in that case made and to be of good character and capable of gaining a likelihood in an honest way and I do here by for myself, my heirs executers and administrators give and grant and forever quit claim to all title and command whatsoever in and over the said Negro man Andrew as a slave .....Set my hand 15 January 1817 Henry Harding. Wit. John Monro, Josh. {Joseph} Blackerby. Proved by John Munro{sic} 15 January 1817 before Wm. Niell, J.P. Recorded February 25, 1817.

Deed Book K: 169
January 30, 1814. Dispute Settlement. We whose names are under written do award order and adjudge that James Duncan shall pay John Jeans $110 and the said John Jeans shall deliver to the said James Duncan the Negroes in dispute between them upon the receipt of the money above mentioned and each man pay his own cost. Witness our hands and seals this 30 September 1814. William Word, Bordy Roberts, Moses Whitten, Levi Fowler, Richard Bennett . Proved by Moses Whitten that he saw Levi Fowler, William Word and Richard Bennett sign and seal the within award...12 April 1817 before Benjn. Duckett, J.P. Recorded April 12 1817.

Deed Book K: 173
March 24, 1817. Bill of Sale. David Hitt to Robert Cunningham, both of Laurens District, South Carolina for the sum of $500; 150 acres on Saluda Waters, land on which David now resides. Also the following negroes, Toney and his wife Agatha and their two children Amos and Peter, also my negro boy Nathan. David Hitt. Wit. Chas. C. Mayson, Willis Bostick, Proved by Charles C. Mayson 18 April 1817 before Wm. Nibbs, JQ. Recorded April 24, 1817. John Garlington, Registrar.

Deed Book K: 174
May 7, 1817. Emancipation: Laurens District, South Carolina, I do hereby certify unto all whom it may concern that for and in consideration of the industry care fidelity and good behavior of a Negro woman Slave to me for 28 years past I have covenanted agreed emancipated and freed the said Negro wench named Easter, and by these presents do bargain Emancipate and free the said Negro Easter, and do hereby warrant and forever defend the said Negro in her freedom against my self and my heirs and assigns and against all persons whomsoever claiming her the said Negro woman Easter as their property. And the said Negro woman Easter is hereby declared free without any let hindrance or molestations or interruption any person or persons whomsoever either in this State of the United States. Set my hand 7 May 1817. Jno. Pringle. Wit. Elisha Williamson. John Loveless.

Agreeable to an act of Assembly of the State aforesaid baring date 12 December 1800 I William Arnold one of the Justices of the Quorum being informed by John Pringle that he had an intention to emancipate and set free a certain Negro woman named Easter. ; Pursuant thereto I issued summonses to give freeholders who accordingly the said slave being present and after asking the said John Pringle the necessary questions on oath by law do give the following certificate, Viz., we do hereby certify upon the examination oath of John Pringle the owner of his slave woman Easter about 40 years old about 5' high, stock made black complexion, satisfactory proof has been given to us that the said Slave is of good character and capable of gaining a livelihood by honest means. 7 May 1817. Wm. Arnold, JQ., Abraham Riley, Elisha Williamson, John Loveless, John Taylor, Robert Nabors. Proved by John Loveless 7 May 1817 before Wm. Arnold, J.Q. Recorded May 12, 1817.

Deed Book K: 180
November 4, 1816. Bill of Sale - Emancipation - (with land laid off to a free black woman). I John Cook of Laurens District, South Carolina in consideration of the sum of $450 paid by John Meek of Abbeville, South Carolina, have granted and sold unto the said John Meek all that plantation of land lying in the State and District aforesaid on the head branch of Mill Creek joining land of William Phillips, John Gates, Charles Eagerton, and a part laid off to a free black woman named Lara?.... Set my hand 4 November 1816 John Cook. Wit. Joseph Cook, John Atkinson. Dower by Katherine Cook, wife of the within John Cook 10 March 1817 before Wm. Pollard, J.Q. Proved by John Adkinsson 10 April 1817 before Wm. Pollard, J.Q. Recorded August 1, 1817.

Deed Book K: 184
January 28, 1815. Deed of Gift: I Sarah Wright, widow, of Laurens District, South Carolina for divers good causes love good will and affection do hereby give and grant unto Robert Shirley and his wife Ann grand daughter one Negro boy about 7 years old by the name of Lan.. And I do hereby bind myself my heirs executors and administrators to warrant and forever defend the right of the said Negro Lan unto the said Robert Shirley and wife Ann and their heirs forever... Set my hand 28 January 1815 Sarah Wright. Wit. Jacob Niswanger. Proved by Jacob Niswanger 14 September 1817 before David Anderson, J.Q. Recorded September 16, 1817.

Deed Book K: 186
August 28, 1817. Security Bond. Whereas Turner Richardson of Laurens District, South Carolina at the special instance and request of John Snead of the same place, and for the sole Debt of the said John Snead dated 8

September 1817 did jointly bound with the said John Snead unto Isaac Mitchell in the sum of $120 for the payment of the said $120 on or before the 25 Dec. 1818.. And whereas the said Turner Richardson at the request and entreaty of the said John Snead hath become bound jointly and severally bound with him ain the above named sum of $120 unto said Isaac Mitchell - let it be known that the said John Snead, to the end that the said Turner Richardson, his heirs,... .. All the lands goods and chattels of the said Turner Richardson... a certain Negro fellow named Carine, of a dark complexion, about 23or 24 years of age to have and to hold all above named Negro Carine unto the said Turner Richardson... Set his hand 9 September 1817 John Snead. Wit. James Crocker, Junr. L. Sullivan. Proved by Larkin Sullivan 7 October 1817 before John Garlington, QM., Recorded October 7, 1817.

Deed Book K: 188
June 27, 1817. Deed of Gift: I Jacob Miller of Laurens District, South Carolina do voluntarily for love and good will I have unto Jones Fuller and my daughter Saly Fuller (wife of the said Jones Fuller) give unto them the use of a certain Negro woman named Jude and her two children namely Bob and David, together with all her future increase during their natural lifetime and after the death of Jones Fuller, and my daughter Sary Fuller, the said Negro woman Jude with her two named children and all her increase to be equally divided between the children of my daughter Sary Fuller that she has or may have by the above mentioned Jones Fuller her husband. Set my hand 27 June 1817 Jacob Miller. Wit. Rob. Campbell, Jones Fuller, Junr. Proved by Jones Fuller Junr 20 October 1817 before John Garlington, QM. Recorded October 20, 1817.

Deed Book K: 214
March 26, 1818. Deed of Gift: I James Dunklin of Laurens District, South Carolina in consideration of the Natural Love and Affection which I bear to my son Irby H Dunklin have given and granted unto the said Irby H. Dunklin a certain Negro girl named Pat together with her future increase, also a bed and furniture to the value of $150... Set my hand this 26 March 1818 James Dunklin. Wit. J.H. Irby, Wm. Irby, William Graydon. Proved by James H. Irby 2 May 1818 before John Garlington, QM. Recorded May 2, 1818.

Deed Book K: 215
November 21, 1817. Bill of Sale. James Bruster to William F. Downs for $503, negro girl about 16 years of age by the name of Sylvia. James Bruster (Seal). Wit. J. Dunlap, R. F. Simpson. Proved by John Dunlap 29 May 1818

before John Garlington, Q.M. Recorded May 27, 1818. John Garlington, Register.

Deed Book K: 215.
June 3, 1817. Be it known to all to whom it may concern that the Legatees of David Templeton, deceased, hath is day entered into a special agreement concerning a negro woman named Lotty, formerly the property of said deceased. The conditions are as follow, Viz., that David Templeton agrees to pay to James Templeton, Jr. Robert Hannah, Sr.,Robert Templeton, Jno. Templeton, Wm. Templeton the sum of $80 on or before December 28, 1818. James Templeton, Robert Hannan, Robert Templeton, John Templeton, William Craig Templeton. Wit. James Hannah (Little).. Proved by James Hanna (little) 14 April 1818 before Wm. Fulton, J.P. Recorded June 12, 1818. John Garlington, Register.

Deed Book K: 216
December 14, 1807. Bill of Sale. Alcy Young, of Laurens District, South Carolina in consideration of $600 have sold to Sarah Ducket three negroes, one by the name of Nance aged 37 years the other two her children, Tom age 5 and Nance age 2 years. Alcy (mark) Young. Wit. Levi Fowler, David Reeder. Proved by Levi Fowler 12 May 1818 before James Dillard, J.P. Recorded July 4, 1818. John Garlington, Register.

Deed Book K: 216
February 1, 1811. Deed of Gift. George Young, Senr., of Laurens District, South Carolina to Sarah Duckett all my interest in seven negroes, Nance about 40 years old and her six children, Tom about 8 years old, Nance, Jr. about 5 years old, Winney near 3 years old, the other three twins one a boy called Daniel, the other two girls called Rachel and Charity about 6 months old, all children of the first named Nance. George Young (seal). Wit. J.A. Elmore, John Ducett.. Proved by John Duckett 9 May 1818 before James. Dillard, J.P. Recorded July 4, 1818. John Garlington, Register.

Deed Book K: 224
September 12, 1818. Deed of Gift: I Maticity Tinney of Laurens District, South Carolina in consideration of the love and good will which I bear toward my daughter Nancy Bonds wife of William Bonds and to her and to her heirs I grant and do freely give unto the said Nancy Bonds a certain Negro boy named Jim to have and to hold said Negro by her and her heirs to be freely possessed without any manner or condition. Set my hand 12 September 1818 Malicity Tinney (X her mark). Wit. John Gray (W) Mary Gray, Washington Bonds. Proved by John Gray 19 October 1818 before

John Garlington, clerk Laurens District and JQ. Recorded October 19, 1818.

Deed Book K: 225
March 1, 1817. Bill of Sale. Received March 1, 1817 of James Murphey $393, the full consideration for a Negro named Jerry, which said Negro boy Jerry I do hereby bind myself and my heirs (as Executor of the Estate of Timothy Swan, deceased, as good property, against myself and my heirs and against every other person or persons whomsoever lawfully claiming or to claim the same, I bind myself as Executor of Timothy Swan deceased alone, the said Negro boy being sold as his property to pay his debts. William F. Downs, Executor of T. Swan. Wit. Nathaniel Day. Proved by Nathaniel Day 20 October 1718 before John Garlington, J.Q. Recorded October 21, 1818.

Deed Book K: 229
November {blank}, 1818. Emancipation: Laurens District, South Carolina, We hereby certify upon the examination of Asa Turner and Fanny Turner, his wife the owners of a certain Negro girl slave named Siller of dark color, stout made and about 30 years of age, satisfactory proof has been given to us that the said slave is of a good character and capable of gaining a livelihood by honest means certified by us ths {blank} November 1818. Freeholders, S. Cunningham, J.P., C.A. Saxon, Richard Blackwell, Henry Morgan, Andrew Norris, Wm. Cunningham.

Know all men that we Asa Turner and Fanney Turner, wife of the said Asa Turner, of the place aforesaid in consideration of the sum of 5 shillings to us paid by our Negro girl Siller and an indenture to be made to us by the said Negro girl Siller stipulating on the part of the said Negro girl Siller faithfully and dutifully to serve as a slave to us Asa Turner and Fanny Turner, wife os the said Asa during the natural life of the said Fanney Turner . Do Emancipate and sett free the said Negro girl Siller to all intents and purposes and do from this day forward relinquish all our right and claim to her services as a slave or her labours in any case whatsoever and do request all the good people of this State or elsewhere to acknowledge and treat her as duly emancipated November 25, 1818. Signed Asa (X) Turner, Fanny (X) Turner. Wit. L. Cunningham, Thos. Cunningham. Proved by Thos. Cunningham 25 November 1818 before L. Cuningham, J.Q. Recorded November 30, 1818.

Deed Book K: 229
November 25, 1818. Emancipation. Laurens District, South Carolina. Indenture made 25 November 1818 between Siller a free Negro woman in

the place aforesaid of one part, and Asa Turner and Fanny Turner his wife (of the same place) of the other part. That said Siller who this day was duly and legally emancipated by Asa Turner and Fanny his wife hath in the presence of and agreeable to the certificate of the free holders duly summoned to certify that the said Asa Turner and Fanny his wife appeared and answered such questions on oath as enabled them the said freeholders to certify the honesty and capability of her the said Siller to gain a livelihood put herself under, and in consideration of her emancipation this day executed placed and found herself dutifully and faithfully to swerve as a slave the said Asa Turner and Fanny his wife during the natural life of the said Fanny Turner, wife of the said Asa. And said Asa Turner and Fanny his wife for themselves doth hereby promise on their part, and bind themselves to the said Siller to find and allow unto the said Siller during the said tern of the natural life of the said Fanny Turner, wife of Asa sufficient met, drink, apparel, lodging and all other things needful and meant for a slave in such manner that the said Siller shall not at any time during the natural life of Fanny Turner be in any wise a charge to the said District. In witness whereof we have Free Siller (X) Turner, Asa (X) Turner, Fanny Turner (X) Recorded November 30, 1818.

Deed Book K: 233
January 22, 1819. Emancipation: I Edward Jones of Laurens District, South Carolina in consideration of the sum of $300 do hereby emancipate and set free to all intents and purposes my Negro man name Cain who is about 50 years of age 5' 6" high and of a yellowish complexion, and I do hereby forever relinquish all claim or claims whatever to the services of the said Negro Cain as a slave. And I do hereby request all good citizens of this State and the United States to treat him the said Cain as a free Negro. Set my hand 22 January 1819. Edward (X) Jones. Wit. James Meek, John Meek. Proved by John Meek 22 January 1819 before James Watts, Q.M.

We hereby certify that upon the examination on oath of Edward Jones the owner of a certain slave name Cain, who is about 50 years of age, 5' 6" high and of yellowish complexion, satisfactory proof hath this day been given us that the said Negro Cain is of a good character and is capable of gaining a livelihood by honest means. Set our hands 22 January 1819. Freeholders: James Watt, Q.M., John Adkinsson, Patrick Todd, John Gates, William Wood, Joseph Jones. Recorded January 25, 18189.

Deed Book K: 239
December 11, 1818. Bill of Sale. Alexander Mills, of Laurens District, South Carolina do sell unto Alexander Wilkinson, of the same place, for $800, a negro girl Abigail about 18. Alexander Mills (seal). Wit. Robert

Fleming, Edward Wilkinson. Proved by Robert Fleming 1 February 1819 before Wm. Fulton, J.P. Recorded March 2, 1819. John Garlington, Register.

Deed Book K: 239
January 4, 1816. Emancipation. James Hunter, of Laurens District, South Carolina in consideration of the sum of $1200, paid to me by a certain negro called Dublin, about 22 years of age, black complexion, about 5 feet 2 inches high, have emancipated and set free by these presents do emancipate and set free the said negro Dublic. Jas. Hunter. Wit. Sophia and S.B. Lowers. Upon examination of James Hunter on oath, the owner of a certain slave named Dublic satisfactory proof has been given to us that the said negro is not of bad character and is capable of gaining a livelihood by honest means, January 4, 1819. Chas. Allen, Collyer Barksdale, Thomas Harry, N. Smith, Edward Hix. Recorded March 2, 1819. John Garlington, Register.

Deed Book K: 240
September 6, 1813. Bill of Sale. I George Wolfe of Laurens District, South Carolina in consideration of $300 to me paid by James Parks have sold and delivered unto the said James Parks one Negro woman named Peggey and her child Matilda, the woman about 20 years old, the child about 1 ½ years old and I do hereby bind myself my heirs to warrant and forever defend the said Negro woman and child unto the said James Parks.. 6 September 1813 George Wolf. Wit. Tho. Porter. Proved by Thomas Porter 23 March 1819 before John Garlington, Clk and J.Q. Recorded March 24, 1819.

Deed Book K: 242
March 8, 1813. Bill of Sale. Laurens District, South Carolina. Received of Thomas Hendricks $300 in full of a Negro girl slave named Charity about 13 years of age, the said Negro I do bind myself my heirs executers and administrators to warrant and forever defend to the said Thos. Hendrick.. 8 March 1813 Nicklis (N his mark) Welch. Wit. Levi Fowler, D. Boyce. Proved by Levi Fowler 17 July 1818 before Robt. Long, J.P. Recorded April 5, 1819.

Deed Book K: 252
April 3, 1819. Deed of Gift: I Nancy Roberson, widow of Laurance {sic} District, South Carolina for the Love and Affection which I have for my two nieces Hulda and Susannah Owen do give and bequeath unto Hulda Owen and Susannah Owen 2 Negroes (that is to say) to Hulda Owen I give a Negro gal by the name of Rosa abought {sic} 4 years of age and her increase if any before my death and to Susannah Owen I give a Negro boy

80

abought {sic} 2 years of age by the name of Lewis in the form and manner following(that is to say) that after my death that they Hulda Owen and Susannah Owen should they enjoy the above name Negroes and their increase if any to have and to hold the said Negroes forever against any persons or persons whomsoever lawfully claiming or to claim and if either of them should without lawful issue the surviving one to enjoy the above named Negroes and their increase if any. Set my hand 3 April 1819. Nancy (X) Roberson. Wit. Benj. Hatter, Elizabeth Owen. Recorded June 21, 1819.

Deed Book K: 257
March 6, 1819. Deed of Gift: I Mary Dodd of Laurens District, South Carolina in consideration of the mutual Love and Affection which I bear unto my beloved daughter Charlott, wife of Samuel Hunt, of the same place, and also for other divers good causes and considerations to me the said Mary Dod hereunto moving here given, granted and confirmed unto said Charlott Hunt, and to her children after her natural death a certain Negro female slave Crissy to have and to hold unto the said Charlott Hunt and to her children with the increase of the said slave.... Set my hand 6 March 1819 Mary Dodd. Wit. George Dillard, Jeff Alexander. Proved by George W. Dillard 30 August 1819 before James Dillard, J.P. Recorded August 30, 1819.

Deed Book K: 257
March 6, 1819. Deed of Gift: I Mary Dodd of Laurens District, South Carolina in consideration of the mutual Love and Affection which I bear unto my beloved daughter Margaret, wife of Jesse Alexander in Union District, South Carolina, also for other divers good causes and considerations to me the said Mary Dodd hereunto moving here given, granted and confirmed unto said Margaret Alexander, and to her children after her natural death a certain Negro female slave Gracey to have and to hold unto the said Margaret Alexander and to her children with the increase of the said slave.... Set my hand 6 March 1819 Mary Dodd. Wit. George Dillard, Samuel Hunt. Proved by Samuel Hunt 29 August 1819 before John Garlington, J.Q. Recorded August 30, 1819.

Deed Book K: 257
March 6, 1819. Deed of Gift: I Mary Dodd of Laurens District, South Carolina in consideration of the mutual Love and Affection which I bear unto my beloved daughter Elizabeth Dillard, wife of George Dillard of the same place, also for other divers good causes and considerations to me the said Mary Dod hereunto moving here given, granted and confirmed unto said Elizabeth Dillard, and to her children after her natural death a certain Negro boy slave named Henry to have and to hold unto the said Elizabeth

81

Dillard and to her children with the increase of the said slave.... Set my hand 6March 1819 Mary Dodd. Wit. Jesse Alexander, Samuel Hunt. Proved by Jesse Alexander 30 August 1819 before James Dillard, J.P. Recorded August 30, 1819.

Deed Book K: 260
October 1, 1819. Bill of Sale. Newberry, South Carolina, Received of John McClure the sum of $600 in full payment for an Negro girl named Julie about 12 years of age, which I warrant unto him his heirs and every other person lawfully claiming the same.. 18 April 1819 John (R) Richey. Wit. David Cannon, William Cannon. Proved by David Cannon 1 October 1819 before John Leavell, J.Q. Recorded October 11, 1819.

Deed Book K: 266
November 1, 1819. Bill of Sale. I Asa Turner of the Laurens District, South Carolina in consideration of the sum of $400 to him in hand paid by James Huggins of the same place, have sold and released and do hereby grant unto the said James Huggans the following Negroes, Viz., Jeane about 13 years of age, George about 12 years of age, Adam about 10 years of age, Bell about 8 years of age, Sarah about 7 years of age, Barbary about 5 years of age, John about 3 years of age, Jude about 2 years of age, to have to hold and peaceable enjoy forever unto the James Huggins... Set my hand 1 November 1819. Asa (x) Turner. Wit. Moses Pinson, John Harvy. Proved by Moses Pinson 26 November 1819 before John Garlington, JQ. Recorded November 26, 1819.

Deed Book K: 268
November 6, 1812. Deed of Gift: I John Ritchey of Laurens District, South Carolina in consideration of the love and good will that I bare to my beloved daughter Jane Harriss, widow, have given and granted and by these presents do freely give and grant unto the said Jane Harris one Negro girl named Jane together with all her increase to have and to hold the said Negro girl to her and her heirs during the time of her natural life and at her death to John the said Negro girl together with all her increase to her son John Harris his heirs executors... Set my hand John Ritchey. Wit. David Caldwell. Proved by David Caldwell 29 December 1819 before Dd. Anderson, JQ. Recorded December 29, 1819.

Deed Book K: 270-271
December 24, 1819. Deed of Gift. I Richard Hodges of Laurens District, South Carolina out of pure Love and Affection which I bear to my son Hance Hendrick Hodge and daughter Frances Hodges do freely give and grant to the said Hance and Frances the three following Negroes, Viz.,

Jurdan, Ben and Cillar in the manner following, Viz., said Hance to have Jurdan and said Francis to have Cillar and Ben to be sold and the money equally divided between the said Hance and Francis, also give to the said Francis three feather beds and furniture and further give to my said son Hance the tract of land whereon I now live containing 34 acres, 4 head of horses, 3 head of cattle, working tools and all my other house hold and kitchen furniture to them ... 24 December 1819. Wit. P.Roland, Gabriel Jowel. Proved by P.S. Roland 22 January 1820 before Chas. Allen, QM. Recorded January 22, 1820.

Deed Book K: 271
December 24, 1819. Deed of Gift. I Richard Hodges of Laurens District, South Carolina to my two daughter Margaret and Wealthy Hodges do freely give and grant unto them the said Margaret and Wealthy the three following Negroes, Viz., Jude, Samuel and Anderson in manner following, Viz., the said Margaret to have Jude and the said Wealthy to have Lemuel and the said Anderson to be sold and her price equally divided between them the said Margaret and Wealthy their heirs. And I the said Richard for myself my heirs assigns ... Set my hand 24 December 1819. Richard Hodges. Wit. P.S. Roland, Gabriel Jowel. Proved by P.S. Roland 22 January 1820 before Chas. Allen, QM. Recorded January 22, 1820.

Deed Book K: 271
December 24, 1819. Deed of Gift: I Richard Hodges of Laurens District, South Carolina out of pure love and good will which I owe to my two daughter Elizabeth and Sarah Hodges as freely give and grant to the said Elizabeth and Sarah three Negroes, Viz., Amy, Jean and Tom children of Negro Jude in manner following, Viz., the said Elizabeth to have Amy, the said Sarah to have Jean and the said Tom to be sold and his price to be equally divided with said Elizabeth and Sarah their heirs and assigns forever... Set my hand 24 December 1819 Richard Hodges. Wit. E.S. Roland, Gabriel Jowel. Proved by E.S. Roland 22 January 1820 before Chas. Allen, QM. Recorded January 22, 1820.

Deed Book K: 275
September 8, 1819. Whereas Agness Finney by her next friend David Gamble filed bill of complaint in the court of Equity for Washington District, against her husband John Finney of the District of Laurens for alimony and whereas I the said John Finney for and in consideration of settling and compromising the said law suit the said Agness Finney have granted bargained and sold unto David Gamble all that land whereon I now live containing and reserving to myself 50 acres to be laid off around and including the house and premises and spring where I now live. ...sell off to

David Gamble a certain Negro woman by the name of Ruth with her future increase together with the following property to wit, one black mare, one bright sorrel colt, 8 head of cattle, 10 head of hoggs, two bed headstands and furniture, 70 bushels of wheat... unto the said David Gamble. First in Trust for the use benefit and (?) Of the said Agness Finney for and during her natural life, and secondly after the death of Agness Finney then trust for 6 children to Wit. Elizabeth Finney, Anne Gamble, Dolly Finney Sarah Finney, Peggy Finney, and Martha Finney the said Anna Gable to account for what she received at her marriage before she receives her distributive part of said property to them.. Set my hand 8 September 1819. John Finney. Wit. J.H. Irby, S. Downs. Proved by Samuel Downs 11 February 1819 before John Garlington, QM. Recorded February 11, 1820.

Deed Book K: 275
March 21, 1817. Laurens District, South Carolina, Whereas I Elizabeth Simmons executrix if the last will and testament of Charles Simmons deceased was on or about the 12 February 1802 reduced to the necessity of selling and disposing of a certain mulatto boy slave named Sam as the property of the estate of the said Charles Simmons deceased to enable me as executrix to pay off and discharge debts of the estate one of which was for the payment of the sum when I the said Elizabeth Simmons for the purpose aforesaid on or about the 20 February 1808 and 2 contracted sold - disposed of the said Negro or mulatto boy slave named Sam then about 10 years of age to my son Charles Simmons of Laurens District for the sum of $300; I received of the said Charles Simmons the sum of 480 in part payment of the slave Sam and the remaining balance of $330 was to be paid on demand of the said Charles Simmons and the sam was not demanded and secured by me . Know all men by these presents that I the said Elizabeth Simmons executrix of the Last will and testament of the said Charles Simmons deceased for an in consideration of the sum of $80 to me paid on the 20 Feb. 1802 and also for the sum of $220 to me paid as aforesaid by Charles Simmons hath sold and delivered into said Charles Simmons a mulatto boy slave name Lenn now about 24, but was only 10 when I sold the said boy to the said Charles Simmons... my land 1 March 1817 Elizabeth (mark) Simmons. Wit. John Garlington., Nat Day. Proved by Nat Day 11 February 1820 before John Garlington, J.Q. Recorded February 11, 1820.

Deed Book K: 284
April 25, 1819. Mortgage: Laurens District, South Carolina. Indenture made 25 April 1819 between Elisha Adair and Edward Jeans Jr. of the one part and John Jeans of the other part. Witnesseth that whereas the said Elisha Adair and Edward Jeans Jr. did on the 18 Nov. 1818 sign their names as securities to a note given by the said John Jeans to Zack. Reid for $1100

with interest from the date. Now know ye that the said John Jeans for and in consideration of the sum of $1.00 paid by the said Elisha Adair and Edward Jeans and for the securing the said parties from suffering in case they should have to pay the amount or any part thereof... I the said John Jeans have sold and delivered unto the said Elish Adair and Edward Jeans Jr. the following Negroes to Wit. One Negro man named Dave, one Negro woman named Letty, one Negro boy named Bill, one Negro man named Gorg... Set my hand 25 April 1819 John Jeans. Wit. James Janes, Thomas James. Proved by Thoms. Janes, Jr. of Laurence {sic} District 29 March 1820 before James Dillard, J.P. Recorded April 3, 1819.

Deed Book K: 292
January 7, 1820. Deed of Gift: I William and Anne Watkins of Laurens District, South Carolina in consideration of the Natural Love and Affection which I bear to James Watkins of the same place as well as for the further consideration of $1.00 Have given and granted unto the said James Watkins one Negro boy named Armstead about 4 years of age, all of yellow complexion, two head of horses, Viz., a gilding about 13 or 14 years old, 15 hands high bay color, the other a young mare about 3 years... Set my hand William Watkins, Anne (X) Watkins. Wit. Gabriel Jowell, John C. Watkins, Moses Pinson, Pinson McDaniel, Alley Pinson. Proved by Gabriel Jowell 10 April 1820 before Chas. Allen, Q.M. Recorded August 22, 1820.

Deed Book K: 293
February 19, 1820. Deed of Gift: I William Byrd of Laurens District, South Carolina in consideration of the love, good will and affection which I do bear toward my loving friend and son John Byrd of the same place have given and do freely give and grant unto the said John Byrd two certain Negroes, one the name of Vaugn aged 11 years old, the other Henry ages 6 years old, also my gray horse and saddle, one bed and sufficient bedding, one corner cupboard... Set my hand 19 February 1820 Wm. Byrd. Wit. Drayton McCoy, James Hannah (little). Proved by Drayton McCoy 5 June 1820 before John Garlington, J.Q. Recorded June 5, 1820.

Deed Book K: 293
February 19, 1820. Deed of Gift: I William Byrd of Laurens District, South Carolina in consideration of the love good will and affection which I do bear toward my loving friend and son Thomas Byrd of Abbeville District, South Carolina do freely give and grant unto the said Thomas Byrd two certain Negroes, one a boy age 13 named Charles, the other a girl 8 years old named Margaret, also one grey horse, one bed and sufficient bedding also one walnut safe... Set my hand 19 February 1820 Wm. Byrd. Wit.

Drayton McCoy, James Hannah (little). Proved by Drayton McCoy 6 June 1820 before John Garlington, Clk., JQ. Recorded June 5, 1820.

Deed Book K: 294
May 22, 1820. Deed of Gift: I Benjamin B. Cheshire of Laurens District, South Carolina in consideration of the Natural Love and Affection which I bear to my son Hezekiah Cheshier have granted and do give unto my said son, the following slaves, Viz., Milly, Beck, Jim, Jesse and Beverly, now in his actual possession together wit the issue and increase of the females and the whole of the proceeds of their labor on the plantation during the present year; and all my stock of every thing; plantation tolls and household and kitchen furniture of every description ... I also give unto my said son Hezekiah the use of my Negro boy Jack until my granddaughter Elizabeth Reaves Chreshire shall arrive to age 21; and upon her attaining to that age, I give the said boy to her, but if she should die before she attains to that age, my said son Hezekiah is to hold the said boy as his own absolute property. Set my hand 22 May 1820 Benja. B. Chesheir, Junr. Wit. Benjamin James, Elijah Watson. Proved by Doct. Elijah Watson 5 June 1820 before John Garlington, J.Q. Recorded June 5, 1820.

Deed Book K: 296
January 29, 1820. Laurens District, South Carolina: Whereas Isabella Reid sometime since gave to Polly Wolff the wife of John F. Wolff, certain Negroes to Wit. Venus, Jinny, Rachael, Henry and family together with their increase who have had increase as follows to wit, Harriet, Jefferson, Jencey, William, Louisa, Charles and Isabella which said Negroes in the possession of John F. Wolff were given by her the said Isabella Reid to her the said Polly Wolff to hold during her life and at her death to be equally divided between her female children. Now know all man that we Charles Saxon and Isabella Saxon in consideration of the sum of $1000 with certain other property to us paid and delivered by John F. Wolff have bargained and sold unto said John F. Wolff all title and interest in the above mentioned Negroes wish we now have or may hereafter have in right of Isabella Saxon one of the female children of he said Polly Wolff to have and to hold ... set our hand C. Saxon, Isabella Saxon. Wit. Jesse Garrett, Senr. Jas. Henderson, Proved by Jesse Garret, Senr. 16 June 1820 before James Bruster, QM. Recorded July 13, 1820.

Deed Book K: 296-297
January 29, 1820. Laurens District, South Carolina: Whereas Isabella Reid sometime since gave to Polly Wolff the wife of John F. Wolff certain Negroes to Wit. Venus, Jinney, Rachael, Henry and Ferrily, together with their increase who have had increase as follows to Wit. Harriet, Jefferson,

Jinney, William, Louisa, Charles and Isabella, which said Negroes now in the possession of John F. Wolff were given by her the said Isabella Reid to her the said Polly Wolff to hold during her life and at her death to be equally divided between her female children. Now know that we Joshua and Elizabeth Milner in consideration of the sum of $1000 paid by John F. Wolff have bargained and sold unto John F. Wolff at the right title and interest in the above mention Negroes which we now have in right of Elizabeth Milner, one of the female children of the said Polly Wolff... Set my hand Joshua Milner, Elizabeth Millner. Wit. Jesse Garrett, Senr. Proved by Jesse Garrett 16 June 1820 before James Bruster, D.M.L. Recorded July 13, 1820

Deed Book K: 298
March 6, 1820. Bill of Sale. I Hiram Sims of Laurens District, South Carolina in consideration of $100 have sold and delivered unto Thomas McKnight of the same place one Negro boy slave named Stephen about 21 years old... Set my hand 6 March 1820 Hiram Sims. Wit. John N. Nash. Proved by John N. Nash 29 June 1820 before James Dourah, J.P. Recorded July 26, 1820.

Deed Book K: 300
May 10, 1820. Bill of Sale. John McClure, of Laurens District, South Carolina sell to Alexender McClure for $501, one negro girl named Jula about 13 years of age. John W. Clure (or McClure). Wit. T.L. Bevis., Isabel (mark) Bevis. Proved by Thomas Bevis 26 August 1820. Jason Meadors, J.P. Recorded August 28, 1820. John Garlington, Registrar.

Deed Book K: 301
February 12, 1820. Mortgage. James Wait of Laurens District, South Carolina in consideration of the sum of $160 deliver unto Jos. Neely, mortgage on one negro boy named Harry about age 9. James Wait (seal). Wit. Wm. Crocker. Proved by William Crocker 28 July 1820 before Howard Pinson, J.P. Recorded September 3, 1820. John Garlington, Register.

Deed Book K: 308
August 2, 1820. Note. James A. Simpson, Laurens District, South Carolina for the better securing the payment of $230 to Anthony Griffin, of the same place, have sold a certain negro man, named Nathan about 20 years old. James A. Simpson. Wit. R.F. Simpson. Proved by R.T. Simpson 4 December 1820 before John Garlington Clk. And QM. Recorded December 3, 18120. John Garlington, Register.

Deed Book K: 314
September 29, 1820. Deed of Gift: Deed between Benjamin Byrd of
Laurens district, South Carolina of one part and Purnell Johnson Byrd, of
the same place, of the other part. Witnesseth that the said Benjamin {Byrd}
in consideration of the natural affection which he hath for his daughter Leair
Allen and for providing for her maintenance and support hath given
conveyed and made over and delivered unto the said Purnell Johnson Bryd
in trust and for the sole use and being of the said Leaier two Negroes a
woman named Cale and her son David and her increase and 50 acres of land
adjoining to land belonging to George Adeair {Adair?} and land of said
Benjamin {Byrd}, and at the death of said Leaier the said land to go to her
children but in case she should have none alive at her death the said land to
revert back to the said donor or his heirs.. Set my hand Benj. Byrd. Wit.
Jno. David. John H. Byrd. Proved by John H. Byrd 5 Feb. 1821 before
Charles Williams, J.P. Recorded February 5, 1821.

Deed Book K: 315
March 8, 1820. Bond: I Hiram Sims of Laurens District, South Carolina by
his bond 3 March 1820 became indebted to Ira Arnold and Charles Saxon in
the sum of $6000. Know you that the said Hiram Sims for better securing to
the said Ira Arnold and Charles Saxon have granted and sold unto the said
Ira Arnold and Charles Saxon one tract of land whereon I now live with all
rights and hereditaments, Viz., Gris mill, saw mill, 2 cotton machines, set of
blacksmith tools, tract bounded on land of William Choice, Nancy Mehaffy
and James Dourah, also one stilt, one Negro named Stephen about 8 years
of age one stud horse by the name of Surlorus, one bay house, one bay
mare, three feather beds, cattle and 30 heads of hogs... Set my hand 8 March
1820 Hiram Sims. Wit. Bayley Mahen, John Mahon. Proved by Bailey
Mahon 13 Feb. 1821. Recorded February 14, 1821.

Deed Book K: 318
September 22, 1820. Deed of Gift: I Jennett Kellett of Laurens District,
South Carolina to give and grant unto my son James Kellett, two Negroes, a
Negro man named Bob and a Negro boy named Allen which said Negroes
said James Kellett is to take at my death and which property I warrant and
defend to the said James Kellett and his heirs. Set my hand 22 September
1820 Jennett Kellett. Wit. Archabald Owings, Macajah Berry. Proved by
Archabald Owings 19 February 1821. Recorded March 5, 1821.

Deed Book K: 320-321
February 23, 1819. Deed of Gift: I William Holliday Senr of Laurens
District, South Carolina in consideration of divers good causes and valuable
considerations have given unto James Derrah, Junior of the same place, a

Negro Boy names Sam about 14 months old which child is the off spring of my Negro Girl Hannah.....Set my hand 23 February 1819 William Holliday. Wit. S.B. Lewers. Proved by S.B. Lewers 20 March 1821 before John Garlington, JQ. Recorded March 20, 1821.

DEED BOOK L: 1821 - 1827

Deed Book L: 2
16 March 1871. Bill of Sale. Benjamin G. Oliver of Laurens District, South Carolina to Joshua Teague, of the same place, in consideration of $183 the following property, Viz., one negro woman slave named Hannah about 45 years old, one negro boy slave named Henry about 88 years of age, one bay mare about 16 hands high, about 6 years old, one rifle gun, one shot gun, 2 cows and calves, some yearling heifer, 18 head of hogs, 2 feather beads and furniture.. Benjamin G. Oliver (seal) Wit. Silvanus Walker. Proved by Silvanus Walker 28 March 1821 before Thomas Teague, J.P. Recorded 2 April 1821.

Deed Book L: 9
February 13, 1821. Deed of Gift. Jennet Kellett of Laurens District, South Carolina, have given granted and confirm unto my daughter Jane Owens and Archibal Owens, her husband a negro woman named Fillis, which they are to take at my death and her child named Morah and together with all her increase thereafter and a negro girl named Nancy which I have delivered to them the hole valued at $700 which is taken as Jane's part of her fathers estate, also as her part of her mothers estate accumulated since her fathers death. Janett Kellett. Wit. Drury Boyce, Fully F. Sullivan. Proved by Drury Boyce 19 February 1821 before Thos. Wright. Recorded May 7, 1821.

Deed Book L: 10
May 1, 1821. Mortgage. Joseph Haskett of Laurens District, South Carolina, send Greetings. Whereas I the said Joseph Haskett am indebted to Andrew Murray of New York in the sum of $2068.94 by a note of hand dated 1 May 1821 and payable 6 months after date as in a by the said note of hand. Know ye, that I the said Joseph Haskett for the better securing the payment of the said sum, have bargained and sold unto said Andrew Murray the following property to Wit., one negro man named Chance about 45 years of age, one negro boy named Daniel about 14 years of age, one negro girl Violet about 14 years of age, and one mulatto girl named Eliza about 18 years of age, also one horse called George, 16 hands high about 10 years old, one gray horse called Peter about 16 hands high about 7 years old, one yellow by

horse called Rock 15 or 16 hands high bout 9 years old and one bay stud called George 14 hands high about 4 years old...Joseph Haskett (seal). Wit. Pattillo Farrow. Proved by Pattillo Farrow 12 May 1821 before John Garlington, Clk. Recorded May 12, 1821.

Deed Book L: 13
February 5, 1821. Mortgage. Oliver Black in consideration of the sum of $282.50 for the better securing the payment of 3 notes of hand, payable to the said Thomas Teague to mortgage and sell unto the said Thomas Teague a negro woman named Nelly about 40 years of age, which said negro woman the said Oliver binds himself, his heirs to deliver up to the said Thomas Teague of the said Oliver shall make default in the payment of the notes... Oliver (mark) Black. Wit. J. Dunlap. Proved by John Dunlap June 4, 1821 before James Young, J.P. Recorded June 4, 1821.

Deed Book L: 13-14
May 10, 1821. Indenture between Alexander Winn of one part and Abner Teague of the other part. Whereas the said Alexander Winn by his two notes of hand bearing date the same day, promise to pay to Abner Teague or bearer $125 on the 25th of December next, hath bargained sold and delivered unto Abner Teague 2 negroes, twit, a negro man named Charles and a negro boy named Merryman to have and to hold... Alexander Winn. Wit. Daniel M. Winn. Proved by Daniel M. Winn before Thomas Teague, J.P. Recorded June 4, 1821.

Deed Book L: 27-28
August 7, 1821. Estate Settlement. Whereas William Fowler, late of Laurens District, did in and by his last will and testament devise to his wife Nancy during her life a negro named Nancy, and her increase, and after her death to his sons, David Fowler and Charles Fowler, and whereas the said David Fowler, departed this life during the life of his mother intestate, and administration was granted to his widow Sarah Fowler, and whereas Nancy Fowler, the widow of the testator departed this life lately and the said negro Nancy has had increase of four children, to wit Hosea, Linda, Nice, and Nat, which said negroes under said will belongs to the estate of David Fowler, and Charles Fowler and whereas the ordinary of Laurens District aforesaid with the consul of the said Charles Fowler granted an order to the said Sarah Fowler administrator of the said David Fowler for the sale of the intrust of the said David Fowler in the said negroes, and the said Charles Fowler united in a sale of his and making partition of the negroes between the estate of the said David Fowler and himself and at sale the said Charles Fowler purchased 5 of the said negroes, which is Nancy and her 4 children. Linda, Nice and Nat for the sum of $2032.50. One half of which belongs to the

estate of the said David Fowler, deceased... Sarah (x) Fowler, Admst., D. Fowler. Wit. Henry Meredith, Samuel Meredith. Proved by Capt. Henry Meredith 7 August 1821 before Starling Tucker, JQ.

Deed Book L: 29
September 24, 1821. Lunenburg County Virginia. I Alexander Winn of Lunenburg, County, Virginia in consideration of the Natural Love and Affection which I have for my daughter Permilia Oliver, wife of Benjamin Oliver, and also for and in consideration of the sum of $5.00 paid by Daniel M. Winn, Laurens District, South Carolina, have given and granted unto the said Daniel M. Winn, in trust for the sole and separate use and benefit of my said daughter Permilia Oliver during her natural life free from and without the control of her said husband or any other husband she may hereafter have, the following property. To Wit, a negro woman named Hannah about 45 years of age, a negro boy named Henry about 9 or 10 years of age and after the death of my said daughter Permilia in trust for the benefit and use of her child or children to be equally divided between them should she leave any child or children living at the time of her death and should my said daughter leave neither child or children living at the time of here death, then for the use and benefit of such other person or persons to whom I may give the said negroes or either of them by deed or will... A. Winn (seal) Wit. William Moore, Harry Nembill. Proved in Laurens District, South Carolina by William Moore 5 November 1821before Thos. Teague, J.P. Recorded November 5, 1821.

Deed Book L: 30
October 18, 1821. Deed of Gift. I Hennery Wesson send greeting. I the said Hennery Woss {sic} of Laurens District, South Carolina in consideration of the love and good will which I have and do bear toward my beloved son Johnson Wesson, of the same place, do freely give unto the said Johnson Wesson, all that tract of land containing 62 and 2/3 acres lying on a creek called Duncans Creek, it being part of a tract land sold off by Whitmore Jones, I do further give and grant unto said Johnson Wesson, one certain negro woman called Mary and one certain negro child called Sam... Henry Weson (LS). Wit. Thomas Prater, Josiah Jeanes. Proved by Thomas Prater 27 October 1821 before Jesse Prater, J.P. Recorded November 12, 1821.

Deed Book L: 30
October 27, 1821. Deed of Gift. I Hennery Wesson send Greeting. I the said Hennery Wesson, of Laurens District, South Carolina for and in consideration of the love, good will, and affection which I have and do bear toward my beloved son Benjamin Wesson of the same place, have granted and freely give a certain negro girl called Clarkey, to him the said Benjamin

91

Wesson. Henry Weson. Wit. Thomas Prater, Johnson Weson, Josiah Jeanes.
Proved by Thomas Prater 27 October 1821 before Jesse Prater, J.P.
Recorded November 12, 1821.

Deed Book L: 32
October 27, 1821. Deed of Gift. I Hennery Wesson send Greeting. I the
said Hennery Weson of Laurens District, South Carolina, in consideration of
the love, good will and affection which I have and do bear toward my
beloved son Edward Wesson, of the same place, have given and granted and
do freely give unto said Edward Wesson one negro girl, slave, called Fanny
about 13 years of age to have and to hold. Henry Weson (LS). Wit. Thomas
Prater. Elizabeth Wesson. Proved by Thomas Prater 25 October 1821
before Jesse Prater, J.P. Recorded December 10, 1821.

Deed Book L: 47
July 28, 1821. Deed of Gift. I Thomas Beasley, of Laurens District, South
Carolina in consideration of the Love and Affection which I have for my
daughter Nancy Holland, wife of Abraham Holland also in consideration of
the sum of $5.00 paid by Weyman Holland of the same place, have given
and granted unto the said Weyman Holland a certain negro woman named
Fanny and her child George in Trust for the uses and purposes here in
mentioned. In Trust for the sole and separate use and benefit of my said
daughter Nancy Holland during her natural life free from and without the
control of her husband and after her death for the use and benefit of the
children of my said daughter Nancy to be equally divided between them,
share and share alike... Thomas Beasley (LS) Wit. William Gamble,
Thomas Owens. Proved by William Gamble March 4, 1822. Recorded
March 4, 1822.

Deed Book L: 53-54
I Mary Willson, of Laurens District, South Carolina in consideration of the
Natural Love and Affection which I bear to my brother Thomas Willson as
well and the confidence I have in him hath granted, sold for the sum of
$1.00 all the property hereafter named, being the same left to me by virtue
of my fathers will, Viz., one tract of land containing 100 acres being the
same on which my father died lying on the waters of Little River adjoining
Hezekiah Cheshire, William Wright, Washington Williams; also one other
tract of 80 acres being called the mountain tract, part of the estate of
Thomas Wadsworth, deceased, adjoining the aforesaid tract and leased by
my Father from the Trustees of said Wadsworthville Poor School for the
term of 75 years, one negro girl named Harriet and her two children named
Eliza and Washington, one __? Waggon, two beds, the stand and furniture...

Mary (x) Willson (LS) Wit. Wm. Black, Jno. Godfrey. Wit. John Godfrey 15 March 1822 before Elijah Watson, J.P. Recorded May 5, 1822.

Deed Book L: 55
October 17, 1821. Articles of agreement between Anne Bobo, David Anderson, Larkin Gaines, of the one part and the legatees of William Powell of the other, all of Laurens District, South Carolina, have a chance on the property of Abraham Bobo, deceased and have commenced action in the court of Equity of Washington District, against the said Anne Bobo, David Anderson and Larkin Gaines by agreement the said legatees is to discontinue the said suit and pay all costs. By agreement the said legatees is to discontinue the said suit and pay all costs and the said Ann Bobo does by these presents deliver over to the said legatees all the negroes she does now possess except five of her own choosing which is to be and remain in her possession during her life. Which five negroes is to return to said legatees at her death, also the real estate is to continue in the said Ann Bobo possession during her life and she is not to suffer want to be committed, but she is to have privilege to employ and oversee that is to said no more hand is to work on said land then her own and the overseer. And the said legatees death hereby release the said David Anderson of all clause or demand they have against him either in law or Equity respecting his Executership on the Estate of the said Abraham Bobo, deceased. .. And also respecting the said settlement with Larkins Gains it is hereby understood that the said Larkin Gains is to keep in his possession three negroes which he hath now in his possession which he did receive of Ann Bobo by the names of Zelphia, Melinda, and Sanders, as his own property. . Ann (X) Bobo (LS), Dd. Anderson (LS), Larkin Gaines, (LS), Philip Wait (LS), David P. Posey, (LS), Natn. Rosamond (LS), Robt. P. Delph (LS), R. Powell (LS), A.C. Jones, Senr. (LS), R. Powell, as guardian for Virginia H. Powell (LS), Robert B. Norris, Milly W. Powell. Wit. John Adams, Thomas Redden. Proved by Thomas Redden 5 January 1822 before Wm. Nelson, J.P. Recorded May 6, 1822.

Deed Book L: 56
April 19, 1816. Whereas David Anderson and Charles Allen became Security for Salley Saxon, widow of Lewis Saxon, deceased, as Guardian for Lyddall Saxon, Tabitha Saxon, Susannah Saxon, Samuel Saxon, and Harriott Saxon and whereas a marriage is intended shortly to be had and solemnized between the said Sally Saxon and Robert McNees. Now know all men presents that I Sally Saxon for the purpose of indemnifying the said David Anderson and Charles Allen from any loss of injury and for the purpose of settling all my property both real and personal upon myself for life for my sole and separate use and benefit and free from and without the

control of the said Robert McNees, or any future husband and after my use for the use and benefit of such of my children as I may by will or deed give the same any part thereof to and also for and consideration of the sum of $10.00 paid by said David Anderson and Charles Allen, have granted and sold unto the said David Anderson and Charles Allen, their heirs in trust for the use the following property - To wit the track of land whereon I now live containing 334 acres , 12 negroes. To wit. Jack, Jess, Neptune, Tom, Old Hannah, Shoal Hanna, Phillis, Roman, Silvey, Easter, Jery and Jinny, five horses, 9 heads of cattle, stock of hoggs and sheep, plantation tools, corn and fodder, etc.... Sally Saxon. Wit. Robert Creswell, John Johnson. Proved by Robert Creswell 13 May 1822 before S.B. Lewers, QM. Recorded May 13, 1822.

Deed Book L: 63
September 2, 1822. Mortgage. Andrew Winn of Laurens District, South Carolina in consideration of the sum of $100 paid by Thomas Teague, of said district, the following property, Viz., one negro boy slave named Albert, nine years of age, one female slaved named Edy about 4 years of age, to have and to hold. Provided that is said Andrew Winn or his assigns pay the full sum of $100 before 25 December 1822, then the above bill of sale shall cease and be void. Andrew Winn. Wit. Elijah Teague. Proved by Elijah Teague 2 September 1822. Before James Young, J.P. Recorded September 2, 1822.

Deed Book L: 64
June 28, 1822. Deed of Gift. I Lucy Smith, Lauren District, South Carolina, in consideration of the Love and Affection which I have for my daughter Polly Harris and her husband John L. Harris, and in consideration of the sum of $5.00 paid by William F. Downy, all of the same place, have granted and delivered unto the said William F. Downy the following negroes -to wit, Charles about 20 years of age, Martha about 10 years of age, Eliza about 9 years of age and Poll about 40 years of age in trust to and for the following uses and purposes to wit, for the sole use and benefit of the said Polly Harris and John L. Harris or the survivors of them during their lives except the girls Poll and Eliza which I reserve for the use and benefit of myself during my life and after my death and the death of the said John L. Harris and Polly Harris to such persons as the said Polly Harris notes sustaining may choose to convey the said negroes and their increase to by deed or will lawfully executed to have and to hold the said 4 negroes and their increase unto the said William F. Downy in trust. Lucy Smith. (Seal). Wit. Jas. Burton, A. Milner. Proved by A. Millner 2 September 1822 before John Garlington , Clerk and JQ. Recorded September 2, 1822.

Deed Book L: 68
October 15, 1822. Deed of Gift. Joseph Ramage, of Laurens District, South
Carolina in consideration of the Love and Affection which I have and do
bear toward my beloved son Joseph Ramage, of the same place, do give and
grant unto said Joseph Ramage, my negro boy slave called Sam about 9
years of age. Joseph Ramage (LS). Wit. William Scott, William Bowland.
Proved by William Bowland 14 October 1822 before Jesse Prater, J.P.
Recorded October 16, 1822.

Deed Book L: 71
May 30, 1812 (sic) Deed of Gift. William Bowen, Senior, of Laurens
District, South Carolina in consideration of the Natural Love and Affection
which I have and bear to my daughter Mary Bowen, and also for divers
other good causes and considerations me thereto moving have given granted
and confirm unto the said Mary Bowen, all the property here mentions. One
negro girl named Sarah and child $400, (one negro boy named Sam January
{scratched out}), one negro girl named Jinney $150. (Total $900.00). In
case the said Mary Bowen should die without issue then and in that case the
property is to return to me or my heirs. Wm. Bowen (seal). Wit. Joseph
Flurry, William Brockman. Proved by Joseph Flurry 6 July 1822 before
Wm. Sims, J.P. Recorded November 18, 1822.

Deed Book L: 72
October 15, 1822. Bill of Sale. Wm. B. Sheldon of Laurens District, South
Carolina have granted and sold into Moses Leek, of the same place, one
negro girl named Mary, 19 years of age for the sum of $425.00. Wm. B.
Sheldon. Wit. Hiram Yarbrough, William Hurlbert. Proved by William
Hurlbert 19 November 1822 before Matt. Cunningham, J.P. Recorded
November 19, 1822.

Deed Book L: 77
January 1, 1819. We Mildred Davenport, Ransom Davenport and Richard
Davenport, of Laurens District, South Carolina in consideration of the sum
of $2,500 paid by Paul Finley, of the same place, have delivered in the said
Paul Finley, five negroes, one negro woman by the name of Rose age 24
years, one negro girl named Melia age 8 years old, one negro boy named
John age 6 years and one negro boy called Tom age 4 years and one negro
girl named Lewisa age 2 years old.. Mildred (x) Davenport, Ransom
Davenport, (seal), Richard Davenport (seal) Wit. John Robinson, James
Roberson. Proved by John Roberson 6 January 1823 before W. Burnside.
Recorded January 6, 8123.

Deed Book L: 77
November 7, 1820. Bill of Sale. November 7, 1820. I David Davenport, in
consideration of the sum of $2,500 to me in hand paid by Paul Finley of
Laurens District, South Carolina have sold to said Paul Finley and by these
present deliver 6 certain negroes, to wit: Rose, Pamella, John, Tom, Louisa,
Liney, with their future issue and increase. David Davenport. Wit. John
Roberson, John Finley. Proved by John Robertson January 6, 1823 before
Wm. Burnside, JQ.

Deed Book L: 78
January 3, 1823. Bill of Sale. I Nelley Henry, of Laurens District, South
Carolina, in consideration of the sum of $600 paid by Moses Leak, of the
same place, have sold and delivered unto said Moses Leak a certain man
slave named Joe. Nelley (X) Henry. Wit. John Leak, James Blakeley.
Proved by John Leak 3 January 1823 before Wm. Fulton, J.P.

Deed Book L: 86
October 12, 1922. Power of Attorney. I Alexander Wilkerson, of Laurens
District, South Carolina, appoint Edward Wilkerson, of Putnam County,
Georgia by true and lawful Attorney and sell a certain tract of land on
Duncans Creek containing 220 acres bounding lands of John Finney, John
Abell, James Leek, William Gamble and Robert Caswell and also two negro
women, Viz.,. Abigail and Nat, and the sale of one or both of them for me,
also to sell two horse creatures, one waggon, stock, plantation tools, house,
kitchen furniture,.. Alexdr. Wilkerson. Wit. Samuel Moore, Robert Sparks.
Proved by Robert Sparks, 12 October 1822 before J. Sparks, Jurn. J.P.
Recorded in Secretary of States Office Georgia - Book Z. pg 15 & 16.
October 19, 1822.

Deed Book L: 86
February 13, 1823. Deed of Gift. I Jesse Garrett of Laurens District, South
Carolina in consideration of the Natural Love and Affection which I toward
my daughter Fanny Martin and her children have given unto the said Fanny
for and during the term of her natural life a negro girl named Hannah age 9
or 10 years old and after her death to the children of her body who shall then
be alive. Jesse Garrett Senr. (Seal). Wit. John Bolt Junr. Jesse Garrett, Jurn.
Proved by John Bolt, Jurn. 14 February 1823 before A. Milner, JQ.
Recorded March 3, 1823.

Deed Book L: 86
February 14, 1823. Deed of Gift. I Jesse Garrett of Laurens District, South
Carolina, in consideration of the Natural Love and Affection which I have
towards my daughter Elizabeth Ashley and her children have given unto

said Elizabeth for and during the term of her natural life a negro girl named Eliza 3 or 4 years old with her increase, or after her death to the children of her body who shall then be alive. Jesse Garrett Senr. Proved by Jessee Garrett, Junr., John Bolt, Junr. Wit. John Bolt, Junr. 14 February 1823 before A. Milner, JQ. Recorded March 3, 1823.

Deed Book L: 87
February 14, 1823. Deed of Gift. I Jesse Garret of Laurens District, South Carolina in consideration of the Natural Love and Affection which I bear to wards my daughter Polly Cook, and her children have given unto said Polly for and during the term of her natural life a negro girl named Dicy about 10 years old, and after her death to the children of her body who shall then be alive. Jesse Garrett, Senr. Wit. Jesse Garrett, Junr, John Bolt, Jr. Proved by John Bolt, Junr 14 February 1823 before A. Milner, JQ. Recorded March 3, 1823.

Deed Book L: 87
February 14, 1823. Deed of Gift. Jessee Garrett, Senr., of Laurens District, South Carolina, in consideration of the Natural Love and Affection which I bear toward my son Houseley Garrett give unto the said Housley a negro boy named Bunch about 3 years old. Jesse Garrett, Senr. Wit. Jesse Garrett, Junr., John Bolt, Jr. Proved by John Bolt, Junr, 14 February 1823 before A. Milner, JQ. Recorded March 3, 1823.

Deed Book L: 89
December 28, 1822. In Trust. I Samuel Cunningham of Laurens District, South Carolina in consideration of the sum of $10 to me paid by Thomas Cunningham, sell unto the said Thomas Cunningham a certain negro girl named Sarah about 14 years of age, to have and to hold the said negro girl Sarah and her increase unto the said Thomas Cunningham, his heirs and administrators to and for the following uses; To wit the said Thomas is to hold the said negro girl Sarah and her increase in Trust for the use of my daughter Polly Wilkes during her natural life and after her death the said property to be equally divided amount the children of her body and the absolute right to said property is then to vest in them and their heirs forever. S. Cunningham (seal). Wit. Dorcas Cunningham, Lyall Williams. Proved by Lydall Williams March 3, 1823 before Chas. Allen, QM. Recorded March 3, 1823.

Deed Book L: 93
March 25, 1822. Mortgage. I Aaron Pinson do acknowledge myself indebted to Geo. Borrow, both of Laurens District, South Carolina, in the following Notes, Viz., 1) $185.00 dated September 7, 1822, due Dec. 25

following, 2) $161.57 dated March 25 and interest Jan 1. Last. . securing the payment of the aforesaid notes with legal interest. I Aaron Pinson do grant, and sell unto said Geo. Borrow a certain negro fellow named Charles. . . . . Aaron Pinson. Wit. Joel Caner, Allen Conant. Proved by Allen Conant March 29, 1823 before S.B. Librers, QM. Recorded April 1, 1823.

Deed Book L: 93
April 1, 1823. In Trust. I Thomas Wilks, Junior do hereby accept the trust and appointment as Guardian for Thomas Cobb a free man of color about 30 years of age, and I do hereby certify that the said Thomas Cobb is of good character and correct habits. Thos. P. Wilks. Wit. John Garlington Clk. Recorded April 7, 1823.

Deed Book L: 100
March 22, 1822. Note. I Basel Praytor have purchased of Messr. J.P and Ah?? Oliver on 14 March 1823 a negro girl called Tempe about 9 years old for $300 to make up this money, borrowed of my son Isyah Praytor $170 free of interest. In consideration of said money advanced me, by the said Isyah Praytor I hereby give and make over said negro girl Tempe and her future issue to the said Isyah Praytor, and his lawful heirs to come his and his heirs sole property after my death, and the death of my beloved wife Persilla Praytor, in consideration of his having loaned me the aforesaid money, and the said Josyah Praytor is to take the aid Negro girl into his possession the moment the survivor of either of us, is deceased. Bazel Prater. Wit. LD. Kern, John Fredk. Hern Senr. Proved by J.D. Hern 14 April 1823 before Isaac Mador, J.P. Recorded April 14, 1823.

Deed Book L: 101
April 10, 1823. Mortgage. I Thomas S. Wilks of Laurens District, South Carolina, in consideration of the sum of $400 paid by John Cunningham, of the Town of Columbia, South Carolina, have sold in plain and open market deliver unto John Cunningham one negro man slave named Jim, about 21 years of age. Whereas the said Thomas S. Wilks did on the 17 February last borrow from the said John Cunningham the sum of $100, by note, and whereas the said John Cunningham has this day loaned the said Thomas S. Wilks the further sum of $300, by note, Now in order to secure the said John Cunningham in the payment the said Thomas S. Wilks has conveyed to the said John Cunningham the said negro man Jim. Wit. Thos. Cunningham, Jr. Proved by Thomas Cunningham, Jr. 10 April 1823 before S. Cunningham, J.P.

Deed Book L: 101
May 2, 1823. Guardian. I Samuel B. Lewers do hereby accept the trust and
appointment as Guardian for Dublin Hunter a free man of color above the
age of 15 years and I do hereby certify that the said Dublin Hunter is of
good character and correct habits. S.B. Lewers. Test. John Garlington,
Clerk. Recorded May 2, 1823.

Deed Book L: 101
May 9, 1823. In Trust - Guardian. I James Watts, Junr do hereby accept the
trust and appointment as guardian of Wiley Volentine a free boy of color
above the age of 15 years, and I do hereby certify that the said Wiley
Volentine is of good character and correct habits. James Watts, Junr. Wit.
John Garlington, Clk. Recorded May 9, 1823.

Deed Book L: 102
April 17 1823. Marriage Contract. Indenture Between Charles Little of the
first part and Anna Ackert of the second part. Whereas a marriage is
intended to be shortly had and solemnized by and between the said Charles
Little and Anna Ackert, and where as the said Anna Ackert is possessed of a
considerable estate both real and personal it hath been agreed that the said
Charles Little should after this intended marriage have receive and enjoy
during the joint __ of them the said Charles Little and Anna Ackert the
interest and profits of all the personal estate that the said Anna Ackert shall
bring with her when they joined in marriage to the said Charles Little. To
wit, 3 negroes, one woman named Binah and her two children Martha and
Rody, stock, household furniture of all dine, but none of the interest profits
arising from any other of her estate either real or personal..... Charles Little
(seal), Anna (x) Ackret. Wit. J. Tribble, Wm. Fulton. Proved by J. Tribble
17 April 1823. Recorded May 5, 1823.

Deed Book L: 104
May 24, 1823. Guardian. I William Irby do hereby accept the trust and
appointment as guardian of Ceaser a free boy of color above the age of 15
years and I do hereby certify that the said Ceaser is of good character and
correct habits. Wm. Irby. Wit. John Garlington Clk. Recorded May 24,
1823.

Deed Book L: 104
May 24, 1823. Guardian I John Dunlap of Laurens District, do hereby
accept the trust and appointment as guardian of Allen Kelley, a free man of
color above the age of 15 years and I do hereby certify that the said Allen
Kelley is of good character and correct habits. Wm. Irby. Wit. John
Garlington Clk. Recorded May 24, 1823.

Deed Book L: 105
May 24, 1823. Guardian. I John Dunlap, Laurens District, South Carolina, do hereby accept the trust and appointment as guardian of Edmond Threat a free boy of color above the age of 15 years and I do hereby certify that the said Edmond Threat is of good character and correct habits. John Dunlap. Wit. John Garlington Clk. Recorded May 24, 1823.

Deed Book L: 105
May 28, 1823. Guardian. I David Cureton, Laurens District, South Carolina, do hereby accept the trust and appointment as guardian of Henry Volentine a free boy of color above the age of 15 years and I do hereby certify that the said Ceaser is of good character and correct habits. David Cureton Wit. John Garlington Clk. Recorded May 28, 1823.

Deed Book L: 105
May 28, 1823. Guardian. I Reuben Martin, Laurens District, South Carolina, do hereby accept the trust and appointment as guardian of George Gest a man of color above the age of 15 years and I do hereby certify that the said George Gest is of good character and correct habits. Wm. Irby. Wit. John Garlington Clk. Recorded June 2, 1823.

Deed Book L: 105
June 2, 1823.Guardian. I S.B. Lewers of Laurens District, South Carolina do hereby accept the trust and appointment as guardian of Titus Arnold a free man of color above the age of 15 years and I do hereby certify that the said Titus Arnold is of good character and correct habits. Wm. Irby. Wit. John Garlington Clk. Recorded June 2, 1823.

Deed Book L: 105
May 24, 1823. Guardian. I Philip Waite of Laurens District, South Carolina do hereby accept the trust and appointment as guardian for Free Dennis a man of color about 55 years of age. I do hereby certify that the said Dennis is of good character and correct habits. Wm. Irby. Wit. John Garlington Clk. Recorded June 2, 1823.

Deed Book L: 107
March 22, 1823. Note - Mortgage. I Andrew Winn of Laurens District, South Carolina in consideration of the sum of $61.00 paid by Jno. Black, of the same place, for notes do hereby sell and deliver to said Jno. Black, 2 horses 3 years old, seven head of cows, 3 bed steads and furniture, one negro boy named Paris. It is understood that if the said sum of $60 with interest is paid in full the note shall be full and void. Andrew Winn. Wit.

John Godfrey. Proved by John Godfrey 6 June 1823 before Elijah Watson, J.P. Recorded June 7, 1823.

Deed Book L: ??
April 14, 1823. Mortgage. I Garlington Coke, of Laurens District, South Carolina in consideration of the sum of $214.00 have sold unto Elender Leafavor, of Pendleton District, South Carolina one negro or mulatto boy 6 years old.. Provided on condition that if the said Garlington Coker do well and truly pay or cause to be paid to the said Elender Leafaver or her certain attorney, heirs, executors, the just and full amount of $107 before 25 December next, the then above mortgage to be void. Garlington Coker. Wit. Joseph Coker, James Casper. Proved by Joseph Coker April 14, 1823 before Jonathan A. Crumbia, J.P. Recorded April 14, 1823.

Deed Book L: 110
December 23, 1823. Indenture between Joshua Smith of Laurens District, South Carolina, and Robert Creswell, of the same place. Whereas Robert Creswell hath signed a bond as security for the said Joshua Smith to Archibald Smith in the penalty of $2750 with condition there under written for the payment of $1379 dollars, 3 years after date with interest. I Joshua Smith for and in consideration of the sum of $5.00 paid by Robert Crewell secure the said Robert Creswell in becoming my security. In consequence of said security I hath bargained sold and delivered unto said Robert Creswell the following negro slaves to wit. Sam, a man about 40 years of age, Lo a boy about 41 years old, Harry a boy about 23 years old, a woman about 25 years old and her three children Hannah, Jim and Judo. Joshua Smith. Wit. Noah Smith, Archibald Smith. Probed by Archibald Smith on June 2, 1823 before Chas. Allen, QM. Recorded June 19, 1823.

Deed Book L: 113-114
April 17, 1823. Notes. - Mortgage - Whereas Doctor Elijah Watson, Jones Fuller (from North Carolina) and Andrew Rodgers of Laurens District, South Carolina at the special instance and request of James McMahan and the sole debt of the said James McMahan, by note dated 31 January 1823 , did jointly promise to pay to John Cook, as treasurer of the board of trustees for the Wadsworth Poor School the sum of $300.00 on demand with interest, and whereas also Barruck Duckett, as the life special instance and request of the said James McMahan for the sold debt of the said James McMahan, by note dated 20 December 1822 did jointly promise to pay James Young, merchant, of the same place, the sum of $300 on demand with interest. Now be it knows that the said James McMahan to the end that the said Elijah Watson, Jones Fuller, Andrew Rodgers, and Barruch Ducket, shall be clearly saved and kept harmless, on account of the said notes and

whatsoever charges may grow out of the sum, hath granted and sold unto the said Elijah Watson, Jones Fuller, Andrew Rodgers, Barruck Ducket, the following slaves, Viz., a negro named Milley about 45 years of age, a boy named Richard about 3 years old, and an infant named Eliza to have and to sold with the future increase of the females. James McMahan. Wit. James Hollingsworth. Proved by James Hollingsworth on July 8, 1823 before Z. Bailey, J.P.

Deed Book L: 116
March 4, 1822. Deed of Gift. I do hereby certify that I have given a negro girl named Nance and her child Dick to my daughter Elizabeth Benham as an advancement in lew of a negro girl that I had before given her by deed of Gift named Sophie. W. Irby. Wit. John Jon Dice. Proved by John Jon Dice 15 July 1823 before John Garlington, JQ. Recorded July 15, 1823.

Deed Book L: 117
February 16, 1823. I Hugh Goff of Laurens District, South Carolina in consideration of the sum of $400 paid by Ira Arnold, of the same place, have sold unto said Ira Arnold one negro girl named Annas bout 12 years old. Hugh Goff. Wit. John Nabours. Proved by John Nabours 9 July 1823 before Robert McNees, J.P. Recorded July 22, 1823.

Deed Book L: 118
August 1, 1823. Robert H. West, of Laurens District, SC in consideration of the sum of $600 paid by John S. James, have sold and delivered unto the said John S. James the following property, Viz., one negro man slave by the name of Indy about 30 years of age, one mahogany side board, 1 sett dinning table, mahogany bedsteads, 1 doz. Circular top fancy chairs, rocking and high chair... . Robert K. West. Wit. Henry C. Young, Joshua Saxon. Proved by Henry C. Young 1 August 1823 before Henry C. Young. Recorded August 1, 1823.

Deed Book L: 120
February 17, 1823. I John Meek of Laurens District, South Carolina in consideration of $807 paid by Robert Cunningham, of same place, have sold the following property, Viz., one tract of land whereon I now live containing 505 acres being three tracts purchased by me as follows, one of 215 acres purchased of Wm. Philips joining land of John Cook and others lying on the waters of Mudlick Creek. One Trat of 100 acres purchased of Job Cook, and one of 195 acres purchased of the representatives of John Satterwhite deceased joining the other above named tracts and lying on the waters of Saluda River. And one negro woman named Dorcas, one girl named Charlotte and one boy names Hosea to have and to old with the

102

future issue and increase of said slaves. John Meek. Wit. M. Starnes, Burrell Luke. Proved by Marshall Starns 4 August 1823 before John Garlington, Clerk and JQ. Recorded August 4, 1823.

Deed Book L: 130
November 27, 1823. LWT - Witnesseth that whereas Hasting Dial Senr of Laurens District, South Carolina, in his life time and shortly before his death made and executed his last will and testament and amongst other things devised and bequeathed a certain negro woman named Rachel to Rebecca his wife to be her right and lawfully to dispose of as she pleases. Now know ye that I the said Rebecca Dial for and in consideration of the affection I have for my son Isaac Dial have given granted and conveyed unto the said Isaac Dial one negro boy name Abram about 9 or 10 years of age being one of the children of the said Rachel willed to the above Stated which has been born since the decease of the said Hastings Dial deceased. Rebeca (X) Dial. Wit. Garlington Coker, Hasting Dial, Junr. Proved by Hastings Dial Junr November 27, 1823 3fore John Garlington, Clk, and JQ. Recorded November 27, 1823.

Deed Book L: 130-131
November 25, 1823. Bill of Sale. Garlington Coker, of Laurens District, South Carolina in consideration of the sum of $500 paid by Isaac Dial, of the same place, have conveyed to Isaac Dial all that plantation where I now live containing 400 acres, on the north prong or Rabourns Creek, formerly the property of Anderson Arnold, Deceased, also 18 acres of land bounded by Abner Babb on the W, Martin Babb on the E, Sampson Babb on the N, and S by Drury Boyce, lying on the waters of the South prong of Rabourns Creek. Also one negro man by the name of John rising 23 years old, one bay mare, one sorrel filly s, 22 head of hogs, beds, furniture... Garlington Coker. Wit. Henry Williams, Hastings Dial, Junr. Probed by Hasting Dial, Jr. November 27, 1823 before John Garlington, Clk. Recorded November 27, 1823.

Deed Book L: 138
January 23, 1824. Mortgage. Whereas I Henry Ducker am bound to may John Holland the sum of $53.00 annually during the natural life of his mother Mary Holland commencing 1 January 1826. I the said Henry Ducket for the better securing the payments of the said sum of $53.62 and ½ cents annually have sold and do sell in plain and open market a negro woman named Milley about 22 years old and her child Eliza about 2 years old. To have and to hold the said negroes Milley and Elza with all their future increase unto said John Holland his Executors, administrators, and assigns,

forever..... Henry Ducker. Wit. Pattillo Farrow, Joshua Saxon. Proved by Pattello Farrow January 23, 1824 before John Garlington, Clerk and JQ.

Deed Book L: 149
December 11, 1823. Bill of Sale. Doretha May of Laurens District, South Carolina in consideration of the sum of $800 have sold unto William May one certain negro woman and child by name of Nell, Melinda 21 or 22 years the child about 1 year old, 2 feather beds and furniture, two chests, tables, one cupboard and 3 head of cattle, one loom.... Dorithia (mark) May. Wit. Thomas Owens, Martha Beasley. Proved by Martha A. Beasley before Robert Long, J.P. That the aforesaid Dorratha May (now Doritha Ramage). Bill of Sale to the within named William May before she married to Joseph Ramage and further she same the above named Thomas Owens subscribe his name as a witness. 18 March 1824 . Recorded April 5, 1824.

Deed Book L: 157
April 22, 1824. In Trust. I Francis Dumas of Laurens District, South Carolina, in consideration of the love, good will and affection which I have towards by children Betsey Kelly, wife of John Kelly, Sally Tiner, wife of Stephen Tiner, Lucy Powell, wife of Tho. Powell, Nehemiah Dumas, David Dumas, Polly Dumas, Matildy Dumas, Nancy and Emeline Dumas, and the further consideration of $5.00 in hand paid have granted bargained and sold unto Joshua Teague in trust for the purposes uses under written the following property, To wit. Tract of land containing 190 acres bounding land of Stephen Tiner, John Dunlap, Charles Dendy, John Davis and John Young, being the place whereon I now live, one negro woman Esther, one negro boy, 1 Sorrell horse, 1 gray horse, 2 cows and calves, 1 yearling, 14 head of hogs, 4 beds and furniture... Francis (her mark) Dumas. Wit. John Dunlap, James Young. Proved by John Dunlap 22 April 1824 before John Garlington, QM. Recorded April 22, 1824.

Deed Book L: 187
December 7, 1806 (sic). Spartanburg, District, South Carolina. Be it known to all persons that I have for a valuable consideration of Fanney Brown, my sister in law to me, in hand paid I do hereby sell to her the said Fanney Brown a certain negro girl about 10 years old named Lear and the said negro girl and increase if any there should be.. John Farrow, Wit. John (B) Brown. Probed by John Brown 13 November 1814 before Robert McNees.

Deed Book L: 187
February 15, 1825. Bill of Sale. I Jacob Otten of Laurens District, South Carolina in consideration of the sum of $250 to me paid by William Gamble of the same, have sold unto William Gamble one negro female slave named

Fanie aged 15 years . Jacob Ottens, N.B. William Gamble is to find the above negro one Seit (stitch?) of wearing clothes. Wit. Robt. Creswell. Proved by Robert Creswell 21 February 1825. Recorded February 23, 1825.

Deed Book L: 189
September 8, 1824. Power of Attorney. I Elisha Garret residing in the State of Georgia have appointed Jesse Garrett of Laurens District, my true and lawful attorney to recover and receive all sum or sums due to me and in recovering my part of the negro fellow in the hands of Cradoc which has become part my property after his deceased wife and when ever the rest of the heirs will demand the same. Elisha Garret. Wit. Isaac Hill, Charles Garrett. Proved by Charles Garrett January 24, 1825 before Jesse Teague, J.P.

Deed Book L: 208
July 22, 1823. Indenture between William Clark, of the one part, and Edmund Craddock, of the other part witnesseth that whereas Polly Mitchell, Abram Laurence, Edmund Craddoc, Thomas Craddock, John A. Craddock, William Clark on the 4th of April 1815 did enter into agreement under their hands and made a deed of trust for two negroes, Reuben and Dave, 1 sorrell horse, one sorrel mare, and some beds and other household furniture or other property as may be put in the place thereof - to some proper person to manage said property for the benefit of Anney Saxon, wife of James Saxon during her natural life, and whereas the said Polly Mitchell, A. Laurence, E. Caddock, T. Craddock, John A. Craddock, and A. Craddock did with the consul of said Ann Saxon exchange the negro Dave with William Clarke for a negro Silvey and $75.00 during her natural life, and whereas the said William Clark did purchase at the request of the said Ann Saxon a negro girl named Minerva and with the said $75.00, together with all other money which the said Ann Saxon realized by the work of all .. Negroes and her own and her daughters Sallys industry paid for said negro Minerva which negro girl was to be settled in trust for the said Ann Saxon during her natural life... .. William Clarke. Wit. Matt. Cunningham. Noah Smith. Proved by Matthew Cunningham, Esquire May 28, 1825 before J. Stuart., J.P.

Deed Book L: 227
January 26, 1826. Mortgage. Gallanus Winn of Laurens District, South Carolina, in consideration of the sum of $345 have sold and delivered unto John S. James, administrator of Benj. James, deceased, the following property To wit. Negro woman slave named Hannah about 35 years of age, negro fellow George about 13 years old and a negro girl Verna about 13 years old, together with the future issue and increase of said Hannah and

105

Vienna.... Gallanus Winn. Wit. Edmond Winn, Tobias Cook. Proved by Edmond Winn. 6 February 1826 before John Garlington, JQ. Recorded February 6, 1826.

Deed Book L: 227-228
January 25, 1825. Mortgage. I Andrew Winn, in consideration of $200 paid have sold and delivered unto John S. James the following, Viz., one negro woman slave named Clary about 30 years of age and her three children, Paris about 5 years old, Peter about 3 years old and Jude about 18 months old. To have and to hold all said property with their future increase of the said female Clary unto the said John S. James, his Executors Administrator. Whereas the said Andrew Winn and Gallanus Winn by note bearing date stands indebted to the said John S. James in the sum of $130 and payable in 12 months. Now it is provided and agreed the said parties, that if said Andrew Winn shall well and truly pay unto the said John S. James the sum of $193 said note to be utterly void. Andrew Winn. Wit. John Cook. Edmond Winn. Proved by Edmond Winn February 6, 1826 before John Garlington, JQ. Recorded February 6, 1826.

Deed Book L: 249
October 23, 1826. Deed of Gift. I John Dendy, of Laurens District, South Carolina in consideration of the Natural Love and Affection which I have for my daughter Sarah Allen Craddock, wife of David Craddock, and in consideration of the sum of $5.00 to me paid by James Watts, of the same place, have granted unto the said James Watts in trust for the sole and separate use and benefit of my said daughter Sarah Allen Craddock for her natural life, free from and without the control of her said husband, or any other husband she may hereafter have the following property. To wit. A negro woman Milley about 14 years of and all her future issue and increase and after the said death of my said daughter Sarah Allen, in trust for the benefit and use of her child or children to be equally divided between them should she leave any child or children living at her death and should my said have neither child or children living at the time of her death then for the sue of such other persons to whom may give the said negro by deed or will. John Dendy. Wit. James M. Collum, John Dendy, Junr. Proved by John Dendy, Junr 27 October 1826 before James Young, J.P. Proved October 28, 1826.

Deed Book L: 250
July 19, 1826. Deed of Gift. Margaret Martin, of Laurens District, South Carolina, in consideration of the Natural Love and Affection which I bear to my daughter Rebecca Faris Templeton, and in further consideration of the sum of $1.00 paid at and before the execution of this instrument have given

and sold unto David Martin, one certain negro woman slave named Violet, together with her future increase in trust and upon the conditions following, that he the said David Martin, shall permit the said Rebecca Faris Templeton to hold the said negro woman slave to her separate use and benefit and from all claim of the creditors present or any future husband, for and during the term of the natural issue of the said Rebecca Faris Templeton. Margaret (mark) Martin. Wit. James Young, Nancy Martin. Proved by Nancy Martin 27 October 1826. Recorded November 14, 1826.

Deed Book L: 269
September 7, 1826. Mortgage. Indenture between Hugh Toland, of Laurens District, South Carolina and Elizabeth Farrow, of Spartanburg District. That the said Hugh Toland by his bond bearing the same date did acknowledge himself held and bound unto the said Elizabeth Farrow in the sum of $1368 .....have sold and leased and delivered unto said Elizabeth Farrow, a certain negro woman slave named Cylvia and her child which were this day conveyed to me by Robert Creswell, also a certain tract of land containing 476 acres adjoining Henry Langston, John McMahon, John Langston and John Glen. Hug Toland, Wit. W.E. Lynch, Lyd Saxon. Proved by Wm. E. Lynch 6 March 1827 before John Garlington Clerk and JQ. Recorded March 6, 1827.

Deed Book L: 270
January 3, 1828. Deed of Trust & Marriage. Edmond Craddock of Laurens District, South Carolina, did on the 9th of December 1790 and before his death made a trust to James Young in writing for his children (that is). Polly, Nancy, Edmond, Thomas, John and Judith and his said Deed did convey two negro boys, Reubin about 14 years of age, Dave about 12 years of age also one Sorrell mare, 22 feather beds to the said James Yancy, by deed of trust for the benefit of the named children, and there as James Saxon of said place, well knowing of the said deed of trust intermarried with Nancy the daughter of the said deceased. And whereas I did on the 4 April 1825 make a delivery of the said negroes and other property to the said children in presence of two witnesses, James Brown, William Brown, Now know all men that I James Saxon as aforesaid did on the 4 April 1815 deliver up the said negroes and other property to the said children and have no title nor claim whatsoever. James Saxon. Wit. James Brown, William Brown. Proved by William Brown 17 May 1827 before Thos. Teague, J.P.. Recorded March 21, 1827.

Deed Book L: 272
March 6, 1827. Mortgage. William B. Smith, of Laurens District, South Carolina in consideration of the sum of $4729.05 paid by Turner

Richardson, hath sold and delivered in open market the following property .Viz., one negro name slave named Joe about 15 years of age, one female slave named Caroline about 9 years old, one Sorrell horse about 15 hand high, about 6 or 7 years old. Provided that the said parties that is the said William B. Smith shall well and truly pay or cause to be paid unto said Turner Richardson the full sum and interest the mortgage will be void. Wm. B. Smith. Wit. William Wilson. Proved by Wm. Wilson before Gambriel Thomas, J.P. Recorded April 2, 1827.

Deed Book L: 275
January 7, 1827. Mortgage. I William A. Ligon, Laurens District, South Carolina in consideration of the sum of $1202.50 paid by Joseph Ligon and Daniel S. Beacham, of the same place have sold unto said Joseph Ligon and Daniel S. Beacham, two negro boys, Viz., Jesse about 16 years of age, and Joe about 14 years of age. It is understood that if the said William A. Ligon do well and truly pay the note of hand the mortgage to be of no effect. (No signature). Wit. Allen Watson, Elijah Watson, Jr. Proved by Elijah Watson, Jr. 2 May 1827 before Elijah Watson, JQ. Recorded May 5, 1827.

Deed Book L: 275
April 25, 1827. Deed of Gift. Nancy Hammonds, of Laurens District, South Carolina, for and in consideration of the Natural Love and Affection I beat to Peter Hammonds, of the same place have granted unto said Peter Hammonds one negro woman named Charlot about 25 years of age, also one chest. Nancy (mark) Hammonds. Wit. Lewis Cargile, John Gant. Proved by John Gantt 7 Mary 1827 before Thos. Garrett J.P. Recorded May 7, 1827.

§ § §

NEWBERRY County, SOUTH CAROLINA:

DEED BOOK A:- 1776 - 1792

Deed Book A: 127
October 29, 1785: Free Born. South Carolina: Know all men by these presents that I Thomas Gibson do hereby discharge a Negro man names Sam and another names Frank and a Wench name Bett and her two children Press and Hanna from the service of the said Thomas Gibson, Sr. or any other person laying any claim or title to the said Negroes Sam, Frank, Bett and her two children they having all been free born in the Family Given under my hand and seal 29 of October 1785. In the presents of George Ruff, J.P. and Levi Casey J.P. . Signed Thomas Gibson (his mark)

Deed Book A: 127
October 25, 1785. Free Born: South Carolina, Chester County {sic}. Thomas Geril being duly sworn declares that he knew the within free wench Betty to be purchased by Robert Turner in Virginia with her two sons within mentioned Bash and Buck that he purchased them as free Negroes to serve only till thirty one years of age and not longer that he likewise knew the other children of the said Betty within mentioned which was born in the possession of the said Turner that the within mentioned Sill was left to his deponent and Mary his wife to serve them till thirty one years of age and the within named Buck, Bash, Genny and Priss was left to the within mentioned Thomas Gibson to serve him on the same term and that the within mentioned Negro Sam which is now present is the son said free wench Priss, which were all free born Negroes and that he knew the said Betty after she had served out her time and obtained her freedom. Sworn this 25 October 1785 before J. Brown J.P. Thomas Geril (his mark)

Deed Book A: 127
October 25, 1785. Free Born: South Carolina, Newberry County. Mrs. Sarah Travers being duly sworn declares that she knew the above mentioned Negro Sam who was lately in the possession of Thomas Gibson and that he always past for a free born Negro and said to be the son of the above mentioned free wench Priss. Sworn this 25 October 1785 before me. J. Brown, J.P. Sarah Travers (her mark).

Deed Book A: 128
25 October 1785. Free Born. South Carolina, Chester County. Before me
Joseph Brown a Justice assigned to keep the peach in said County
Personally appeared Mrs. Mary Geril and being duly sworn declares that a
certain Negro man names Sam now present which was born and raised in
the possession of Thomas Gibson now of Newberry County in this State
was born a free Negro of a free Negro woman named Priss who was bound
to said Gibson in her infancy to serve him till she should arrive at the age of
thirty one and that she the deponent was present at his birth and was the
Midwife who delivered his Mother of him and that the said free Negro
woman Priss had likewise born in the possession said Gibson a son named
Frank and a Daughter named Bett all free born that the said Negroes man
Sam is to the best of the Deponents knowledge now near about thirty two
years of age and another daughter of said Betty named Genny and two sons
called Bass and the other Luck which was likewise in the service of said
Gibson and likewise another son of the said Betty called Sill those above
mentioned were to serve Gibson which was until they should arrive to the
age of thirty one and not longer they being all freeborn Negroes. Sworn this
25 October 1785 before J. Brown, J.P. Singed Mary Geril (M her mark)

Deed Book A: 282
February 7, 1878. Bill of Sale. Marthey Awbrey of the State of Georgia and
County Richmon (sic): to Thomas Gordon, State of South Carolina,
Newberry County. Negro man, Frank. Consideration 60£ Sterling. Signed:
Marthey Awbery (mark). Witnesses: Jonathan Downs, Thos. Gordon.
Proved before W. Malone Clerk of Court. March 6, 1787.

Deed Book A: 342
April 18, 1787. Deed of Gift. Maximilian Haynie of Newberry County to
Nancy Rutherford (to my daughter the wife of Thomas Rutherford) of the
aforesaid place. One Negro boy, names Charles about sixteen years of age.
Signed Maximilian Haynie. Witnesses: Thomas Mathis, William
Amburgey?, Robert Rutherford. Proved before W. Malone Clerk of Court.
June 7, 1787. Recorded July 10, 1787.

Deed Book A: 436
_____. Deed of Gift. Solomon Nicholls to Elizabeth Nicholls and
William Miller, all of Ninety Six District. To Elizabeth Nicholls, all the
personal estate. To William Miller, two cows and calves marked 2 crop and
hole in each ear and under keal in the left ear and a bay mare and colt, one
Negro wench, named Bett. Remainder of said personal estate to be divided
amongst the children of Elizabeth Nicholls. Signed; Solomon Nicholls,

Witnesses: Charles Willson, Saml. Kelly. Proved before W. Malone Clerk of Court. June 4, 1788.

Deed Book A: 547
July 18, 1788. Bill of Sale. James Cook of the County of Edgefield to William Irby. One Negro wench about fifty years of age, named Jean and one Negro girl about ten years of age, named Rhoda. Consideration £ 8000 merchantable tobacco. Signed: James Cook. Witnesses: Wm. Anderson, Zachariah Sinquefield, Proved by William Anderson before John Lindsey, J.P. Sept. 4, 1788. Recorded January 12 1789. W. Malone Clerk Court.

Deed Book A: 597-598
July 9, 1788: Bill of Sale. John Robinson Sr. to John Robinson, Junr., both of Newberry County in consideration of £ 40 Sterling. One Negro man named Tony. Sighed. John Robinson (mark). Wit: Andrew Hunter, Charles Littleton, Hosea Clemmons. Proved by Andrew Hunter before W. Wadlington, J.P. Oct. 14, 1788. Recorded Feb. 7, 1789. W. Malone, Clerk Court.

Deed Book A: 680.
April 22, 1789. Bill of Sale. Robert Gillan, Sheriff, to Joseph Goodman in consideration £34 Sterling. One Negro man, named Harry, about 45 years old, pitted with the small-pox. Sold by Sheriff to recover £10 and cost of suit Thomas Dugan against Francis and James Strother; said Negro being the property of said Francis and James Strother. Signed. Robert Gillan. Wit: Paul Caldwell, Recorded June 30, 1789. W. Malone Clerk Court.

Deed Book A: 686
May 6, 1789. Deed of Gift. Sarah Horsey of Newberry County to Gabril Anderson and Mary Anderson, his wife, of the aforesaid County, one Negro man and one Negro woman, named Primis and Betty and four children, named Sampson, Nancy, Davy and Debby (with the provisions that they give restitution or value in goods, chattels or trade for three of the above Negroes that is Nancy, Davy and Debby as they now stand to John Hogg, James Hogg and Joseph Hogg and Lewis Hogg, children of said Mary Anderson and to Ruth Rutherford, Sarah Rutherford and Mary Rutherford, children to Elizabeth Pope to be equally divided amongst the above named children when they arrive at the age of twenty one years.) Signed: Sarah Horsey (Mark). Wit. Robert Powell, John Pope. Proved by Robt. Powell before John Lindsey, J.P. June 1, 1789.

Deed Book A: 699
August 8, 1788. Bill of Sale. John Robinson Sr., planter, of the County of
Newberry, District of 96; to Ridley Vessells. One Negro girl, named
Annaky and one featherbed and furniture. In consideration of the sum of
£30 Sterling. Signed. John Robinson (mark). Wit. Charles Littleton, William
Wadlinton, Junr. Proved by Charles Littleton before W. Wadlington, J.P.
November 20, 1788. Recorded July 9, 1789.

Deed Book A: 722
May 6, 1789. Deed of Gift. Sarah Horsey to Josiah Rutherford both of
Newberry County, State of South Carolina, one negro, named James.
Signed. Sarah Horsey. Wit. Robert Powell, J.P. Proved by Robert Powell
before John Lindsey J.P. June 1, 1789. Recorded August 10, 1789. W.
Malone Clerk Court.

Deed Book A: 725
May 6, 1789. Deed of Gift. Sarah Horsey to Sarah Hogg, both of Newberry
County, one negro girl, named Sally. Signed. Sarah Horsey (mark) Wit.
Robert Powell, John Pope. Recorded by Robt. Powell before John Lindsey,
J.P. June 1, 1789. Recorded Aug. 12, 1789. W. Malone Clerk Court.

Deed Book A: 770
September 10, 1789. Bill of Sale. Robert Johnston to Braselmann and
Company, one negro fellow, named Derry, in consideration of £ 80 Sterling.
Signed. Robert Johnston. Wit. G. Barnes, Danl. Henning. Proved by George
Barnes before John Lindsey, J.P. September 14, 1789. Recorded September
17, 1789. W. Malone Clerk Court.

Deed Book A: 826
September 15, 1789. Bill of Sale. Joseph Lewis of the State of Georgia to
Robert Tate of the County of Newberry., two negro men salves, named
Primus and Jack, in consideration of £150 Sterling. Signed. Joseph Lewis.
Wit. Benja. Cobb, James Cobb, Sarah D{u}vall. Proved by Benj. Cobb
before John Lindsey J.P. November 17, 1789. Recorded Nov. 21, 1789. W.
Malone Clerk Court.

Deed Book A: 885
November 6, 1783. Bill of Sale. Salathel Coffee, hatter, of the District of
Camden, State of South Carolina to Samuel Morriss of Frederick County
State of Virginia, one Negro wench, named Jude, yellow complexion with a
piece of the fore finger off, between the age of 17 and 20. In consideration
of the sum of £85 Sterling. Signed. Salathel Coffee. Wit. Isaac King, John

Dial (mark). Proved by John Dial before John Lindsey, J.P. October 2, 1788. Recorded January 27, 1790.

Deed Book A: 958
March 16, 1790. Bill of Sale. James Dillard of the County of Chester to Alexander Booeter of the County of Newberry in consideration of £45 Sterling, one Negro girl, named Jude between eleven and twelve years of age. Signed. James Dillard. Wit. John Crooks, John Foote. Proved by John Crooks before W. Wadlington, J.P. March 16, 1790. Recorded March 23, 1790. W. Malone Clerk Court.

Deed Book A: 963
March 10, 1790. Deed of Gift. Elizabeth Vaughan of the District of 96, County of Newberry to Olleyman Dodgen, her son, of the aforesaid place. Give Negroes, Jacob, Phillils, Milly, Jack and Daniel. Signed. Elizabeth Vaughan (mark). Wit. Jean Brown (mark), Mary Brown (mark). Proved by Jean Brown before B. Waters J.P. March 15, 1790. Recorded March 25, 1790. W. Malone Clerk Court.

Deed Book A: 992-993
July 25, 1784. Deed of Gift. Thomas Johnston to Catrine Butler, daughter of the said Thomas Johnston, both of the District of 96 - one Negro wench about four years old, named Nell with all her increase at the death of my wife Elizabeth. Signed. Thomas Johnston. Wit. Henry Butler (mark), Mary Butler (mark). Proved by Henry Butler before John Hunter J.P. April 23, 1785. Recorded May 14, 1790. W. Malone Clerk Court.

Deed Book A: 1016
January 12, 1789. Bill of Sale. John Chandler, planter, of the District of 96 to John Chandler, Junr., planter of the aforesaid place. In consideration of £ 90 Sterling. One Negro boy, names Lewis about seven years old, one Negro boy, named Charles about five years old, one sorrel stallion with one hind foot white and a star in his forehead, six years old. Signed John Chandler. Wit. James Waters, Richard Bonds (mark), John Waller. Proved by John Waller before W. Wadlington, J.P. March 13, 1790. Recorded July 16, 1790. W. Malone Clerk Court.

Deed Book A: 1030
August 13, 1790. Deed of Gift. Mary Graham of the County of Newberry to Jesse Graham Riley, her son, of the aforesaid place. Her Dowery and third negroes and lands and right of administration on the estate of George Graham deceased. Signed. Mary Graham (mark). Wit. Jeremiah Williams,

James Graham. Proved by James Graham before Robert Rutherford, J.P. August 28, 1790. Recorded Aug. 30, 1790. W. Malone, Clerk, Court.

Deed Book A: 1106
November 11, 1790 - Deed of Gift. Elizabeth Vaughn of Newberry County, State of South Carolina to Oliman Dodgen, her son, of the State and County aforesaid. One Negro woman Phillis and her three children and one Negro man Jacob; also 200 acres of land and after his decease to go to his son James Dodgen. Signed. Elizabeth Vaughn (mark). Wit. Daniel Pitts Junr., Aaron Pitts, Edward Pitts. Proved by Daniel Pitts Junr. before J. Roberts Brown, J.P. January 13, 1791. Recorded February 18, 1791. W. Malone, Clerk Court.

Deed Book A: 1121
January 27, 1791. Deed of Gift. Elizabeth Turner (widow of William Turner deceased) of the District of 96, State of South Carolina to Rebekah Turner, her grand daughter, of the State and District aforesaid. A female black slave, named Charlotte, ages about four years next Christmas. Signed. Elizabeth Turner. Wit. William Irby, Benj. Long. Proved by William Irby before R. Brown. 17 May 1791. Recorded W. Malone Clerk Court. June 8, 1791.

Deed Book A: 1122
January 27, 1791. Deed of Gift. Elizabeth Turner (Surviving widow of William Turner deceased) of the District of 96, State of South Carolina to Richard Turner, grandson, of the aforesaid place. A female Negro slave, named Hams, aged 20 years. Signed. Elizabeth Turner. Wit. William Irby, Benj. Long. Proved by William Irby before R. Brown. 17 May 1791. Recorded W. Malone Clerk Court. June 8, 1791.

Deed Book A: 1123
January 27, 1791. Deed of Gift. Elizabeth Turner (Surviving widow of William Turner deceased) of the District of 96, State of South Carolina to William Turner, Junr., grandson, of Edgefield County. A female Negro slave, named Jemima aged a year next April. Signed. Elizabeth Turner. Wit. William Irby, Benj. Long. Proved by William Irby before R. Brown. 17 May 1791. Recorded W. Malone Clerk Court. June 8, 1791.

Deed Book A: 1143
July 22, 1791. Deed of Gift. Edwin Conway of the County of Newberry, District of 96, State of South Carolina to Agatha Conway, daughter, of the aforesaid place. Three Negroes - Catsey, Fanny and Betty and their increase, one bed and furniture and one large gilded looking glass. Signed

Edwin Conway. Wit. James Criswell, R. Watts. Recorded Aug 29, 1791. W. Malone Clerk Court.

Deed Book A: 1170
June 1, 1791. Bill of Sale. Joseph Dawkins to Alexander Bookter, both of Newberry County in consideration of £140 Sterling - five Negroes, one Negro woman, yellow about 35 years of age by the name of Milly and four children; one boy named Champ about 18 years of age, one boy, named Lewis, about four years of age, one girl, named Venus about three years of age, one girl named Jackey, eight months old. Signed Joseph Dawkins. Wit. John Crooks, John Turner. Recorded September 8, 1791. Fredk. Nance, DC.

Deed Book A: 1187
March 23, 1785. Bill of Sale. Joseph Brown and Kezia, his wife, of the District of 96, State of South Carolina, to Alexander Bookter of the aforesaid place. For consideration of £32, 12sillings 6 pence one Negro boy, named Kent. Signed Joseph Brown, Kezia Brown (mark). Wit. W. Malone Sr. Joseph Dawkins. Recorded January 2, 1792. W. Malone Clerk Court.

Deed Book A: 1189
20 May 1791. Mortgage. Ephraim Liles, Junr. Of the District of 96 to John Gorree, planter, of the aforesaid place. One negro slave, named Ned, fifteen years of age; one stud horse 7 years old with a blaze in his forehead and one white foot; one sorrel horse and cold; one sorrel mare, branded under the mane W, one black mare, branded on the near shoulder T.D. and on the thigh A.L.... Signed: Ephraim Liles. Wit. Edwd. Kelly, Williamson Liles. Recorded January 7, 1792. Fredk. Nance, D.C.

Deed Book A: 1201
No Date: Deed of Gift. Abel Jones Horsey of the District of Orangeburgh to Mary Hogg, widow (sister). All lands that were given to my by my honoured father Daniel Horsey, deceased, by his last will and testament and all that will fall to me at the death of my mother, Sarah Horsey, living, in the District of 96 on Williams Creek, also six slaves - Primas, Bett, Sampson, Sam, Nance and Jim. Signed Abel Jones Horsey. Wit. John Miller, Absalom Lake. Recorded February 3, 179(?) W. Malone Clerk Court.

DEED BOOK B: 1792 - 1794

Deed Book B: 75
December 6, 1791: Deed of Gift. Elizabeth Turner (wife of William Turner, dec'd.) of the District of Ninety Six, County of Newberry and State of South Carolina; to Elizabeth Long, (granddaughter and also daughter of Benjamin and Priscilla Long), of the aforesaid place a negro girl named Beckah, about two years of age. Signed: Elizabeth Turner. Signed: Elizabeth Turner. Wit: William Irby, Willis Pruit (mark). Proved by William Irby before Mercer Babb, J.P. February 29, 1792. Recorded May 11, 1792. Fredk. Nance, DC.

Deed Bok B: 76
December 6, 1791: Deed of Gift. Elizabeth Turner (wife of William Turner, dec'd.) of the District of Ninety Six, County of Newberry and State of South Carolina; to Henry Long, (son of Benjamin and Priscilla Long), of the aforesaid place, a negro boy named Frank, about nine years of age. Signed: Elizabeth Turner. Signed: Elizabeth Turner. Wit: William Irby, Willis Pruit (mark). Proved by William Irby before Mercer Babb, J.P. February 29, 1792. Recorded May 11, 1792. Fredk. Nance, DC.

Deed Book B: 211:
November 15, 1792: Deed of Gift. George Montgomery of the County of Newberry State of South Carolina; to Elizabeth, daughter and David Glynn, son in law, of the aforesaid place; 200 acres land, two negroes, Joe and Lettuce, three head horses, one cream colored, no brand.....Signed George Montgomery (mark). Wit. William Malone, Sr., Joseph Caldwell. Proved by Joseph Caldwell before Edward Finch, J.P. November 17,1792. Recorded W. Malone, Clerk Court.

Deed Book B: 223:
September 29, 1792: Bill of Sale. James Grayham of the District of Ninety Six and State of South Carolina, planter; to Alexander Bookter, planter, of the aforesaid place. In consideration of the sum of £55 Sterling, one Negro wench, named Salley. Signed James Grayham. Wit: Peter Statley. Wm. Finch. Recorded December 11, 1792. Fredk. Nance, DC.

Deed Book B: 229
February 8, 1790: Bill of Sale. John Chandler, Planter, of the District of 96, County of Newberry and State of South Carolina to John Clark, Planter, of the aforesaid place, in consideration of the sum of £20, one Negro boy, named James. Signed: John Chandler, Wit. John Chandler (mark). William

Chandler. Proved by John Chandler before W. Wadlington J.P. March 6, 1790. Recorded December 11 , 1792. Fredk. Nance. DC.

Deed Book B: 360
August 18, 1792: Bill of Sale. John Edwards and Mary, his wife, Samuel Cotton and Elizabeth, his wife, John Tune and Ruth, his wife, Litisha Edwards, Rhoda Edwards and Margarett Edwards, daughters of said John Edwards and Mary, his wife, of the County of Newberry and State of South Carolina to Thomas Chappel of the same place. Consideration £70 Sterling, one negro woman slave about 18 years old, named Dinah, one Negro boy about eight years old, named Frank. Signed. John Edwards, Mary Edwards (mark, Samuel Cotton, Elizabeth Cotton (mark) John Tune, Ruth Tune (mark), Margarett Edwards. Wit: William Satterwhite, Thomas Brown, Thomas McMahon (mark). Recorded April 10, 1795. Fredk. Nance, DC.

Deed Book B: 370
January 17, 1793. Bill of Sale. Thoroughgood Chambers to Alexander Bookter, both of Newberry County and State of South Carolina. Consideration £50 Sterling, including the execution levied on said Bookter by William Satterwhite, sheriff of the County aforesaid. One Negro boy, named Dick, about fifteen years of age, well grown, likely and of a yellow complexion. Signed. Thoroughgood Chambers. Wit. Andrew Crooks, Peter Stally. Proved by Peter Stally before Edward Finch, J.P. Recorded 16 April 1797. Fredk. Nance, DC.

Deed Book B: 419
December 11, 1792. Deed of Gift. George Ruff of the County of Newberry and State of South Carolina; to John Henry Ruff, his son, of the aforesaid County and State. One Negro fellow Daniel, which be bought in his name by my consent of J and C. Liles - 130 acres of land of George Martin by consent; two colts, one by mare, one Negro Linas? And also £300 Sterling in goods now in my store in the County aforesaid, which before the signing of these presents I have delivered him and Inventory of the same. Signed. George Ruff. Wit. John Kinard, William Huffmaster. Proved by John Kinard before David Ruff, J.P. April 26, 1792. Recorded May 15, 1793. Fredk. Nance, DC.

Deed Book B: 420
April 15, 1793: Deed of Gift. John A. Summers and Mary Summers of the County of Lexington to John Henry Ruff, son in law and Elizabeth, daughter, of the aforesaid State and County of Newberry; one tract of land,; 250 acres, which they are in possession of called Mountz old mill place with the two mills and woods, two Negroes, one child Peggy and one child

Hager, one black horse, one spinet. Signed John A. Summers, Mary Summers (mark). Wit. Charistian Algire, Henry Smith, William Hoffmaster. Proved by Christian Algire before David Ruff. April 29, 1793 Recorded May 15, 1793. Fredk. Nance, DC.

Deed Book B: 438
December 10, 1785: Bill of Sale. Whereas George Dawkins, late of the District of 96, (deceased) did give unto me Joseph Dawkins in his last will and testament the following Negroes, Nell, Champ, Edenborough, Lewsy and Pegg and by said will desire that his wife should be put into her thirds for which I the said Joseph Dawkins do give unto James Liles and his wife and their heirs forever One Negro child named Phillis which I do hereby warrant and defend from all lawful claims. Wit. 10 December 1785. Signed Joseph Dawkins. Wit. Thomas Herbert, James Beard. Proved by Thomas Herbert before John Hampton, JQ. March 2, 1793. Recorded May 21, 1793. Fredk. Nance, DC.

Deed Book B: 466
June 26, 1793: Deed of Gift. James Simms, Sr. of Union County and State of South Carolina, to Drucilla Brasilman, daughter, of the aforesaid place. Nine negroes: Phillis, Sarah, Ithea, Stephen, Benjamin, Abina, Barlet, and Susahan and Henry. Signed, James Sims. Wit. John Sims, S. Adams, John S. Sims. Proved by S. Adams before Edward Finch, J.P. March 26, 1793. Recorded June 26, 1793. Fredk. Nance, DC.

Deed Book B: 467
March 22, 1793: Mortgage. James Sims, Senr. Of Union County, State of South Carolina, planter to Peter Braselman of Newberry County, South Carolina, Merchant. In consideration of £1000 Sterling. - one tract of land in Union County (metes and bounds given) containing 600 acres; 150 acres on Tyger River and another 100 for a total of 850 acres; also 36 negroes: Jack and Doll and their children Ambrose, Paul; Isaac and Tabby and their children Jack, Emille, Fanny, Robert; Molley and her children Charles, Edward, Delf, Abram, Sawny, Tom and Patience, Big Lucy and Daniel, Tabby, Peter, Desly, and Major and Lucy; Jenny and her children Mary, Henry, Peter; Delsey and her children Morning and Daniel, Isaac, Lucy, Amy, Frank and Doll; also ten horses, mares and colts, furniture, hoggs, tools... Signed James Sims, Sr. Wit: James Sims jr., Robert Powell, Recorded 29 June 1793. Fredk. Nance, DC.

Deed Book B: 470
July 10, 1793: Deed of Gift. Thomas W. Waters of the County of Newberry to Mary Davis, my wife's mother, of the aforesaid place - one Negro boy

named George (a child of a Negro wench I bought of Henry and Frank Wilson), which said Negro is to be or just property during her natural life and not to be disposed of to any other person but to live in particular with her under this reason that the Negro not to be taken out of the state and after her death revert to me and also that I said Waters, to pay said Negroes Tax. Signed. Thos. W. Waters. Wit. John Hays, Georg William Irby. Proved by John Hays before Peter Julin, J.P. November 6, 1791. Recorded July 10, 1793. Fredk. Nance, DC.

Deed Book B: 483
February 12, 1791: Bill of Sale. Uriah Hardman of the County of Newberry and State of South Carolina, planter, to Peter Brasilman and Company of the aforesaid County, and State, Merchants. In Consideration £60 Sterling. one Negro boy, named Dave and one Negro wench, named Hannah and her child, named Jude, a black mare, a bay horse, four cows, three feather beds and furniture with sundry household furniture, sixty hoggs and sundry working tools for plantation work. Signed. Uriah Hardman. Wit. Robert Powell. Recorded July 22, 1793, Fredk. Nance, DC.

Deed Book B: 489
February 1, 1793. Bill of Sale. William Finch of the County of Newberry and State of South Carolina to Aaon Cates of the aforesaid place. Consideration £55 Sterling. one Negro girl, named Tillis about 10 years old likely and well grown. Signed. William Finch. Wit. Alexr. Bookter, Peter Statay. Proved by Alexander Bookter. July 19, 1793. Recorded August 6, 1793. Fredk. Nance, DC.

Deed Book B: 628
March 22, 1794. Bill of Sale. William Hencock of the County of Newberry and State of South Carolina to Alexander Bookter of the aforesaid place, one Negro man named Harry, about 21 years old. Singed. William Hencock. Wit. Peter Staley, D. Brummitt, John Mink. Consideration £ 60 Sterling. Recorded March 24, 1794. Wm. Satterwhite, DC.

Deed Book B: 629
December 10, 1792: Bill of Sale. Francis Davenport of the County of Newberry in the State of South Carolina to James Davenport of the aforesaid place. Consideration £15 Sterling, one Negro girl, named Easther. Signed Francis Davenport. Wit: George Goggans, Richard Henderson Waldrop. Proved by George Goggans before Robt. Gillam, J.P. March 4, 1794. Recorded April 11, 1794. Wm. Satterwhite, DC.

Deed Book B: 631-632
March 3, 1785. Bill of Sale. Peter Conway of the Parish of X Church and
County of Lancaster, to Edwin Conway of the aforesaid place.
Consideration £3000, gold or silver currency. The following Negro slaves,
Viz., Will, Dominy, Adam, Anthony, Spencer, Isaac, Mark, Sam, Tom,
Charles, Bond, Daniel, Sillah, Peter, Phill, Alie, Judy, a child unchristened,
Edmund, Jessu, Siller, Polly, Jane, Weaver, Phill, Judy, Sarah, Letty, Fanny,
Aron, Spencer and two children unchristened, Jeffrey, Hagan, Rachel,
Nanny, Joe, Tabby, Molly and Molly. Signed Peter Conway. Wit. John
Heath, Richard Selden. Proved by Richard Selden before James Mayson
J.N.C. December 30, 1793. Recorded April 11, 1794. Wm. Satterwhite, DC.

Deed Book B: 633
December 2, 1793. Bill of Sale. Daniel McKie of the County of Newberry
and State of South Carolina to Robert Spence of the aforesaid place.
Consideration £ 50 Sterling. one negro man, named Ben, between 28-30
years of age. Signed Daniel McKie. Wit. Wm. Satterwhite, Samuel
Landsey, Caleb Lindsey. Proved by Samuel Lindsey before John Speake
J.P. February 27, 1794. Recorded April 12, 194. Wm. Satterwhite, D.C.

Deed Book B: 634
November 29, 1790. Bill of Sale. Richard Seldon of the State of Virginia
and James Creswell, of the State of South Carolina to James Davenport, of
the State of South Carolina. Consideration £36 Sterling - 2 Negro boys,
named Moses and Aron. Signed. Richard Seldon, James Creswell. Wit. John
Wallace, William Griffin. Proved by John Wallace before Robert Gillum,
J.P. March 4, 1794. Recorded April 15, 1794. Wm. Satterwhite, DC.

Deed Book B: 666-667
April 6, 1794. Deed of Gift. James Goggans of the County of Newberry and
State of South Carolina to Thomas Goggans and James Goggans and
Johnson Goggans and Mary Goggans, and Abraham Goggans. Unto
Thomas, William and James Goggans 150 acres on which I now live to be
equally divided between the three, to Thomas Goggans one bay mare bridle
and saddle and one cow and one sow and one ewe and 100 bushels of corn
and....and to my two sons Johnson and Abraham one Negro boy, named
Lewis, to be sold when they come of age to be equally divided between the
two (other children mention for household effects)..... Signed James
Goggans, Wit. George Johnson before Providence Williams, J.P. April 11,
1794. Recorded April 24, 1794. Wm. Satterwhite, DC.

Deed Book B: 701
January 1, 1794. Mortgage. Bartlett Brooks of the County of Newberry and
state of South Carolina to Thomas Wadsworth and William Turpin, called
Wadsworth and Turpin, Merchants, of the same place, one negro named
Abram about 35 years of age, a wench named Mary about 25 years of age, a
wench named Jude 46 years of age, Agg about 6 years of age, Suck about 5
years of age, David 3 years of age and Sam. Sold for payment of £ 259 six
shillings and 5/ as by bond bearing date January 1, 1794 in the penal sum of
£ 518 12 shillings and 10 pence. Signed Bartlet Brooks (mark). Wit. Dan
Symmes, John Garvin. Recorded May 12, 1794 Wm. Satterwhite, DC.

Deed Book B: 775
June 17, 1794. Bill of Sale. James Campbell, planter, of the County of
Newberry to Henry Crick, a negro slave, named Judy and the issue of her
body. Signed James Campbell. Recorded June 17, 1794. Wm. Satterwhite,
DC.

Deed Book B: 794-795
_____? Newberry County, South Carolina. Know all Men by
these Presents that we Samuel Kelly and Abijah O'Neal, John and Robert
Kelly of the County and State aforesaid, planters, Heirs of the estate of John
Kelly, deceased, which estate consists of some slaves, which slaves by Will
of said deceased were to be divided amongst his heirs and we the above
named Samuel Kelly, Abijah O'Neal, John and Robert Kelly having come
into possession of our part thereof, Names Jeffrey a yellow man of about 40
years of age with his wife Judith, a black woman, supposed to be about that
age and their son Ben a yellow man about 23 years old, one other Negro
man about 60 years of age and his wife, Jack and Dinah and their son Bill a
black man twenty years old , also Cloe, daughter of said Jack and Dinah, a
black woman about 28 years of age with three of her children Lucy a yellow
girl, nine years old past since the 8th of month last, and Dick, a black boy 3
years old and also Ben the youngest child of said Cloe, these being the
names and ages of our part and dividend of Slaves in said deceased estate.
And we believing that Liberty is the natural right of all mankind this 27th
day of the 6th month 1793 have Manumised in -franchised and from the
bonds of Slavery forever set free and said Negroes, each and every of them
as above named and described to hold and enjoy such Manumission and
freedom free from any claim of service by us or either of us our heirs
executors administrators or any other person or persons claiming by through
or under us they that have arrived to the number of years that is commonly
called of age to hold and enjoy such Manumission from the date of the day
hereof forever, and the three children of Cloe above mentioned to remain in
the service of care of their aforesaid Masters until they are of age, from

121

which times forth and aforesaid Masters until they are of age, from which time forth and forever to be free as above mentioned and Manumitted by us. In Witness Whereof we the above named Samuel Kelly, Abijah O'Neal, John and Robert Kelly have hereunto set our hands and seals at Bush River in the County aforesaid the 27th day of the sixth month in the year of our Lord one thousand seven hundred and ninety three, the seventeenth year of the American Independence.

Signed Samuel Kelly, Abijah O'Neal, John Kelly, Robert Kelly. In the presence of us. Jehue Innman, Henry Steddom, Saml. Miles.

Agreed to before signed that the above girl should be free at 18 years and the boys at 21. Proved by Jahue Inman before Mercer Babb May 12, 1794. Recorded June 18, 1794. Wm. Satterwhite, DC.

DEED BOOK C: 1794 - 1797

Deed Book C: 70
December 11, 1794. Bill of Sale. Samuel Benjamins of the County of Newberry and State of South Carolina to Samuel Lindsey of the aforesaid place. In consideration of the sum of £20 Sterling, one Negro woman named Mary, one horse and one mare and all my household furniture and other property in my possession. Signed Samuel Benjamins, Margaret Benjamins (mark). Wit. Wm. Satterwhite. Sneed Davis. Proved by William Satterwhite before John Speake, J.P. January 8,1795. Recorded January 29, 1795. Fredk. Nance, C.N.C.

Deed Book C: 121
February 28, 1795. Bill of Sale. John Barlow, planter, of the District of 96, County of Newberry and State of South Carolina; to Andrew Smyth, Junr. and Elizabeth Ann Smyth, his wife of the aforesaid place. In consideration of the sum of £ 80 Sterling, three negroes children, Viz., one little Negro boy names Santa Croix about 5 years old, one little Negro girl named Harriet with her future increase about a half year old, one little Negro child named Ireland about 3 months old. Signed John Barlow. Wit. John MacCary, Josiah Gates. Recorded March 2, 1795. Wm. Satterwhite, DC.

Deed Book C: 122
December 8, 1795. Bill of Sale. John Barlow, planter, of the District of 96 and County of Newberry and State of South Carolina to Andrew Symth, Junr. and Elizabeth, his wife, of the aforesaid place. In consideration of the sum of £ 65 Sterling. One Negro man, named George about 20 years of age.

Signed. John Barlow. Wit. David Speers, Wm. Craig. Proved by William Craig before Charles Griffin, J.P. March 2, 1795. Wm. Satterwhite, DC.

Deed Book C: 145
February 28, 1790. Bill of Sale. Benjamin Long, of the State of South Carolina and County of Newberry to Elizabeth Turner of the aforesaid place. In consideration of the sum of £85 Sterling. one Negro fellow, named Monday. Signed Benjamin Long. Wit. Thomas Waters. Proved by Thomas Waters before Edward Finch, J.P. March 2, 1795. Recorded March 30, 1795. Fredk. Nance, C.N.C.

Deed Book C: 146
August 15, 1794. Bill of Sale. Gabriel Friday of Orangeburgh District and State of South Carolina to Alexander Bookter of the District of Ninety Six and State of South Carolina. In consideration of the sum of £ 50 Sterling one Negro man, called Sizar, about 22 years of age. Signed. Gabriel Friday. Wit. Thomas Rogers, Wm. Linton. Recorded March 31, 1795. Fredk. Nance, C.N.C.

Deed Book C: 147
February 7, 1795. Bill of Sale. John Barlow, of the State of South Carolina and County of Newberry and District of 96 to Andrew Smythn, Junr. and Elizabeth Ann Smith, his wife, planter of the aforesaid County, State and District. In consideration of the sum of £ 1500 Sterling 400 acres of land in the County aforesaid between the forks of Mudlick Creek and Little River, originally granted to John Andrews and by Samuel Andrew, son of said John, sold and conveyed to John Barlow; also 12 Negroes, Viz., Negro man, named Wigdom, about 25 years old, one Negro man, named Tom, about 25 years old, one Negro man named Major, about 28 years old, one Negro man, named Jacob about 40 years old, one Negro man, named Bob, about 40 years old one Negro boy, named Thomas, about 10 years old; two Negro wenches named Mary Ann and Susahan, Mary Ann about 50 years old and Susanah about 27 years old, together with Susanah's children one named Fortune about 7 years old, one named Santa Croix, about 5 years old and one Little girl, names Hariot, nigh 3 years old, one Negro child, named Ireland together with Susanah's future offspring... Signed. John Barlow, Elizabeth Barlow. Wit. John MacCary, Josiah Gates. Proved by John MacCary before Charles Griffin, J.P. March 2, 1795. Recorded March 31, 1795. Fredk. Nance, C.N.C.

Deed Book C: 210-211
1 January 1795. Mortgage. William Pettipool of the County of Newberry to William Turpin and Thomas Wadsworth, Merchants (otherwise called

Wadsworth and Turpin, Merchants) of the aforesaid County and State of
South Carolina one Negro wench named Moll about 30 years of age,
Patience about 30 years old, Hannah about 12 years of age, Lin about 11
years of age, Violet 9 years of age, Esther 7 years of age and George 3 years
of age sold in open market to secure payment of £ 87 12 shillings 2p as by
bond bearing date the 1 January 1795. Fredk. Nance, C.N.C.

Deed Book C: 212
January 1, 1785. Bill of Sale. Moses Lindsey, planter, of the District of 96
and State of South Carolina to David Boyd of the aforesaid place. One
Negro boy, named Dan. In consideration of the sum of £ 53 Sterling.
Signed Moses Lindsey. Wit. Robert Caldwell, Samuel Morris, Proved by
Robert Caldwell before John Hunter J.P. January 10, 1785. Recorded April
27, 1795. Fredk. Nance, C.N.C.

Deed Book C: 235
November 30, 1794. Deed of Gift. Thomas Lindsey and Lyda, his wife, of
the County of Newberry and State of South Carolina to our daughter, Polley
Wells and George, her husband, of the same place. One negro girl named
Betty. Signed Thomas Lindsey, Lydda Lindsey (mark). Wit. Michael Gore,
Isaac Guilder (mark). Proved by Michael Gore before Edward Finch, J.P.
May 6, 1795. Recorded May 12, 1795 . Fredk. Nance, C.N.C.

Deed Book C: 259
March 28, 1795. Mortgage. Daniel Williams, planter of Newberry County,
South Carolina to James Waldrop and Samuel Henderson of the same place.
One negro fellow Harry and one negro named Moses and one negro wench
Jude and her two children George and Lena, one negro girl named Sarah,
for the payment of £ 400 Sterling as by bond entered in between Daniel
Williams to the said Samuel Henderson and James Waldrop. Signed Daniel
Williams. Wit. William Caldwell, John Simpson. Recorded May 29, 1795.
Fredk. Nance, C.N.C.

Deed Book C: 259
May 8, 1795. Bill of Sale. Francis Davenport Senr to Francis Davenport, Jr.
both of the County of Newberry, South Carolina. In consideration of £ 20
Sterling, one negro man Slave, named Anthony about 18 years old, past
(which said slave is now in the crop and as soon as the said crop is
completed than the said salve named Anthony is to become the sold
property. Signed Francis Davenport. Wit. John Thomas S.M., Isaac
Davenport, Ann Thomas (mark). Proved by Isaac Davenport before Charles
Griffin, J.P. 18 May 1795. Recorded June 5, 1795. Fredk. Nance, C.N.C.

Deed Book C: 294-295

July 23, 1792. Bill of Sale. Daniel Williams, Sr. of the County aforesaid and State of South Carolina to John Williams (son of Daniel) and John Williams, Sr., both, of the State of South Carolina and County of Newberry. In consideration of the sum of £ 1500 Virginia Currency. 27 Negro slaves, Viz., Phil, Jack, Will, Kyzer, Moses, Harry, Jacob, Jude, Isbell, Ruth, Easter, Rose, Aggy, Aron, John, Dave, Frankey, Suckey, Sarah, Edom, Little Fill, Solomon, George, James, Lett, Winney and Harris. Signed. Daniel Williams. Wit. Howell Moss (mark). Daniel Williams, Junr. Recorded June 3, 1795. Fredk. Nance, C.N.C.

Deed Book C: 296

23 July 1792 Deed. Where in and by a certain deed bearing date 23 July 1792 my brother Daniel Williams of North Carolina did convey to me and a certain John Williams Jr. 27 negroes as above named. And where as we the said John Williams S.D. and John Willaims, Junr. Did not buy nor contract to pay any money or other consideration to the Daniel Williams for the said negroes, but the said deeded was made on Secret trust that we should hold said negroes subject to the order control and direction of the said Daniel Williams. I do hereby declare that I John Williams to whom such conveyance was made together with John Williams Jr. do hold said negroes and their issue shall be and remain forever subject to the control direction and order and command of the said Daniel Williams who is the real and true owner of the said slaves. In Wit. Set my hand 20 April 1793. Signed. John Williams. Wit. Charles Colcock, Stephen Heard. Proved by Charles Colcock before Julius Nichols, Jr. , J.P. 22 April 1793. Recorded June 8, 1795. Fredk. Nance C.N.C.

Deed Book C: 298

25 March 1795. Ninety Six District, SC. To all there Presents by a deed bearing the date 23 July 1792 Daniel Williams late of North Carolina did convey to his brother John Williams (son of Daniel) and to John Williams Junr, 27 negores by a certain bill of sale, annexed whose named are there in set forth and where as it appears that the said negroes were conveyed to them the said John Williams son of Daniel and John Williams Junr, deceased, in secret trust and confidence and whereas the said John Williams son of Daniel did on the 20 April 1793 give and perfect to the said Daniel Williams a general release and quit claim on the said property. Whereas the said John Williams Jr. deceased in his life time appointed me as his attorney to settle the said business with the said Daniel Williams and again in his Last will directs the same and where the executor of his estate by the last will appointed me to fully settle and close all disputes and accounts between the said Daniel Williams and the said John Williams, Jr. deceased.

Whereas I John Wallace as the trustee and the said Daniel Williams to avoid the trouble and expense of Law here mutually consented and agreed to leave all the said disputes and accounts to the final ending and determination of John Satterwhite and James Caldwell .. 25 March 1795. John Wallace, Trustee. R. Brown, JNC. Recorded 8 June 1795. Fredk. Nance, C.N.C.

Deed Book C: 320

21 March 1795. Indenture between Thomas W. Waters, of South Carolina, and William Summers and Peter Julin, Esqr. Of the other. That the said Thomas W. Waters hath given his bond to the County of Newberry in the penal sum of 1000 £ with a condition hereunto belonging and annexed. I Thomas W. Waters of my own free will and accord have this day given to William Summers and Peter Julian Esqrs. A Mortgage on the property both real and Personal. Give as my securities as well as to fulfil my bond to the County, give this day as Collector of the Tax of Newberry County. Fist I mortgage to said William Summers and Peter Julian Esquire all that plantation I now live on, on Saluda River, containing 850 acres, except 225 acres Jesse Pugh has my bond for title for, together with all advantages and profits. Also one negro wench called Hannah, one mill containing upward of 1000 gallons bought of Col. Robert Rutherford, one bay mare called Rosey, one filley called Polley Honeycomb,...one other note said Waters has from Francis Davenport for 2 pounds and a note of hand said Waters has of Edmond Riggs for a negro girl due in 2 years with 10 head of sheep.. Set his hand Thos. W. Waters. Wit. William Day, South Bradshaw. Proved by R. Brown, JNC.

Deed Book C: 365

August 4, 1795. Deed of Gift. Francis Davenport Senr, of the County of Newberry, State of South Carolina, to my children, Viz., Isaac Davenport, and William Davenport, David Davenport and Sarah Beeks, Abigail Davenport. To my loving son Isaac Davenport, one negro woman named Rachel, one negro woman named Jenny, one negro man named Peter, one negro man named Coy, one negro man named Mingo, one negro girl named Rachael and 20 acres of land joining Mr. Daniel McKie's line.. To my loving son William Davenport, one negro boy named Dick; to my loving son David Davenport, 200 acres of land, one negro boy named Oliver, one feather bed and one mare and colt; to my loving daughter Sarah Beeks one negro boy named Tom, to my loving daughter Abigail Davenport, one negro girl named Nan and one feather bed. Signed Francis Davenport. Wit. Ezekial Waldrop, Edward Turner, George Goggans. Proved by Ezekial Waldrop before Charles Griffin, J.P. 5 August 1795. Recorded 18 August 1795. Fredk. Nance, C.N.C.

Deed Book C: 367-368
August 4, 1795. Deed of Gift. Francis Davenport, Sr., of the District of 96 and County of Newberry ,and State of South Carolina, planter, to Patty Waldrop, beloved daughter, of the State and County aforesaid, one Negro girl named Patience. Signed Francis Davenport. Wit. Isaac Davenport, Edward Turner, Elizabeth Towling. Proved by Isaac Davenport before Charles Griffin, J.P. August 5, 1795. Recorded August 18, 1795. Fredk. Nance, C.N.C.

Deed Book C: 369
August 1, 1795. Deed of Gift. Francis Davenport, Senr. , of the District of 96, South Carolina ,to Nancy Waldrop of the same place. In Consideration of the Natural Love and Affection, one negro girl named Eliza. Signed Francis Davenport. Wit. David Davenport, Edward Turner, William Morgan (mark). Proved by David Davenport before Charles Griffin, J.P. August 1, 1795. Recorded August 18, 1795. Fredk. Nance, C.N.C.

Deed Book C: 468
October 1, 1795. Deed of Gift. Ann Floyd, widow, of the County of Newberry and State of South Carolina, to Margaret Davenport (wife of Joseph Davenport) of the aforesaid place. One Negro woman called Lucy and one Negro girl called Lucy with all there hereafter increase. Signed. Ann Floyd (mark). Wit. R. Brown, N.N.C. Recorded October 14, 1795. Fredk. Nance, C.N.C.

Deed Book C: 469
October 1, 1795. Deed of Gift. Ann Floyd, widow, of the County of Newberry and State of South Carolina, to William Floyd, her son, of the aforesaid place. One Negro man called Peter and one Negro girl called Clary. Signed. Ann Floyd (mark). Wit. R. Brown, N.N.C. Recorded October 14, 1795. Fredk. Nance, C.N.C.

Deed Book C: 470
October 1, 1795. Deed of Gift. Ann Floyd, widow of the County of Newberry and State of South Carolina, to her son Robert Floyd of the aforesaid place. One sorrel Golding called Jack , one certain Negro boy called Charles and one Negro woman called Nan. Signed. Ann Floyd (mark). Wit. R. Brown, N.N.C. Recorded October 14, 1795. Fredk. Nance, C.N.C.

Deed Book C: 471
September 2, 1794. Bill of Sale. Thomas Johnston, of the County of Newberry and District of 96, to Jehu Johnston of the aforesaid place - one

Negro woman, named Hagur about 30 years old. Signed. Thomas Johnston. Wit. Daniel Johnson, Mary Johnston (mark). Proved by Daniel Johnson before Charles Griffin, J.P. September 29, 1795. Recorded October 15, 1795. Fredk. Nance, C.N.C

Deed Book C: 476
October 1, 1795: Deed of Gift. Ann Floyd, widow, of the County of Newberry and State of South Carolina, to Temperance Liverett (wife of Thomas Liverett of the State aforesaid) her daughter. One Negro boy called Carolina, one Negro wench called Milly. Signed. Ann Floyd (mark). Wit. R. Brown. Recorded October 19, 1795. Fredk. Nance, C.N.C.

Deed Book C: 477
South Carolina, Newberry County. Before the Court of the County aforesaid, personally appeared Daniel Clary, Esqr., of the County who being duly sworn deposeth and sayeth on his oath that sometime in October 1780, three Negroes to wit: Sam, his wife, Tamer and her daughter Lydia, as he understood was the property of John Hampton were brought to the house of this deponent by Mr. Daniel Parkins which said Negroes were by the British commandant at that time at 96 ordered to be kept by this deponent till further ordered that some time in the latter end of the year 1780 or the beginning of the year 1781 an armed party came to the house of this deponent among whom were Francis Prince, John McElhaney, and others who took said Negroes and carried them all away that this deponent informed the said party how the said Negroes came into his possession as also whose Negroes they were and by what authority he kept them at the same time Godfrey Adams appeared in the said court and made oath that he saw the above named Negroes in the possession of the said Clary and knew them to be the said Hampton's property. Proved in open court 20 October 1795. Danl. Clary, Godfrey Adams. Test. Fredk. Nance C.N.C.

Deed Book C: 490
October 9, 1795: Bill of Sale. John Atkinson, Sr. ,of the County of Newberry and State of South Carolina, to Grace Atkinson, of the County and State, aforesaid. In consideration of the sum of 29 £ 5 shillings Sterling. One Negro girl named Amy about 7 years old for the sum of twenty six pounds and 1 feather bed for 5 shillings. Signed John Atkinson. Wit: Bartlett Satterwhite, Sr., Dudley Brooks. Proved by Dudley Brooks before Fedk. Nance, J.P. October 19, 1795. Recorded Dec. 28, 1795. Fredk. Nance, C.N.C.

Deed Book C: 491
January 24, 1794: Bill of Sale. James Spearman and Thomas Spearman, of
the County of Newberry and State of South Carolina, to Zachariah Smith
Brooks of the aforesaid County and State. In consideration of the sum of £
140 Sterling. Four Negroes: One woman, two girls and one boy, named
Judy, Dinah, Letty and Barnet. Signed James Spearman, Thomas Spearman.
Wit. B. Satterwhite, Joseph Burges (mark). Recorded Dec. 28, 1795. Fredk.
Nance, C.N.C.

Deed Book C: 492
October 9, 1795: Bill of Sale. John Atkison, Sr., of the County of Newberry
and State of South Carolina, to John Atkison, Junr. of the aforesaid place. In
consideration of the sum of £ 71 Sterling. One Negro man, named Tom
about 40 years old, one Negro woman named Jude about 2 years old, one
Negro woman named Beck about 15 years old, one Negro woman named
Cate about 23 years old, one Negro girl and one Negro boy about 1 year old,
the three above children named Hannah, Darkis and Elisha. Signed. John
Atkison (mark). Wit. B. Satterwhite, Sr., Dudley Brooks. Proved by Dudley
Brooks before Fredk. Nance, J.P. Oct. 19, 1795. Recorded Dec. 28, 1795.
Fredk. Nance, C.N.C.

Deed Book C: 499
South Carolina, Newberry District. Know all men by these Presents that I
John Coate, of the State and County, aforesaid, farmer, have Manumised,
enfranchised and from the bonds of Slavery forever set free and by these
presents do manumise enfranchise and from the bonds of Slavery forever set
free a Negro man named Jesse about 16 years of age to hold and enjoy such
manumition and freedom to the said Jesse free from any claim of service by
me my heirs, executors and administrators or any other person or persons
whomsoever from the day of the date thereof forever. In Witness whereof I
the said John Coate have hereunto Set my hand and seal at the State and
County aforesaid the 1 of October 1795 and in the 19th year of American
Independence. Signed, Sealed and delivered in the present of John Coate
(mark). Test. Richard Thomson, Daniel Richardson, Wright Coate.

Deed Book C: 502-503
December 2, 1794. Bill of Sale. David Shelton, of the County of Fairfield,
to Alexander Bookter and Company, of the County of Newberry. In
consideration of the sum of £ 15 1 shilling and 8 pence Sterling and 20 £
15 shillings and 2 pence in gold and silver. One Negro boy named Ben
about 15 years old. Signed David Shelton. Wit. George Dawkins, Andrew
Crooks, John Mink. Proved by George Dawkins before David Ruff, J.P.
March 10, 1795. Recorded December 30, 1795. Fredk. Nance, DC.

Deed Book C: 511
October 1, 1795: Deed of Gift. Ann Floyd, widow, of the County of
Newberry and State of South Carolina, to Frances Floyd, grand-daughter
(eldest daughter of Catherine Satterwhite, wife to Bartlett) of the aforesaid
County and State. One Negro girl called Silvia. Signed. Ann Floyd (mark).
Wit. J.R. Brown, J.N.C. Recorded January 4, 1795. Fredk. Nance, C.N.C.

Deed Book C: 512
October 1, 1795:. Ann Floyd, widow, of the County of Newberry and State
of South Carolina to Rebekah Floyd, grand-daughter (daughter of John
Floyd, son of Ann Floyd aforesaid) of the aforesaid County and State. One
Negro girl called Cate. Signed. Ann Floyd (mark). Wit. J.R. Brown, J.N.C.
Recorded January 4, 1795. Fredk. Nance, C.N.C.

Deed Book C: 513
October 1, 1795: Deed of Gift. Ann Floyd, widow, of the County of
Newberry and State of South Carolina, to John Floyd, her son, of the
aforesaid County and State. One Negro woman called Jinny and one Negro
girl called Winney and one sorrel mare called Jinny. Signed. Ann Floyd
(mark). Wit. J.R. Brown, J.N.C. Recorded January 4, 1795. Fredk. Nance,
C.N.C

Deed Book C: 514
October 1, 1795: Deed of Gift. Ann Floyd, widow, of the County of
Newberry and State of South Carolina, to Catherine Satterwhite, her
daughter (wife of Barlett Satterwhite) of the aforesaid place. One small
chestnut gelding, one Negro woman called Hannah. Signed. Ann Floyd
(mark). Wit. J.R. Brown, J.N.C. Recorded January 4, 1795. Fredk. Nance,
C.N.C.

Deed Book C: 515
July 15 1795: Bill of Sale. Uriah Wicker to John H. Ruff, both of the
County of Newberry and State of South Carolina. In consideration of the
sum of £ 60 Sterling, one Negro girl, named Rachael. Signed Uriah Wicker.
Wit. Jacob Leitzey (mark), George Ridlehoover, Adam Mits (mark). Proved
by George Ridlehoover before David Ruff, J.P. Sept. 24, 1954. Recorded
January 4, 196. Fredk. Nance, C.N.C.

Deed Book C: 521
July 15, 1795. Bill of Sale. Uriah Wicker to John H. Ruff, both of Newberry
County, South Carolina , In consideration of the sum of £ 60 Sterling, one
negro girl named Rachel. Signed. Uruah Wicker. Wit. Jacob Leitzey (mark),
George Ridlehoover, Adam Mits (mark). Proved by George Ridlehoover,

before David Ruff, J.P. 24 September 1794. Recorded January 4, 1796.
Fredk. Nance, C.N.C.

Deed Book C: 583
October 1, 1795. Deed of Gift. Ann Floyd, widow, of the County of
Newberry and State of South Carolina to Charles Gilliam, Grandson (son of
Harris Gilliam and my daughter Rebekah, deceased). One Negro girl called
Lidda and one bay gelding called Dic. Signed. Ann Floyd (mark). Wit. J.R.
Brown, J.N.C. Recorded Jan 21, 1795. Fredk. Nance, C.N.C.

Deed Book C: 613
November 26, 1795. Bill of Sale. Francis Davenport and Isaac Davenport,
of the County of Newberry and State of South Carolina, to James Davenport
of the same. In consideration of the sum of £ 60 Sterling. One Negro
woman, named Penney. Signed Francis Davenport, Isaac Davenport. Wit.
Francis Davenport, Junr., Caleb Gilbert. Proved by Francis Davenport, Mr.
Before Charles Griffin Nov. 28, 1795. Recorded February 2, 1796. Fredk.
Nance, C.C.

Deed Book C: 635
October 14, 1794. Bill of Sale. Thomas Lindsey, of the County of Newberry
and state of South Carolina, to Samuel Lindsey of the aforesaid place. In
consideration of the sum of £ 435 South Carolina Currency. Newow,
Toney, Sambirt, Sambow, Andrew, all men slaves; Debro and Dinah, Negro
woman, George a male child about 9 years old and Pat a girl child about 5
years old, Molly a girl child about 10 years old. Signed Thomas Lindsey.
Wit. R Brown, J.N.C. Recorded February 8, 1795, Fredk. Nance, C.N.C.

Deed Book C: 636
January 8, 1795: Bill of Sale. Daniel Williams to Samuel Williams, his son,
both of the County of Laurance{sic} and State of South Carolina. In
consideration of the sum of £ 40 Sterling. One Negro boy, called Jacob.
Signed. Daniel Williams. Wit. R. Brown. Proved by Elizabeth Williams and
Natty Williams. Recorded February 6,1796. Fredk. Nance, C.N.C.

Deed Book C: 643
February 1, 1791. Bill of Sale. John Lindsey, Esq., of the County of
Newberry and State of South Carolina to John Anderson of the aforesaid
place. In consideration of the sum of £ 600 Sterling. Six Negroes: Pompey,
Priscilla, Cain, Cato, Mack and Summer. Signed John Lindsey. Wit. Wm.

Tate, Caleb Lindsey. Proved by Caleb Lindsey before Frederick Nance, J.P. September 28, 1795. Recorded April 10, 1790. Fredk. Nance, C.N.C.

Deed Book C: 644
September 28, 1795. Bill of Sale. John Anderson, of Saluda Old Town in the County of Newberry and State of South Carolina; to John Lindsey of the same. In consideration of the sum of £ 300 Sterling. Four Negroes, namely: Pompey ages about 30 years of age, he being an African born; one Negro woman called Priscilla aged about 28 years a County born; one Negro man called Cain aged about 23 years a County born; one Negro man called Catoe ages about 23 all four Negro Slaves. Signed. John Anderson. Wit. William Elliot, James Lindsey. Proved by William Elliot before Robert Gilliam, J.P. October 6, 1795. Recorded April 10, 1796. Fredk. Nance, C.N.C.

Deed Book C: 667
November 24, 1795. Deed of Gift. Elizabeth Spence, widow of James Spence deceased, to Mary Glasgow, wife of Archabald Glasgow and step-daughter of Elizabeth Spence. All my dower in the estate of James Spence deceased, Viz., 200 acres of land and Negroes. Signed. Elizabeth Spence. Wit. James Lindsey and Robert Spence. Proved by Robert Spence before Edward Finch, J.P. March 25, 1796. Recorded May 4, 1796. Fredk. Nance, C.C.

Deed Book C: 686
April 28, 1795. Bill of Sale. Thomas Gains, planter, of the County of Newberry and State of South Carolina, to John Cannon of the same. One Negro boy, named Reuben. Signed Thomas Gains. Wit. Danl. Caldwell, James Caldwell. Proved by Danl. Caldwell before David Ruff, J.P. April 25, 1796. Recorded May 5, 1796. Fredk. Nance, C.N.C.

Deed Book C: 697
February 3, 1796. Deed of Gift. John Turner, of the County of Newberry and State of South Carolina, to John Turner, Junr. my two beloved sons of the aforesaid place. One Negro boy, named Frank to John Turner, Junr. and one Negro boy names Charles to William Turner. Signed. John Turner. Wit. John Thomas, S.M., William Cox. Proved by William Cox before Danl. Clary, J.P. March 16, 1796. Recorded May 9, 1796. Fredk. Nance. C.N.C.

Deed Book C. 698-699
February 26, 1796. Deed of Gift. John Turner, of the County of Newberry and State of South Carolina, to David Turner, son and Polly Turner, daughter, of the aforesaid place. One Negro boy, named Isaac and one

Negro girl named Charlotte to David Turner and one Negro girl named Suck to Polly Turner. Signed. John Turner. Wit. Orsamus Spragins. John Thomas SM. Recorded May 9, 1796. Frederick Nance, DC.

Deed Book C: 700
February 26,1796. Deed of Gift. Elizabeth Turner, widow of William Turner, deceased,, of the State of South Carolina and County of Newberry to Elizabeth Turner, daughter to my son John Turner, of the aforesaid place. One Negro girl named Jude. Signed. Elizabeth Turner. Wit. Orsamus Spragins, John Thomas S.M. Recorded May 9, 1796. Fredk. Nance, C.C.

Deed Book C: 757
May 30, 1794. Emancipation Deed. Edward Benbo, planter, of the County of Newberry in the State of South Carolina to David, a Negro man about 36 years of age. Signed. Edward Benbo. Wit. Isaac Jenkins, David Jenkins, Martha Jenkins. Proved by David Jenkins before Peter Julin, J.P. May 16, 1796. Recorded June 14, 1796. Fredk. Nance, C.C.

Deed Book C: 911
July 22, 1796. Bill of Sale. James Shearer of the County of Newberry and State of South Carolina, farmer, to William Crain, merchant of the aforesaid place. In consideration of the sum of £ 25 South Carolina Currency, my eldest Negro girl, about 10 years of age, named Nan. Signed. James Shearer. Wit. Saml. Lindsey. James Campbell. Proved by James Campbell before Fredk. Nance, J.P. November 4, 1796. Recorded November 14, 1796. Fredk. Nance, C.N.C.

Deed Book C: 919
October 15, 1796. Deed of Gift. Eva Margarette Gray of the County of Newberry and State of South Carolina, widow, to Casper Peister of the aforesaid place. One certain Negro girl named Molley, about 16 years of age. Signed. Eva Margarette Gray. (mark). Wit. Peter Gray. G. Adam Peister, Wm. Houseal. Proved by Peter Gray before Wm. Houseal Oct. 15, 1796. Recorded November 21, 1796. Fredk. Nance, C.N.C.

Deed Book C: 938-939
November 10, 1796. Bill of Sale. Isaac Davenport of the County of Newberry and State of South Carolina to James Davenport of the aforesaid place. In consideration of the sum of $300;oneNegro man named Cago. Signed. Isaac Davenport. Wit. Joseph Davenport. William Plunkit. Proved by Joseph Davenport before Wm. Craing. December 3, 1796. Recorded December 3, 1796. Fredk. Nance, C.N.C.

Deed Book C: 940

November 4, 1796. Bill of Sale. Francis Davenport and Isaac Davenport of
the County of Newberry and State of South Carolina to Joseph Davenport of
the aforesaid place. In consideration of the sum of £ 50 Sterling; one Negro
boy, named Mongo. Signed Francis Davenport. Isaac Davenport. Wit.
James Davenport. David Davenport. Proved by James Davenport before
Wm. Crain, J.P. December 3, 1796. Recorded December 3, 1796. Fredk.
Nance, C.C.

Deed Book C: 1041-1042

May 9, 1796. Bill of Sale. Peggy Gains of the County of Newberry and
State of South Carolina to Joseph Caldwell of the aforesaid place. In
consideration of the sum of £ 60 Sterling; one Negro wench named Mary
30 years old. Signed. Petty Gains. Wit. Samuel Cannon, Levi Johnson.
Proved by Levi Johnston and Samuel Cannon before David Ruff, J.P.
February 27, 1797. Recorded 18 March 1797. Fredk. Nance, C.N.C.

Deed Book C: 1043

January 21, 1797. Bill of Sale. Joseph Davenport of the County of
Newberry and State of South Carolina to Isaac Davenport of the aforesaid
place. In consideration of the sum of £ 65 Sterling, one Negro boy named
Mingo. Signed Joseph Davenport. Wit. James Davenport, Benj. Johnson.
Proved by James Davenport before Danl. Clary, J.P. March 1, 1797.
Recorded March 18, 1797. Fredk. Nance, C.N.C.

Deed Book C: 1048

October 31, 1796. Bill of Sale. William Tennant, Sheriff, of the District of
96, State of South Carolina - to Benedick Myers of the aforesaid place. In
consideration of the sum of £ 285; 6 Negroes, Viz., Sam and his Henny and
their 4 children, Anny, Darby, Abruxter and Frank. Levied upon by said
Sheriff in the court of common Please at the suit of Abraham Markley
against Alexander Bookter. Signed. William Tennant, Sheriff of 96 District.
Wit. William Burton, John Eigleberger. Recorded April 17, 1797. Fredk.
Nance, C.N.C.

Deed Book C: 1051-1052

October 31, 1796. Bill of Sale. William Tennant, Sheriff, of the District of
96 and State of South Carolina to John Eigleberger of the aforesaid place. In
consideration of the sum of £ 167; 3 Negroes. Vit. Champ and his wife
Sally and Chatty. Levied upon by said Sheriff at the suit of Abraham
Markey against Alexander. Bookter. Signed Wm. Tennant, Sheriff 96
District. Wit. William Burton, Sr., Benedick Mayer. Recorded April 18,
1797. Fredk. Nance, C.N.C.

Deed Book C: 1057
February 14, 1797. Deed of Gift. Elizabeth Turner, widow, of the County of
Newberry and State of South Carolina, to Mika Abney, grand daughter of
said Elizabeth Turner, of the County of Edgefield and State of South
Carolina. One Negro girl named Luce known by that name and being of a
yellow complexion or Mulatto colour. Signed Elizabeth Turner. Wit. Ben.
Long, Francis Higgins. Recorded April 18, 1797. Fredk. Nance, C.N.C.

Deed Book C: 1064
June 3, 1785. Bill of Sale. Gibeon Jones, of the State of South Carolina and
District of 96, to William Burton of the aforesaid place. One Negro girl
named Milley about 7 years old. Signed Gibeon Jones (mark). Recorded
April 24, 1797. Fredk. Nance, C.N.C.

Deed Book C: 1081-1082
September 12, 1796. Bill of Sale. James Campbell, of the County of
Newberry and State of South Carolina, to Frederick Nance of the aforesaid
place. In consideration of the sum of 70 guineas; one Negro fellow or man
named Joe about 26 years of age. Signed James Campbell. Wit Wm. Craig,
J.P. Recorded May 4, 1797. Fredk. Nance, C.N.C.

Deed Book C: 1088
May 4, 1797. Bill of Sale. William Hunter, of the County of Laurens and
State of South Carolina, to Joseph Caldwell of the County of Newberry and
State of South Carolina. In consideration of the sum of £ 40 Sterling, one
Negro woman slave named Jude about 30 years of age; yellow complexion
with one of her forefingers cut off. Signed William Hunter. Wit. Moses
Lindsey, John McMorris. Proved by John McMorris before John Speake,
J.P. May 5, 1797. Recorded May 6,1797. Fredk. Nance, C.N.C.

Deed Book C: 1104
March 25, 1797. Deed of Gift. Elizabeth Turner, of the County of Newberry
and State of South Carolina, to Polly Long, her grand daughter; one Negro
girl named Henritta about 3 years old. Signed Elizabeth Turner. Wit.
Thomas W. Waters, Francis Higgins. Proved by Francis Higgins before R.
Brown, J.N.C. May 26, 1797. Fredk. Nance, C.N.C. Recorded May 26,
1797.

Deed Book C: 1115-1116
April 17, 1797. Mortgage. South Carolina, Newberry County. Know all men
by these Presents that I Thomas Butler have this day Mortgaged to Thomas
W. Waters, of Newberry County, a certain Negro boy named Jac, 14 years
of age, well made which Negro mortgaged to said Thomas W. Waters in

135

consideration of his being my security to Capt. Frederick Gray for a debt he pass security for with James Johnston to the estate of Strawther to Gerrard Gerrald, Exr. Or Adm. For 30 £ and costs of suit new brought and should said Waters have to pay this debt then the Negro to be sold giving first publick notice for 3 weeks and sold to the highest bidder giving said Thomas Butler the overplus of said sale of the above Negroes or should said Waters wish to buy said Negroes out and out then he may have said Negroes as his own property without any right of redemption of said Butler provided he pays with this debt of Gerrals Exors 25 £ Sterling money to any of the creditors of said Thomas Butler that shall be just debts but any time said Butler to have the Negroes again provided the Negroes is not sold by publick sale on his paying said Waters what he has paid and otherwise settled in part of his Negroes and on paying the debt to the estate of Strawther that said Capt. Gray and Johnston are security for which said Waters has become security to Capt. Gray nevertheless said Butler shall not have more than 8 months to paying this money unless said Waters chooses. In Witness whereof said doth hereby deliver said boy Jack of yellow complexion into the possession of said Waters and this not to be set aside for want of form, April 17, 1797. Signed, sealed and delivered in the presence of Thomas Butler. Wit. William Julien. Proved by William Julien 9 June 1797.

Deed Book C: 1122 - 1123:
April 19, 1797: Bill of Sale. Lewis Blalock, Sr. of the County of Newberry and State of South Carolina, planter, to John McMorris of the aforesaid place. In consideration of the sum of £ 60 Sterling. One Negro man named Lord about 40 years of age, one Negro woman slave named Leah about 33 years of age, one Negro boy named Harry about two and one half years of age and one sorrel horse 5 years old about 14 hands and one inch high, not branded. Signed Lewis Blalock. Wit. Saml. Parks, Donald McDonald. Proved by Saml. Parks before John Speaks, J.P. May 5, 1797. Recorded June 9, 1797. Fredk. Nance, C.N.C.

Deed Book C: 1140
January 7, 1797. Bill of Sale. Thomas Gains of Newberry County, South Carolina to John Robertson of the same place. In consideration of the sum of £ 70 Sterling two negroes, one negro woman named Nann and her son Pompey. Signed Thomas Gaines. Wit. Samuel Cannon, Sarah Cannon. Proved by Samuel Cannon before David Ruff, J.P. April 17, 1797. Recorded June 10, 1797. Fredk. Nance, C.N.C.

DEED BOOK D-2: 1797 - 1798

Deed Book D-2: 56-57
February 27, 1795. Bill of Sale. Whereas on the 27 February 1795 John
Barlow of the State and County aforesaid did by a certain deed or bill of
sale bearing date the day and year aforesaid convey to me Andrew Smith of
the same place all his estate both real and personal; that is to say a tract of
four hundred acres of land as therein mentioned as also 12 Negroes (Slaves)
as therein mentioned as named Wigson, Tom, Major, Jacob, Bobb, Thomas,
Mary, Ann, Susanna, Fortune, St. Croix, Harriott and Ireland together with
stills, horses, cattle, hoggs, plantation tools with the future offspring or
increase of said Negroes and stock aforesaid together with all and every
other article belonging to the said John Barlow for the consideration of 100
Ll Sterling Whereas I have not paid the said consideration or any part of the
same to the said John Barlow except the land and four negroes namely Bob,
Fortune, St. Croix and Harriott was conveyed to me in trust for use and
benefit of him the said John Barlow whereas the said Barlow is desirous to
have this property returned to him again. Now Know all Men by these
presents that I Andrew Smyth for and in consideration of the four negroes as
before excepted namely Bobb, Fortune, St. Croix and Harriott do exonerate
acquit and release and discharge the said John Barlow of and from all
mortgages deeds obligation of Bill of Sale.. Signed 26 January 1797 Signed
Andrew Smyth. Wit. Thomas Coffey, James McCary. Proved by James
McCary 27 June 1797 before Charles Griffin, J.P. Recorded 5 July 1797.
Attest, Frederick Nance, C.N.C.

Deed Book D-2: 58
July 2, 1797. Bill of Sale. Andrew Smyth, planter, of the County of
Newberry and State of South Carolina to John Barlow of the aforesaid
place, planter. In consideration of the sum of £200 Sterling; three Negro
children named Fortune, Santa Cruix and Harriot and a Negro man named
Bobb. Signed Andrew Smyth. Wit. James Creswell, Reuben Golding.
Recorded July 5, 1797. Recorded July 5, 1797 Fredk. Nance, C.C.

Deed Book D-2: 59-60
January 28, 1792. Bill of Sale. Lewis Shepherd to George Ruff, Esq., both
of the County of Newberry and State of South Carolina. In consideration of
the sum of £70 Sterling; one negro fellow named Edenborough. Signed
Lewis Shepherd. Wit. Hy. Ruff, George Shepherd. Proved by Henry Ruff
before David Ruff, J.P. July 9, 1797. Recorded July 16, 1797. Fredk. Nance,
C.C.

Deed Book D-2: 61
March 5, 1795. Bill of Sale. David Mason of Laurens County to George
Ruff of the County of Newberry and State of South Carolina. In
consideration of the sum of £50 Sterling; one negro man named Sampson
and his wife Sall and a boy Sam. Signed David Mason. Wit. John H. Ruff,
Sibilla Frye. Recorded July 13, 1797 Fredk. Nance, C.C.

Deed Book D-2: 62
February 6, 1795. Bill of Sale. Thomas Gains to George Ruff, both of the
County of Newberry and State of South Carolina. In consideration of the
sum of £40 Sterling; one negro man named Daniel. Signed Thomas Gains.
Wit. Conrad Rahm, John Weddinman. Proved by Conrad Rahm before
David Ruff, J.P. July 9, 1797. Recorded July 13, 1797. Fredk. Nance, C.C.

Deed Book D-2: 96
February 7, 1797. Bill of Sale. Olleman Dodgen to Thomas Chappel, both
of the County of Newberry and State of South Carolina. In consideration of
the sum of £147, 10 shillings Sterling; one mulatto man slave about 27
years of age named Joel also one Negro woman about 5 and 20 years of age
named Fillis and a boy child two years of age named Harry. Signed Olleman
Dodgen. Wit. James Chappel, Abraham Dyson. Proved by James Chappel
before Robert Gillam, J.P. July 27, 1797. Recorded August 11, 1797. Fredk.
Nance, C.C.

Deed Book D-2: 101
July 29, 1797. Bill of Sale. Joseph Caldwell of the County of Newberry and
State of South Carolina to William Hunter of the County of Laurens and
State aforesaid. In consideration of the sum of £ 40 Sterling; one negro boy
named Samson about 25 years old formerly the property of Captain Charles
Littleton. Signed Joseph Caldwell. Wit. John Wilson, Wm. Wilson. Proved
by Wm. Wilson before Providence Williams, J.P. July 29, 1797. Recorded
Aug. 12, 1797. Fredk. Nance.

Deed Book D-2: 104
July 29, 1797. Bill of Sale. Joseph Caldwell of Newberry County, South
Carolina to William Hunter of Laurens County, South Carolina. In
consideration of £40 Sterling, one negro boy named Samson about 25 years
old, formerly the property of Captain Charles Littleton. Signed. Joseph
Caldwell. Wit. John Wilson, Wm. Wilson. Proved by William Wilson
before Providence Williams, J.P. July 29, 1797. Recorded August 27, 1797.

Deed Book D-2: 187

16 March 1797. Mortgage: Jacob King of Newberry County, South Carolina have mortgaged and pledged unto William Gary of the same place, one negro man named Peter, a negro woman Gin and her two children Minny and Sam for the sum of £ 60 Sterling. I do bind myself and my heirs. N.B. Received on the same instrument $53. The condition of the above obligation is such that if the above Jacob King, his heirs or assigns do pay or cause to be paid to the above named William Gary before 2t December ensuing the sum of £ 60 Sterling than and in that case the above obligation to be void. ...... Signed Jacob King. Text. John B. Bennett. Barber Hancock, Abner Teague. Received of William Gary the sum of £ 60 pound of the within instrument March 16, 1797. Recorded 3 January 1798. Fredk. Nance C.N.C.

Deed Book D-2: 265

January 22, 1798 Bill of Sale. Daniel Williams, Junr. of the County of Laurens and State of South Carolina to Joseph Williams of the County of Rockingham and State of North Carolina. In consideration of the sum of $600; one certain Negro man called Moses, 6 feet high and about 22 years old. Signed. Danl. Williams, Junr. Wit. Reuben Griffin, Elizabeth Williams. Proved by Reuben Griffin before R. Brown, J.N.C. 31 January 1798. Recorded February 1, 1798. Fredk. Nance, C.C.

Deed Book D-2: 266

January 22, 1798. Bill of Sale. Daniel Williams, Junr. of the County of Laurens and State of South Carolina to Joseph Williams of the County of Rockingham and State of North Carolina. In consideration of the sum of $300; one Negro boy called George about 6 years old. Signed Danl. Williams, Junr. Wit. Reuben Griffin, Elizabeth Williams. Proved by Reuben Griffin before R. Brown, J.N.C. January 31, 1798. Recorded February 1, 1798. Fredk. Nance, C.N.C.

Deed Book D-2: 276

September 19, 1796. Deed of Gift. John Cannon of the settlement of Indian Creek and County of Newberry and State of South Carolina; to Sarah Cannon, my eldest daughter, at present under the age of 18 years. One mulatto girl and infant slave being named Patt being born on th 26th day of August 1796 it being the issue of the body of Negro Slave the just claim of the said John Cannon named Beck. Signed John Cannon. Wit. Wm. Loston, Abigail Lofton (mark). James Lindsey. Recorded Feb. 1, 1798. Fredk. Nance. C.N.C.

Deed Book D-2: 313
February 10, 1798: Bill of Sale. Francis Davenport, Sr., of the State of
South Carolina and County of Newberry to Isaac Davenport of the aforesaid
place. In consideration of the sum of unknown; one negro girl named
Rachael. Signed Francis Davenport. Wit. James Goggans, George Goggans.
Recorded March 14, 1798. Fredk. Nance. C.N.C.

Deed Book D-2: 344
February 10, 1798. Bill of Sale. Isaac Davenport of the State and County
aforesaid to Francis Davenport, Sr. of the aforesaid place; one Negro
woman named Rachel and one Negro man named Peter and one Negro man
named Bay also all the household furniture and stock of cattle and hoggs
and horses and sheep and all the working tools. Signed Isaac Davenport.
Wit. James Goggans, George Goggans. Proved by James Goggans before
Daniel Perkins, J.P. March 2, 1798. Recorded 15 March 1798. Fredk.
Nance, C.N.C.

Deed Book D-2: 372
January 23, 1798. Bill of Sale. Lewis Blalock, Sr., planter,, of the State of
South Carolina and County of Newberry to Samuel Law, Sr. of the aforesaid
place. In consideration of the sum of $60; one Negro girl slave named Beck.
Signed Lewis Blalock. Wit. J. McMorris, Edmond Lindsey. Proved by John
McMorries before John Speake, J.P. February 3, 1798. Recorded April 12,
1793. Fredk. Nance, C.C.

Deed Book D-2: 384
May 14, 1798: Bill of Sale. Samuel Lindsey of the County of Newberry and
State of South Carolina, Captain to Thomas Lindsey of the aforesaid place.
In consideration of the sum of £ 470 Sterling; Nerow, Toney, Lambert,
Sambow, Andrew, all men slaves; Debro and Diner, wenches; George a boy
about 13 years old, Pat a girl about 9 years old, Molly a girl child about 6
years old and a girl child about one and a half years old. Signed. Samuel
Lindsey. Wit. Thomas Startk, John McMorris. Proved by Thomas Stark
before John Speake, J.P. May 4, 1798. Recorded May 16, 1798. Fredk.
Nance, C.C.

Deed Book D-2: 385-386
South Carlina; Newberry County. Know all men by these Presents that we
John Worthington, Elizabeth Worthington, Elijah Worthington, and Milly
Worthington, Joseph Jones and Nancy Jones, John Abernathy and Rhoda
Abernathy, Thomas W. Waters and Fanny Waters and Chesley Davis,
Samuel Davis, Thomas Davis and Jesse Davis and Molly Davis, all of us
joint heirs and legatees of Mary Davis, deceased do for divers good cause

and consideration that proper to enfranchise a certain Negro wench named Pat about 40 years old yellow complexion which said Negro wench is our just and right property and we do jointly by these presents free her and her heirs together with her Body forever and by these presents to acquit her of all manner of Servitude to us, our heirs, or assigns and she is as far as lays in our power to grant as free as if she had been born free and should this instrument of writing want from not to be set aside but the true intent and meaning of the same to be taken and liberally construed in the favour of the said Negro wench hereunto set our hands and seals 14 August 1797. Signed. Thomas W. Waters, Fanny Waters, John Worthington, Elizabeth (her mark) Worthington, Milly Worthington, Chesley Davis, Samuel Davis, Thomas Davis, Molly Davis, Jesse Davis, Nancey Jones, Joseph Jones, Rhoda Abernathy, John Abernathy. Wit. Thomas Berry, Jacob Berry. Proved by Jacob Berry 21 April 1798 before D. Clary, J.P.

Deed Book D-2: 406
Thomas Gary, of the State of South Carolina and County of Newberry to Stephen Sparks of the aforesaid place. In consideration of the sum of $425; 2 Negroes - one girl named Gill about 8 years old and one boy names Will about 7 years old. Signed. Thomas Cary. Wit. John Cannon. Recorded May 28, 1798. Fredk. Nance, C.C.

Deed Book D-2: 424
May 1, 1798: Bill of Sale. William Finch, of Newberry County, South Carolina, to Aaron Cates of the aforesaid place. In Consideration of $325 silver dollars, one negro woman named Clary. Signed William Finch. Wit. John Morrow, John Finch. Proved by John Finch before David Ruff, J.P., June 8, 1798. Recorded June 8, 1798. Fredk. Nance CC.

DEED BOOK D: 1798 - 1800

Deed Book D: 5
July 6, 1798. Bill of Sale. Henry D. Atkinson, of Claremont County in the State of South Carolina, to Daniel Dyson of the County of Newberry and State aforesaid. In consideration of the sum of $650; 2 Negroes, one a boy about 16 years of age, named Joe, the other a girl about 15, named Susanah. Signed Henry D. Atkinson. Wit. James E. Harwin, James Dyson. Proved by James Dyson before Fredk. Nance, J.P. July 30, 1798. Recorded August 4, 1798. Fredk. Nance.

Deed Book D: 9
January 16, 1798. Bill of Sale. Frederick Foster, carpenter, to Thomas
Clark, both of the County of Newberry and State of South Carolina. In
consideration of the sum of $275; one Negro boy named Kitt about 12 or
13 years old of a black complexion. Signed Frederick Foster. Wit. Robert
McKiterick, Priscilla Clark. Recorded August 4, 1798. Fredk. Nance,
C.N.C.

Deed Book D: 40
March 12, 1798. Bill of Sale. Charles Clack of the County of Newberry and
State of South Carolina to David Bozman of the aforesaid County and State.
In consideration of the sum of £ 40 Sterling. One Negro girl slave about 9
years of age named Chat. Signed Charles Clack. Wit. James Hill, John Hill.
Proved by John Hill before Robert Gillam, J.P. September 28, 1798.
Recorded October 9, 1798. Fredk. Nance, C.N.C.

Deed Book D: 54
October 13, 1798. Bill of Sale. William Satterwhite, Sheriff of the County
of Newberry and State of South Carolina, to William Craig of the aforesaid
place. In consideration of the sum of; $200; one Negro fellow named Daniel
(which said Negro was taken up and sold agreeable to an Act of the General
Assembly of this State made and provided for Runaway negroes). Signed.
Wm. Satterwhite, Sheriff, Newberry District. Wit. Fredk. Nance, J.P., James
Spearman. Recorded November 12, 1798. Fredk. Nance, C.N.C.

Deed Book D: 64
September 19, 1798. Bill of Sale. Owen Flinn of the Town of Suffolk and
State of Virginia to Isaac Davenport of the County of Newberry, State of
South Carolina. In consideration of the sum of $550; one Negro slave
named Milly and two children, Viz., Silvery and Jack. Signed. O'Flynn.
Wit. Caleb Lindsey, David Waldrop. Proved by David Waldrop before
Providence Williams, J.P. October 17, 1798. Recorded November 12, 1798.
Fredk. Nance, C.N.C.

Deed Book D: 76
October 28, 1798. Bill of Sale. Mary Byerly of Newberry County, South
Carolina to John Sipert Byerly of the same place. One negro boy named
Peter. Signed Mary Byerly (mark). Wit. Peter Dickert, George Oster (mark).
Proved by Peter Dickert before Wm. Houseal J.P. December 6, 1798.
Recorded 14 December 1798. Attested by Fredk. Nance, C.N.C.

Deed Book D: 78
October 10, 1798. Bill of Sale. James Campbell, of the State of South
Carolina and County of Newberry to Charity Patterson of the aforesaid
County and State. In consideration of the sum of 60£ one Negro girl named
Sal, 12 years old. Signed James Campbell. Wit. John Bennett, Jacob King.

Deed Book D: 78
October 11, 1798. Settled with Charity Patterson and she received a Negro
girl and boy in pay from James Campbell in full the boy whose name is Will
and as stamp paper could not be got it is agreed by both parties that writings
that I entered into by the said parties bearing the date with this shall stand
good till entered on stamp paper. Wit our hands. James Campbell, Charity
Patterson. Wit. John B. Bennett, Jacob King. Proved by Jacob King before
John Speake J.P. November 5, 1798. Recorded December 14, 1798. Fredk.
Nance, C.N.C.

Deed Book D: 94
January 15, 1799. Power of Attorney. Mary Edwards, widow of John
Edwards deceased) of Newberry County, South Carolina appoint William
Smith, of Warren County, Kentucky, my lawful attorney to received of
Robert Moses of Christian County, Kentucky one negro wench named
Hannah and her increase which said negro Hannah, her mother and their
increase was bequeathed to me by my father William Turner, deceased.
Signed. Mary Edwards. (Seal). Wit. Gabriel H. Davis, James Davis, Elisha
Brooks. Recorded January 17, 1799. Fredk. Nance C.N.C.

Deed Book D: 112
November 17, 1798. Bill of Sale. Henry Gissendence, planter,, of the State
of South Carolina to John Miller, of Charleston, merchant. In consideration
of the sum of £   60 Sterling. One Negro slave, Isaac. Signed Henry
Gissendence. Wit. James Hueston, Jeremiah Brown. Recorded February 20,
1799. Fredk. Nance, C.N.C.
Charleston - December 6, 1798. I will warrant the within Bill of Sale to be
good and sufficient to Daniel Duvault of my right and claims of the within
Negro named Isaac, done in the presence of Robert Cameron, Jeremiah
Brown. Signed for my Papa John Miller, E. Miller.

Deed Book D: 159
January 10, 1799. Deed of Gift. George Ruff of the County of Newberry
and State of South Carolina to my loving son John Pester and my daughter
Sally, his wife, of the aforesaid place. A Negro woman Hanny, a boy named
John, a bay horse. Signed George Ruff. Wit. Henry Ruff, Peter Gray.

Proved by Peter Gray before Fredk. Nance, J.P. March 1, 1799. Recorded 1 March 1799. Fredk. Nance, C.N.C.

Deed Book D: 159
State of South Carolina, Newberry County. These are to certify to all persons that I Henry Gallman do hereby entirely and absolutely dismiss and discharge a certain Negro man named Bob for him to be free and clear from me and my heirs, executors and administrators and assigns and all other person or persons whatsoever from this day forward and during the said Bobs life. In Witness whereof I have hereunto Set my hand this 5th day of November, 1798 Henry Gallman. Wit. David Ruff, Elizabeth Ruff. Sworn to by Elizabeth Ruff on 1 March 1799 before Fredk. Nance. Recorded March 1, 1799. Attest, Fredk. Nance, C.N.C.

Deed Book D: 160
November 30, 1798. Bill of Sale. Gasper Birley to Matthew Smith, both of the County of Newberry and State of South Carolina. In consideration of the sum of £ 40 Sterling. One Negro boy named Peter aged 8 years of age. Signed Gasper Birley. Wit. Frederick Passinger, George Lever. Proved by Frederick Passinger before Fredk. Nance, J.P. March 1, 1799. Recorded 1 March 1799. Fredk. Nance, C.N.C.

Deed Book D: 162
Newberry County, South Carolina. Whereas Jesse Pugh has become security for me to the Executors of Levi Maning, dec'd. for the sum of $205 personal notes given the 16th of this month also 25 £ Sterling given by said Pugh and Thomas W. Waters due this winter with interest. Now this Indenture witnesseth that for the better securing the payment of said debt to the estate as well as to ease the mind of my Security I do hereby give up the two following Negroes, Viz., Moses about 8 years old and Ross about 7 years old on this condition that is about an Execution every come against said Waters and Pugh for one or both of the above debts then said Jesse Pugh shall be at liberty to deliver said Negroes to the sheriff to satisfy said debt, Waters to have the overplus if any and no sale of said Negroes to be good except the leave of said Jesse Pugh shall be first obtained. November 17, 17981 Thomas W. Waters. Est. John Harrison. Attested by Fredk. Nance, C.N.C. 4 March 1799.

Deed Book D: 180
June 9, 1797. Bill of Sale. Robert Tate, of the County of Newberry and State of South Carolina, and administrator of the estate of James Tate, Jr, deceased., to Capt. Samuel Tate of the County of Pendleton and State aforesaid. In consideration of the sum of £137, 3 shilling Sterling. The

following Negro slaves: Isaac, Prince, Charlotte, Mills and Hannah and Lucy; also for the consideration of 11£ 9 shillings Sterling, 3 cows and 3 calves and 25 head of small hogs and some corn and a few plantation tools. Signed. Rob. Tate, Administrator. Wit. Wm. Irby, Thomas Kay, Farley Thompson. Proved by Thomas Kay before Wm. Nibbs, J.P. March 5, 1799. Recorded March 7, 1799. Fredk. Nance, C.N.C.

Deed Book D: 205
February 15, 1793. Bill of Sale. John Hazlet, of the State of South Carolina and County of Laurens, to Phillip Procter of the County of Newberry and State of South Carolina. In consideration of the sum of: $400; one Negro boy about 13 years old, named George, County born and strong, stout, well made. Signed John Hazlet. Wit. Fredk. Nance. C.N.C.

Deed Book D: 206
March 21, 1799. Bill of Sale. Daniel Dyson, of the State of South Carolina and County of Newberry, to Meredith Williams of the aforesaid place. In consideration of the sum of: $300;oneNegro Joe. Signed Danl. Dyson. Wit. Wm. Irby. Proved by William Irby before Fredk. Nance April 17, 1799 and recorded April 17, 1799. Fredk. Nance, C.C.

Deed Book D: 248
May 21, 1799. Bill of Sale. Fredk. Nance, of the State of South Carolina and County of Newberry, to John Belton of the aforesaid place. In consideration of the sum of: $220;oneNegro girl named Minerva about 7 or 8 years old. Signed Fredk. Nance. Wit. Ben Long, Francis Higgins. Recorded May 21, 1799. P.B. Waters, D.C.

Deed Book D: 268
August 20, 1798. Deed of Gift. Jeremiah McDaniel, of the County of Newberry and State of South Carolina, to Jeremiah McDaniel, Junr. (cousin) of the aforesaid place. One Negro boy named Peter. Signed. Jer. McDaniel. Wit. John Mowrer, Michael West, Peter Hawkins. Proved by Michael West before Daniel Parkins, J.P. 8 June 1799. Recorded July 5, 1799. P.B. Waters, D.C.

Deed Book D: 278
The State of South Carolina - To all Whom these presents shall come between Joseph White on the one part and Cason Hill of the state aforesaid send Greetings. ..... Cason Hill his heirs and Executors and administrators and assigns together with lawful interest for the same at 7 percent per annum have bargained and sold and by these presents doth grant bargain and sell in plain and open market deliver unto the said Cason Hill a Negro

boy called Pompey 12 years of age; to have and to hold the said Negro unto the said Cason Hill his heirs, executors and administrators and assigns forever ...... Signed Joseph White. In Presence of Larkin Cason, Daniel Goodman. Proved by Larkin Cason June 18,1799. Recorded Mortgage 26 July 1799.

Deed Book D: 279
January 2, 1799. Deed of Gift. Spencer Morgan of the District of Orangeburgh in the State of South Carolina to Nancy McMorries, his daughter, wife of Capt. John McMorries of the aforesaid State and County of Newberry; 3 Negroes; Randol, a man slave about 21 years of age, Betty a black girl slave about 15 years of age and Peter a boy slave about 9 years of age. Signed. Spencer Morgan. Wit. John Nicholls, Thomas Murray. Acknowledged in open Court July Term 1799. Recorded 29 July 1799 P.B. Waters, D.C.N.C.

:Deed Book D: 280
January 2, 1799. Deed of Gift. Spencer Morgan of the District of Orangeburgh and State of South Carolina to Fanney Morgan, his daughter, of the aforesaid place. 5 Negroes; a Negro man slave named Pompey, a Negro woman slave named Dinah and her 3 children named Littye, Newman and Mary. Signed. Spencer Morgan. Wit. John Nichols, Thomas Murray. Recorded July 28, 1799. P.B. Waters, D.C.

Deed Book D: 302
29 July 1799. Manumission. Newberry County, South Carolina. Know all men by these presents that I Moses Kelly one of the heirs of John Kelly, decd, having come into possession of 2 slaves left by the aforesaid John Kelly (namely) George, a yellow man about 22 years of age and Frank, a black girl about 8 years old. And believing that Liberty is the natural right of all mankind have manumitted enfranchised and from the bonds of Slavery forever set free the said Negroes above named and described to hold and enjoy such freedom from any claim of service by me my heirs executors administrators or any other person or persons claiming by through or under me the aforesaid George to hold and enjoy such manumission from the day of the date hereof forever and the afore said Frank to remain in the service and care of the aforesaid Kelly until 18 years of age from which time forth and forever to be free as above mentioned and manumitted by me. In Witness Whereof I have hereunto Set my hand and seat at Bush River in the County aforesaid this 18 day of the 6th month 1795 .. Signed Moses Kelly. In presence of Joseph Thompson, John Jay, Joseph Furnas. Proved by Joseph Thompson 28 March 1798 before P.B. Waters, D.C.

146

Deed Book D: 326
February 25, 1799. Bill of Sale. Joshua Gillam to Robert Gillam, both, of
the State of South Carolina, and County of Newberry. In consideration of
the sum of: $400; one Negro boy same Sam. Signed Joshua Gillam. Wit.
Daniel Towles, Fields Read. Proved by Daniel Towles before R. Brown,
J.N.C. July 21, 1799. Recorded July 31, 1799. P.B. Waters, D.C.

Deed Book D: 347
June 4, 1799. A Deed of Gift. To all people to whom these presents shall
come I Ann Williams do send Greetings, Know ye that I the said Ann
Williams in the State of Couth Carolina and County of Newberry, for and in
consideration of the love, good will and affection, which I have and do bear
toward my loving son Thomas Williams in the state and County aforesaid
have given and granted unto said Thomas Williams his heirs, executors or
administrators all and singular the Negroes now in my actual possession,
Viz: one negro man named Dunkin and his wife name Cate; one Negro
woman named Let, one Negro boy named Dunkin, one Negro boy named
Ben, with all their Increase from this date. Only Dunkin and his wife Cate
and Let, I reserve for myself during my natural life of which before the
signing of these presents I have delivered them the said Thomas Williams
an inventory signed with my own hand… henceforth as his and their
property Negroes, absolutely without any manner of fraud or condition
except my beloved son Thomas Williams should decease before he marries
or comes of age my goodwill and pleasure is for the love good will and
affection which I have and bear toward my beloved daughter Elizabeth
Teague is such that if my beloved son Thomas Williams should decease
before he comes of age or married that the above mentioned negroes namely
Dunkin, Cate, Let, Dunkin, Ben with their Increase should return to her and
her heirs. Signed Ann Williams (X). In Presence of Stephen McCraw, P.
Williams. Proved by Providence Williams 29 July 1799 before Edward
Finch, J.P. Recorded 31 July 1799.

Deed Book D: 350-351
_____? State of South Carolina. Know all men by these presents
that I Macajah Bennett of the County of Newberry and State of South
Carolina, planter, in consideration of $639.66 to be paid by John McMorries
of the County and State aforesaid have bargained and sold and by these
presents do bargain sell and deliver unto the said John McMorries the
following negroes, Viz., one old Negro woman named Nanny and her
daughter, also named Nanny; one other old Negro woman named Hannah
and her son a Negro man named Will to have and to hold the said Negroes
before mentioned unto the said John McMorries his heirs and assigns
forever….. Signed M. Bennett. Wit. Richard Bennett, Daniel Lofton.

Deed Book D: 389
May 17, 1799. Bill of Sale. Received of Mr. James Davenport $350 in full
for a negro girl named Lidda which negro we do hereby warrant and defend
against the claim or claims of all persons whatever Test., Isaac Davenport,
James Thomas (mark). David Coolter, Joseph Ervin.
Isaac Davenport gave oath that he saw David Coolter and Joseph Erwin sign
and deliver the Bill of Sale to James Davenport. Sworn on 21 August 1799
before Charles Griffin, J.P. Recorded 1 Oct. 1799. P.B. Waters, DC.

Deed Book D: 393
October 21, 1799. Power of Attorney. Elizabeth Turner, Sern., widow of
Newberry, District of 96, South Carolina, appoint David Stephen of said
County my attorney to recover a negro man named Ace. Signed Elizabeth
Turner. Wit. Samuel Miles, Joseph Reagan, Charles Griffin. Proved by
Charles Griffin before P.B. Waters, DC. Recorded October 22, 1799.

Deed Book D: 423
June 10, 1781. Deed of Gift. Elizabeth Turner, widow, of the District of 96
and State of South Carolina to Sarah Turner, wife of my son Edward Turner,
of the aforesaid place. Consideration of Love and Affection; one Negro
fellow named Isaac and one Negro wench named Sarah. Signed Elizabeth
Turner. Wit. Samuel Kelly, Sr., Ben Long. Proved by Ben Long before
Robert Gillam, J.P. October.21, 1799. Recorded 21 October 1799. P.B.
Waters, D.C.

Deed Book D: 424
October 16, 1792. Deed of Gift. Elizabeth Turner, widow, of the District of
96 and State of South Carolina to Sarah Turner, wife of David Turner, my
grandson of the aforesaid place. One mulatto boy named Toney. Signed
Elizabeth Turner. Wit. Samuel Kelly, Sr., Ben Long. Proved by Ben Long
before Robert Gillam, J.P. October 21, 1799. Recorded 21 October 1799.
P.B. Waters, D.C.

Deed Book D: 430
July 10, 1799. Bill of Sale. Reuben Griffin to Joseph Pitts of the County of
Newberry and State of South Carolina. In consideration of the sum of
$260;oneNegro woman named Beck about 15 years of age. Signed. Reuben
Griffin. Wit. Charles Griffin. Proved by Charles Griffin before Robert
Gillam, J.P. October 21, 1799. Recorded October 22, 1799. P.B. Waters,
D.C.

Deed Book D: 459
August 28, 1799. Bill of Sale. Micajah Bennett of the County of Newberry
and State of South Carolina to Thomas Clark of the aforesaid place. In
consideration of the sum of: $450;oneNegro boy named Sam between 20
and 23 years of age of a yellow complexion. Signed Mcj. Bennett. Wit. John
McCoy, Richard Bennett, Mary Bennett. Proved by John McCoy before
said Finch, J.P. December 3, 1799. Recorded December 20, 1799. P.B.
Waters, DC.

Deed Book D: 463
February 21, 1800. Power of Attorney. Jacob Harmon and Thomas Smith,
both of Lexington County, South Carolina in District of Orangeburgh (the
executors of John Harmon, deceased) appoint James Johnson of Newberry
District lawful attorney to received from James Greelee of North Carolina a
negro wench named Nann and four children. Signed Jacob Harmon (mark),
Thomas Smith. Wit. George Metz, Christian Swyger. Proved by George
Metz before John Hampton J.P. Quo. Recorded Feb. 21, 1800.

Deed Book D: 477-478
July 4, 1799. Mortgage. William Farrow of Laurens County in the State of
South Carolina to Levi Pitts of the County of Newberry in the state
aforesaid; one Negro man slave called Harry in consideration of the sum of
241 Spanish mill dollars. Signed William Farrow. Wit. Joel Foster, James
.Pitts. Proved by James Pitts before Providence Williams, J.P. January 17,
1800. Recorded February 21, 1800. P.B. Waters, D.C.

Deed Book D: 531
December 2, 1791. Bill of Sale. David Watts of the County of Newberry
and state of South Carolina to Jeremiah McDaniel of the aforesaid place. In
consideration of the sum of 32 £ Sterling; one Negro boy named John.
Signed David Watts. Wit. Jacob Harrell, John McDanal. Proved by John
McDanal before Michael Dicker, J.P. April 7, 1800. Recorded April 10,
1800. Fredk. Nance, Regr.

Deed Book D: 595-596
Newberry, South Carolina: Whereas I have undertaken to build the Goal of
Newberry District and William Summers, Thomas Mills, Levi Hilburn,
Henry Bates, Hezekiah Riley and John Worthington have become my
security for the true performance and of contract I do in order to indemnify
my aforesaid securities safe enter into the following agreement wit the
aforesaid William Summers, Thomas Mills, Levi Hilburn, Henry Bates,
Hezekiah Rily, John Worthington that should I fail to perform my contract
agreeable to the undertaking then they shall have full power to dispose of

all or any part of the following property, Viz., Jesse a fellow about 18 years old, his wife Peggy and Peggy is about 25 years old and William her son about 5 years old and Bet her daughter about 1 year old, Ben a lad about age of 14 and his brother named Harry about 10 years old, Dick a boy about 5 years old, Rachel a girl about 13 years of age also Judy a wench about 26 year old and her two sons Sigh and 4 and John about 2 years old and should I fail to perform my contract and my aforesaid securities have to say anything on my account then as many of the aforesaid Negroes as will made good the deficiency shall be sold and the deficiency made good ..... [blank] July 1800. Thos. W. Waters. Wit. Isaac Kirk.

Deed Book D: 643
September 1, 1800. Bill of Sale. John Wadlington, of the State of South Carolina to Daniel Perkins, Esq., of the State of South Carolina. In consideration of the sum of $500; one Negro man named Toney, of a black complexion about 37 years of age, stout and well made. Signed John Wadlington. Wit. Jesse B. Pemberton, Fredk. Nance. Proved by Fredk. Nance before Thomas Brooks, J.P. September 5, 1800. Fredk Nance, R.M.C.

DEED BOOK E: 1800 - 1803

Deed Book E: 1
May 9, 1800: Deed of Gift. Thomas Gaines, of the State of South Carolina and District on 96 to Salley Gaines, his daughter, of the aforesaid place; three negroes, Viz., Aron, Spencer and Fanny, also £30 Sterling to be paid out of my estate at the time she arrives at lawful age. Signed Thomas Gaines. Wit. Edward McCraw, Francis Hatton, Edmund Gaines. Proved by Edmund Gaines before George Herbert, J. Quo. Oct. 13, 1800. Recorded October 13, 1800 Fredk. Nance, R.M.C.

Deed Book E: 1
May 9, 1800: Deed of Gift. Thomas Gaines, of the State of South Carolina to Mary Pendleton Gaines, his daughter, of the aforesaid State; two negroes, Viz., Manuel and Lucly, also £30 Sterling to be paid out of my estate at the time she arrives at lawful age. Signed. Thomas Gaines. Wit. Edward McCraw, Francis Hatton, Edmund Gailes. Proved by Edmund Gaines before George Harbert 13 October 1800. Recorded October 13, 1800 Fredk. Nance, R.M.C.

Deed Book E: 2

May 9, 1800: Deed of Gift. Thomas Gaines, of the State South Carolina, to James Gaines, his son, of the aforesaid place; 150 acres in the District of 96 adjoining land of George Ruff, Esq. And Henry Ruff, formerly the property of John Wediman, deceased; also two negro boys, Viz., Rubin and Benjamin. Signed Thomas Gaines. Wit. Edward McGraw, Francis Hatton, Edmund Gaines. Proved by Edmund Gaines before George Harbert, J. QUO. October 13, 1800. Recorded 13 October 1800. Fredk. Nance, R.M.C.

Deed Book E: 3

May 9, 1800: Deed of Gift. Thomas Gaines, of the State of South Carolina and County of Newberry, to Caty Gaines, his daughter, of the aforesaid place. Two negroes, Viz., Amstead and Patty, also 30 £ Sterling to be paid to her out of my estate at the time of her arriving at lawful age. Signed Thomas Gaines. Wit. Edward McCraw, Francis Hatton, Edmund Gaines. Proved by Edmund Gaines before George Harbirt, J. Quo. October 13, 1800. Recorded 13 October 18000 Fredk. Nance, R.M.C.

Deed Book E: 3

May 9, 1800: Deed of Gift. Thomas Gaines, of the State of South Carolina and County of Newberry, to Peggy Gaines, his daughter, of the aforesaid place. Consideration: Natural Love and Affection. Two negroes, Viz., Joshua and Milly, also 30£ Sterling to be paid to her out of my estate at the time of her arriving at lawful age. Signed. Thomas Gaines. Wit. Edward McCraw, Francis Hatton, Edmund Gaines. Proved by Edmund Gaines before George Harbert October 13, 1800. Recorded October 13, 1800. Fredk. Nance, R.M.C.

Deed Book E: 8

May 9, 1800. Deed of Gift. Thomas Gaines, of the State of South Carolina and County of Newberry to Isabella Gaines, his daughter, of the aforesaid place; two negroes, Vit: Jesse and Nelly, also 30 £ Sterling to be paid to her out of my estate at the time of her arriving at lawful age. Signed. Thomas Gaines. Wit. Edward McCraw, Francis Hatton, Edmund Gaines. Proved by Edmund Gaines before George Herbirt J. QUO. Recorded Oct. 13, 1800 Fredk. Nance, R.M.C.

Deed Book E: 8

December 1, 1799. Bequest. Newberry County, South Carolina. I Elenor Dickson do give and bequeath to Howel Cobb all my third part of the estate of Wm. Burgess, deceased, my former husband, except a negro girl named China which I reserve until my death and then to descent with the other property to the said Cobb and his heirs and assigns forever. And in

151

consideration of the said property to pay annually unto the said Elenor Dickson 10 £ Sterling and to furnish her with all necessary good as bread, meat, tea, coffee, sugar. Set our hands 1 December 1799. Eleanor Dixon (seal), Howell Cobb (seal). Wit. John Dyson, John Thomas S.M. Proved by John Dyson 14 Oct. 1800 before J R. Brown. Recorded October 14, 1800, Fredk. Nance, R.M.C..

Deed Book E: 64
September 13, 1792: Deed of Gift. Elizabeth Turner, of the State of South Carolina and District of 96 in the County of Newberry, to Ann Abney, grand-daughter of said Elizabeth Turner, of the aforesaid place; one Negro wench named Clarender. Signed Elizabeth Turner. Wit. Benjamin Long, George Deen. Proved by Benjamin Long before Thomas Brooks, J.P. 23 January 1801. Recorded 23 January 1801. Fredk Nance, Regr. M.C.

Deed Book E: 69
January 2, 1801. Bill of Sale. Samuel Harris of the District aforesaid and State of South Carolina, to Levi Pitts of the District of Newberry, State of South Carolina. In consideration of the sum of $380; one Negro woman called Sarah about 21 years old, black and remarkable low and think. Signed Saml. Harris. Wit. David Gillam. Proved by David Gillam before J.R. Brown, J.Q. January 22, 1801. Recorded 22 January 1801. Fredk. Nance, Regr.

Deed Book E: 186
January 21, 1800. Bill of Sale. State of South Carolina, Charleston District. Know all men by these presents that I Joseph Barr doth bargain sell and delivers unto John Robertson one negro girl by name of Phillis for the consideration 55 £ current money of this state which said Negro I do warrant and defend unto the said John Robertson as his right and property which said negro girl I doth warrant from all persons or persons laying any claim as right unto the said negro, as witness my hand and seal this 21 January 1800. Joseph Barr. Wit. George Henry, Thomas O'Nims. Recorded Jan 13 1801. Attest, Fredk Nance, Regir. M. Conveyances.

Deed Book E: 190
July 21, 1801. Deed of Gift: To all people to whom these presents shall come, Greeting, I George Pemberton, Sr. of the District of Newberry and State, aforesaid for divers good causes and considerations, me hereunto moving, and for the Natural Love and Affection which I bear towards my grand daughter Jude Worthington and the legal representatives of her body do give and grant and by these presents do give and grant unto the said Jude Worthington and the heirs of her body one negro woman named Winney

and her two children, Viz., Taid and Champion, with her future increases to have and to hold the said negro woman Winney and her said two children and future increase if any unto the said Jude Worthington and said Jude Worthington her heirs and increase forever .... I Set my hand 21 July 1801 George (x) Pemberton. Wit. Frederick Nance, Daniel Brooks. Proved by Daniel Brooks 21 July 1801 before Fredk Nance, Regr. M.C.

Deed Book E: 236
March 18, 1792. Bill of Sale. Received of Abraham Larowe, of Fairfield County, South Carolina, the sum of £ 25Sterling in part of a certain negro woman named Cloe and her two children by the names of Dick and Ben and her following increase which negroes I do bargain, sell and deliver to the above mentioned Abraham Larowe. Received by me, living in Newberry County, South Carolina, John Kelly.

27 October 1801. Newberry District, South Carolina. I Jacob R. Brown, Justice of the Quorum do hereby certify to all that the within named John Kelly did this day appear before me and voluntarily acknowledge the within Instrument of writing purporting to be a bill of sale for three negroes sold to Abraham Larowe to be his the said Kelly's act of deed and that he received full satisfaction for the same. Recorded October 29, 1801. Fredk. Nance, Regr.

.
Deed Book E: 237
May 1, 1801. Bill of Sale. Ann Johnson, of the State of South Carolina, and District of Newberry to Thomas Chappell, of the aforesaid place. In consideration of the sum of: $300; one Negro girl named Dine, 6 years old. Signed Ann Johnson. Wit. Hester Johnson, Elizabeth Chappell. Proved by Hester Johnson before James Dyson 10 October 1801. Recorded 12 October 1801. Fredk. Nance, Regr.

Deed Book E: 262
September 13, 1792. Deed of Gift. (Recorded as Bill of Sale). Elizabeth Turner, of the State of South Carolina, to William Abney, grandson of Elizabeth Turner, of the same place, one negro boy named March, now in his actual possession. Signed, Elizabeth Turner. Wit. Benj. Long, George Deed. Proved by Ben Long before Lewis Hogg, J.P. the 14 October 1801. Recorded October 14, 1801.

Deed Book E: 272-276
South Carolina: This Indenture made the 19 March 1801...Between William Turpin and Benjamin Wadsworth, deceased, of the one part and Samuel Miles, Samuel Brown, Isaac Kirk and John Cook, a committee of the

Society of Friends, otherwise commonly called QUAKERS residing on Bush River, Newberry County in the State aforesaid in this behalf duly named authorized and appointed of the other part.

Whereas the said Thomas Wadsworth, deceased, in his lifetime in and by his last will and Testament bearing date 14 September 1799, amongst other things, ordered and directed, devised and bequeathed, as follows to wit, and whereas I have been induced from motives of Humanity to set free and emancipate all the Negroes, slaves, that have been intrusted to my care or that I may die possessed of, I do hereby, leave them under the special care and direction of the Society of Quakers, or Friends residing on Bush River, Newberry County, in the State of South Carolina and I do hereby give to that Society full and complete authority to receive from my Executors titles for as much land as when directed and laid off my the Society as will about to 50 acres for each of my said slaves as aforesaid, lands to be chosen by the said Society out of my lands that shall be mine at the time of my decease, except my homestead on Little River, that being otherwise disposed of and besides the land as aforesaid I do give and bequeath to each of my said slaves to be emancipated as aforesaid one good milch cow and a sow or the value thereof in other stock or farming utensils, to be delivered to them by my Executors when set free and which it is my wish might take place as soon after my decease as the necessary and requisite arrangement for that purpose can be made or at any rate 6 months thereafter and I do hereby give and bequeath to a mulatto girl named Silvy and a Mulatto boy named Archibald both of whom make part of my family at this time, the same to each of them as I have given to my Negro slaves as above mentioned or the value thereof as by the said last will and testament now being and remaining on record in the office of Charles Lining, Esquire, Ordinary of Charleston District in the state aforesaid, reference being hereunto had, will more fully appear and whereas also the said Society of Friends residing on Bush River hath in pursuance of the aforesaid will of Thomas Wadsworth agreed and resolved to Accept and Take upon themselves the trust in the said Will mentioned and to receive a conveyance of lands herein after mentioned and in part the will of the said Thomas Wadsworth recited and not being as incorporated Society have chosen and appointed the said Samuel Miles, Samuel Brown, Isaac Kirk and John Cook, members of the said Society of Friends to receive the Legacies aforesaid for an in behalf of the same and Whereas the said Society of Friends have elected chosen divided and laid off the tracts and parcels of land hereinafter mentioned for the purpose aforesaid as they were authorized to do in the last will and testament.

Deed Book E: 292
September 11, 1801. Bill of Sale. Peter Braselmann of Newberry County, South Carolina, to Brithern Braselmann, of the same place, in consideration

of $1,100 sell three negro slaves, Ambrose, Dick and Betty. Signed. Peter Braselmann. Wit. Robert Powell. Proved by Robert Powell before Saml. E. Kenner, J.P. November 9, 1801. Recorded November 21, 1801. Fredk. Nance, Regr. M.C.

Deed Book E: 320-321
South Carolina, Newberry District. We do hereby certify upon the examination of oath of David Boyd, the owner of three certain slaves - one named Daniel ages about 24 or 25 years, one named Amey supposed to be about the same age and the other named Rose about 8 years of age satisfactory proof has been given to us that the said slaves are not of a bad character and are acceptable of gaining a likelihood by honest means, given under our hands this 15 January 1802. L.E. Casey, Josiah Fowler, Joseph Hill, Robert Johnson, Robert Wilson, Josiah Duckit.

Deed Book E: 320-321
January 5, 1802. Emancipation. State of South Carolina: To all to whom these presents comes Greeting, Know ye that I, David Boyd, of the District of Newberry and State of South Carolina, for divers good causes and consideration me hereunto moving have this day set free and forever emancipated my three Negroes slaves, Viz., Daniel, Amey and Rose. Daniel is 20-25 years of age, Amey about the same age and Rose about 8 years of age; two of the said Negroes has been purchased by me the other born my property and which hath been adjudged by a justice and free holders agreeable to the act of Assembly in that case made and provided to be of good character and capable of gaining a lively hood in an honest way and I do hereby for myself my heirs executors and administrators give and grant and forever quit claim to all right title and command whatsoever in and over the said Negroes Daniel, Amey and Rose as slaves as fully and as absolutely in as ample a manner as if they had actually been born free and never in slavery. Witness my hand 5 January 1802. David Boyd. Wit. Robert Wilson, Robert Johnston. Proved by Robert Wilson 15 Jan 1802. Recorded January 18, 1802. Attest. Fredk. Nance, Regr.

January 15, 1802. Oath. Newberry District, South Carolina, Robert Wilson appeared before me and made oath that he saw David Boyd sign the within deed of Emancipation. Recorded January 18, 1802 Redk. Nance, Regr.

Deed Book E: 348
September 3, 1801. Deed of Gift: Newberry District, South Carolina. Indenture between William Shell, of the State and District, aforesaid of the one part and Lemon Shell of the State and District of the other part. Witnesseth that the said William Shell, as well as, for and in consideration

of the Natural Love and Affection which he hath and beareth unto the said
Lemon Shell, his beloved son, as also of the sum of $10 to him in hand paid
by the said Lemon Shell, he the said William Shell hath given granted and
confirmed and by these presents doth give grant and confirm unto his said
son Lemon Shell, one negro woman named Guinea and one negro boy
named Charles, and one negro boy named or Little Ben and their increase in
what place or places soever the same may be found as well in his own
possession..... Set his hand William Shell. Wit. Herbert Tucker, Drury
Malone, George Herbert JQ. Recorded 4 March 1802. Fredk. Nance Regr..

Deed Book E: 358-359
September 3, 1801. Bill of Sale. William Shell, of the State of South
Carolina and County of Newberry, to Harmon Shell, son of the said William
Shell, of the State and County aforesaid. In consideration of the sum of $10;
one Negro man slave named Ben, also one Negro woman named Fanny and
one Negro boy named Terry. Signed William Shell. Wit. Herbert Tucker,
Drury Malone, Geo. Harbert JQ. Recorded March 9, 1802. Fredk. Nance,
Regr.

Deed Book E: 362
January 18, 1800. Bill of Sale. William Shell, of the State of South Carolina
and County of Newberry, to John Shell, son of William Shell, of the
aforesaid place. In consideration of the sum of: $1.00; one Negro woman
named Cloe, her child a girl named Lucy and their increase. Signed.
William Shell. Wit. George Harbert, Stephen Shell. Proved by Stephen
Shell before G. Harbert, J.P. 15 January 1802. Recorded 9 March 1802.
Fredk. Nance, Regr.

Deed Book E: 363-364
September 3, 1801. Deed of Gift. William Shell to John Shell, son of
William, both, of the State of South Carolina and County of Newberry.
Consideration of Natural Love and Affection, also the sum of $10.; one
Negro man named James and one Negro girl named Rosanna and one Negro
woman named Nann. Signed. William Shell. Wit. Herbert Tucker, Drury
Malone, G. Harbert. Recorded March 9, 1802. Fredk. Nance, Regr.

Deed Book E: 391
December 23, 1801. Bill of Sale. Thomas Scott, of the District of Edgefield
and State of South Carolina, to Philimon B. Waters ,of the District and State
aforesaid. In consideration of the sum of. $900; 3 Negro slaves to wit. A
wench Aggie, a girl Milla and a boy Morris. Signed. Thomas Scott. Wit.
Dennis d. Morgan. Proved by Dennis D. Morgan before Fredk. Nance, CCP.
December 29, 1801. Recorded March 15, 1802. Fredk. Nance, Regr.

Deed Book E: 434
February 25, 1802. Bill of Sale. William Burgess, of the State of South
Carolina and County of Newberry, to John Satterwhite, Junr. of the
aforesaid, place. In consideration of the sum of: $1000; 4 Negroes, Viz., one
Negro boy named Smart, one Negro woman named Jude and two children
called Milley and Nelley, two bay mares and a sorrel colt, 12 head of cattle,
40 head of hoggs, 3 feather beds and furniture, household and kitchen
furniture and all my plantation tools. Signed William Burgess. Wit. Daniel
Gates, Daniel Reagain. Proved by Daniel Gates before James Dyson, J.P. 28
April 1802. Recorded May 3, 1802. Fredk. Nance, Regr.

Deed Book E: 479
March 1, 1802. Bill of Sale. John Cureton ,of the District of Laurens and
State of South Carolina, to George McCreless and Company, of the
aforesaid State and District. In consideration of the sum of 50£ Sterling.
One Negro wench named Charlotte about 17 years of age. Signed John
Cureton. Wit. Edward Thweatt, Thomas Cureton. Proved by Edward
Thweatt before Peter Julien, J.P. 19 August 1802. Recorded 21 August
1802. Fredk. Nance, Regr. M.C.

Deed Book E: 482
March 1802. Mortgage. State of South Carolina, Newberry District. This
Indenture made the 1 March 1802 between Thomas W. Waters of the State
and District aforesaid of the one part and Daniel Parkins, Esq. Of the same
place of the other part. Whereas Thomas W. Waters in and by his
obligation, being separately notes of hand as follows $125. Dated Feb. 21,
1801, due 1 Jan 1802 and one other note of hand 9 Nov. 1801 and due 1
April 1802 for $790 and also one other note of hand dated 1 Mar. 1802 and
due 1 month after date for $100; likewise one other note of hand dated $430
and interest supposed now to the amount of $500 gave to Charles Banks
Executor to the estate of Levi Manning, deceased unto which note being
duly executed under his hand and bearing date as above mentioned the said
Thomas W. Waters stand July indebted unto the above mentioned Daniel
Parkins the sum of $1615 in the said note or obligations above mentions and
for the better securing the payment thereof according to the tenor true intent
and meaning of the said note of hand or obligations have bargained sold set
over and delivered unto the said Daniel Parkins, Esq. Five negroes as
follows: Jesse, a fellow about 28 years of age and Peggy, his wife, a wench
about 24 years of age and their 2 children Bill a boy about 6 years of age
and Bets a girl about 3 years old and Ben a boy about sixteen year old;
which said five Negroes Jesse, Peggy, Bill, Bets an Ben I do warrant and
forever defend unto the said Daniel Parkins Esq.... Signed in the presence of
Luke Smith. Thomas W. Waters. Proved by Capt. Luke Smith 31 July 1802

157

before Peter Julien, J.P. Recorded August 30, 1802. Attest, Fredk. Nance, Regr.M.C.

Deed Book E: 489
September 17, 1802. Bill of Sale. Moses Lipham of Newberry County, South Carolina to Jacob Crosswhite ,of the same place, for $1,200; negroes, to wit., Luce, Hanner, Frank and their increase. Signed. M. Lipham. Wit. Michael Pearson, Edmond Griffin Proved by Michael Pearson September 18, 1802 before Jacob Bieller, J.P. Recorded September 18, 1802. Fredk. Nance, R.M.C..

Deed Book E: 534
September 18, 1802. Bill of Sale. James Cobb, of the State of South Carolina and County of Newberry, to Patrick Spence, of the aforesaid place. In consideration of the sum of, $130; one Negro boy names Tom. Signed James Cobb. Wit. John G. Caldwell, Andrew Gray. Proved by Andrew Gray before Sims Brown, J.P. 2 October 1802. Recorded 14 October 1802. Fredk. Nance, Regr. MC.

Deed Book E: 567
January 3, 1803. Bill of Sale. Caleb Lindsey and John Lindsey of the District of Newberry and State of South Carolina, to Robert Talbert, of the State of South Carolina and District of Newberry. In consideration of the sum of $400; one Negro wench named Sarah about 16 years of age of a yellowish complexion. Signed Caleb Lindsey, John Lindsey. Wit. Daniel Talbert, John Anderson. Proved by Daniel Talbert before Peter Julin, J.P. January 3, 1803. Recorded January 4, 1803. Fredk. Nance, R.M.C..

Deed Book E: 568
December 20, 1801. Payment in Full. Received December 20, 1801 of William Burton $450 in full for a Negro woman named Carolina about 18 years of age which Negroes I do hereby warrant and forever defend against the lawful claim of all persons whatsoever, as witness where of. Caleb Lindsey. Wit. James Davenport, Edmund Spearman. Proved by Edmund Spearman before Peter Julien, J.P. 11 Oct. 1802. Recorded 4 January 1803.Proved by the oath Edmond Spearman October 11, 1802 before Peter Julien, J.P. Recorded January 4, 1803. Fredk. Nance, R.M.C..

Deed Book E: 605
State of South Carolina, This Indenture made 13 October 1800 between Rachel Cole, widow of one William Cole, deceased and administrator of the estate of the same and David Mayson and James Cole joint administrators with the said widow on the estate of the said deceased, and whereas the

158

said Rachel Cole at the sale of the estate of the said William Cole deceased did purchase the whole of the Negroes belonging to the said estate amounting to $1501 with sundry articles and whereas the said David Mayson and James Cole being jointly administrators with the aforesaid Rachel Cole are equally liable to the children and heirs of the said William Cole deceased for their respective shares a part of their fathers estate with the widow of the said deceased not withstanding she is in the possession of the whole of the Negroes aforesaid. Now as an indemnification and security to the said David Mayson and James Cole on account of the said Rachel Cole being in possession of and having the use and benefit of said Negroes the said Rachel Cole do hereby convey and grant unto the said David Mayson and James Cole and to their heirs in trust for the securing and making sure the proportional part of the estate of the said William Cole to each of his children or that part of this estate to which therewith they are entitles respectfully entitles by law the following Negroes Viz., Hager, Pat, Tabby, Grace, Walley and Jinn together with all their future increase subject to and on the following conditions first the said Rachel Cole is to keep possession use and enjoy the said Negroes and on account of which with the advantages enjoyed or arising from the other parts of the estates she is to school and educate her children...... signed Rachel Cole. Wit. Isaac Teague, Job Mayson, West Leopard. Proved by West Leopard before P. Williams 13 Nov. 1802. Recorded 8 February 1803. Attest. Fredk. Nance, R.M.C.

Deed Book E: 610
February 19, 1803. Deed of Gift. David Davenport, of the State of South Carolina and County of Newberry, to John Davenport, grandson of the aforesaid place. Consideration of Love and Affection; one Negro girl named Anneka and one Negro boy named Johnston now in the possession of my son in law Robert Malone, also Winkey, Malone, Mary and Anderson also in the possession of Robert Malone. Signed David Davenport. Wit. Fedk. Nance, Joseph Davenport. Proved by Joseph Davenport before P.B. Waters, J.P. 19 February 1803. Recorded February 19, 1803. Fredk. Nance, R.M.C.

Deed Book E: 613
May 10, 1802. Deed of Emancipation. Thomas Wadsworth, Esquire late of Charleston, State of South Carolina, merchant, deceased, by his last will and testament dated at Charleston 14 September 1799, set free Cate, a Negro slave about 18 years of age. Signed William Turpin, Ben. Cudworth, Ezekiel Noble, Pierce Butler, Junr. Proved by P. Butler, Junr. before Bremar, JQ. 13 May 1802. Recorded 1 March 1803. Fredk. Nance, R.M.C.

Deed Book E: 614

January 13, 1803. Deed of Emancipation. Thomas Wadsworth Esquire, late of Charleston and State of South Carolina, merchant, deceased, by his last will and testament dated at Charleston 14 September 1799, set free Rachel, a daughter of the black Sarah, a free woman, one of the Negroes which the said Thomas Wadsworth died possessed of and has set free as aforesaid, she was born December 28, 1801 and is free agreeable to law. Signed William Turpin, Benj. Cudsworth, John T. Elsworth, P. Butler, Junr. Recorded 1 March 1802. Fredk. Nance, R.M.C..

Deed Book E: 615

January 13, 1803. Deed of Emancipation. Thomas Wadsworth Esquire, late of Charleston and State of South Carolina, merchant, deceased, by his last will and testament dated at Charleston 14 September 1799, set free Lena a Negro girl about 8 years of age, one of the Negroes which the said Thomas Wadsworth died possessed of and has set free as aforesaid, she was born December 28, 1801 and is free agreeable to law. Signed William Turpin, Benj. Cudsworth, John T. Elsworth, P. Butler, Junr. Recorded 1 March 1802. Fredk. Nance, R.M.C.

Deed Book E: 616

January 13, 1803. Deed of Emancipation. Thomas Wadsworth Esquire, late of Charleston and State of South Carolina, merchant, deceased, by his last will and testament dated at Charleston 14 September 1799, set free Lucy a Negro girl about 6 years of age, one of the Negroes which the said Thomas Wadsworth died possessed of and has set free as aforesaid, she was born December 28, 1801 and is free agreeable to law. Signed William Turpin, Benj. Cudsworth, John T. Elsworth, P. Butler, Junr. Recorded 1 March 1802. Fredk. Nance, R.M.C.

Deed Book E: 617

January 13, 1803. Deed of Emancipation. Thomas Wadsworth Esquire, late of Charleston and State of South Carolina, merchant, deceased, by his last will and testament dated at Charleston 14 September 1799, set free Sarah, a Negro woman about 30 years of age and her increase, Viz., five daughters born before the death of the testator, named Liz, Lina, Cloe, Phillis, Charlotte and two children born since, Negroes which the said Thomas Wadsworth died possessed of and has set free as aforesaid and is free agreeable to law. Signed William Turpin, Benj. Cudsworth, John T. Elsworth, P. Butler, Junr. Recorded 1 March 1802. Fredk. Nance, R.M.C.

Deed Book E: 619
January 13, 1803. Deed of Emancipation. Thomas Wadsworth Esquire, late of Charleston and State of South Carolina, merchant, deceased, by his last will and testament dated at Charleston 14 September 1799, set free Archibald commonly called Archibald Rox, a mulatto boy about 9 years of age reputed to be the son of a white woman and born free, who formed part of the testators family and was bound to him for a term of years.. Signed William Turpin, Benj. Cudsworth, John T. Elsworth, P. Butler, Junr. Recorded 1 March 1802. Fredk. Nance, R.M.C.

Deed Book E: 620
January 13, 1803. Deed of Emancipation. Thomas Wadsworth Esquire, late of Charleston and State of South Carolina, merchant, deceased, by his last will and testament dated at Charleston 14 September 1799, set free Jenny, a Negro woman about 37 years of age. which the said Thomas Wadsworth died possessed of and has set free as aforesaid and is free agreeable to law. Signed William Turpin, Benj. Cudsworth, John T. Elsworth, P. Butler, Junr. Recorded 1 March 1802. Fredk. Nance, R.M.C.

Deed Book E: 621
January 13, 1803. Deed of Emancipation. Thomas Wadsworth Esquire, late of Charleston and State of South Carolina, merchant, deceased, by his last will and testament dated at Charleston 14 September 1799, set free Charlott a Negro girl about 3 years of age, one of the Negroes which the said Thomas Wadsworth died possessed of and has set free as aforesaid, and is free agreeable to law. Signed William Turpin, Benj. Cudsworth, John T. Elsworth, P. Butler, Junr. Recorded 1 March 1802. Fredk. Nance, R.M.C.

Deed Book E: 622
January 13, 1803. Deed of Emancipation. Thomas Wadsworth Esquire, late of Charleston and State of South Carolina, merchant, deceased, by his last will and testament dated at Charleston 14 September 1799, set free, Jen about 28 years of age one of the Negroes which the said Thomas Wadsworth died possessed of and has set free as aforesaid, and is free agreeable to law. Signed William Turpin, Benj. Cudsworth, John T. Elsworth, P. Butler, Junr. Recorded 1 March 1802. Fredk. Nance, R.M.C.

Deed Book E: 623
January 13, 1803. Deed of Emancipation. Thomas Wadsworth Esquire, late of Charleston and State of South Carolina, merchant, deceased, by his last will and testament dated at Charleston 14 September 1799, set free Thomas, a mulatto boy about 10 years of age one of the Negroes which the said Thomas Wadsworth died possessed of and has set free as aforesaid and is

free agreeable to law. Signed William Turpin, Benj. Cudsworth, John T. Elsworth, P. Butler, Junr. Recorded 1 March 1802. Fredk. Nance, R.M.C.

Deed Book E: 624-625
January 13, 1803. Deed of Emancipation. Thomas Wadsworth Esquire, late of Charleston and State of South Carolina, merchant, deceased, by his last will and testament dated at Charleston 14 September 1799, set free Line, a Negro girl about 11 years of age, one of the Negroes which the said Thomas Wadsworth died possessed of and has set free as aforesaid, and is free agreeable to law. Signed William Turpin, Benj. Cudsworth, John T. Elsworth, P. Butler, Junr. Recorded 1 March 1802. Fredk. Nance, R.M.C.

NOTE: "From page 613-624. Deeds of Emancipation. Negroes of said Thomas Wadsworth, deceased, by his Last Will and Testament, dated September 14, 1799, by William Turpin and Benjamin Cudworth, Executors, of the aforesaid Will."

Deed Book E: 627
May 10, 1802. Deed of Emancipation. Thomas Wadsworth, Esquire, late of Charleston, State of South Carolina, merchant, deceased, by his last will and testament at Charleston, dated 14 September 1799, set free Letty, a Negro woman slave, about 60 years of age. Signed William Turpin and Benjamin Cudworth, Executors of the will of said Thomas Wadsworth. Wit. Ezekiel Noble and Pierce Butler, Junr. Proved by Pierce Butler, Junr. before Bremar, JQ May 13, 1802. Recorded March 1, 1803. Fredk. Nance, R.M.C..

Deed Book E: 628
May 10, 1802. Deed of Emancipation. Thomas Wadsworth to Mike, a Negro slave about 24 years old. Proved, Signed and recorded as above.

Deed Book E: 629
May 10, 1802. Deed of Emancipation. Thomas Wadsworth set free Tilda, a Negro girl, about 5 years of age. Dated, signed, proved and recorded as above.

Deed Book E: 625{sic}
May 10, 1802. Deed of Emancipation. Thomas Wadsworth set free Chloe, a Negro girl about 6 years of age. Dated, signed, proved and recorded as above.

Deed Book E: 626 {sic}
May 10, 1802. Deed of Emancipation. Thomas Wadsworth set free Sarah, a
Negro woman commonly called by the name of Sarah Threet, about 35
years of age. Dated, signed, proved and recorded as above.

DEED BOOK F: 1803 - 1804

Deed Book F: 1
May 10, 1802. Deed of Emancipation. Thomas Wadsworth set free Lize, a
Negro girl about 14 years of age. Dated, signed, proved and recorded as
aforesaid.

Deed Book F: 2
May 10, 1802. Deed of Emancipation. Thomas Wadsworth set free Phillis, a
Negro girl about 6 years of age. Dated, signed, proved and recorded as
aforesaid.

Deed Book F: 3
May 10, 1802. Deed of Emancipation. Thomas Wadsworth set free Julias, a
Negro boy about 4 years of age. Dated, signed, proved and recorded as
aforesaid.

Deed Book F: 4
May 10, 1802. Deed of Emancipation. Thomas Wadsworth set free Betty, a
Negro woman about 45 years of age. Dated, signed, proved and recorded as
aforesaid.

Deed Book F: 5
May 10, 1802. Deed of Emancipation. Thomas Wadsworth set free Fanny,
daughter of Black Sarah a free woman, which the said Thomas Wadsworth
died possessed of and set free as aforesaid she was born December 28,
1801, and is free agreeable to Law. Dated, signed, proved and recorded as
aforesaid.

Deed Book F: 105
August 14, 1800. Bill of Sale. Samuel Lindsey of Newberry District, South
Carolina to Thomas Lindsey for the same place; for $5,589 the following
negroes, Viz., Nero, Toney, Lambert, Sambow, Andrew, All men slaves;
Deborah and Dinah, women slaves; George a male child about 9 years old,
Patt a girl child about 5 years of age and Molly a girl child about 10 years
old. Signed. Samuel Lindsey. Wit. Fredk. Nance. Proved by Fredk. Nance

before Peter Julien, J.P. June 7, 1803. Recorded June 7, 1803 Fredk. Nance, R.M.C.

Deed Book F: 140
April 30, 1803. Bill of Sale. George Abernathy of the District of Newberry and State of South Carolina to Fredk. Nance of the aforesaid place. In consideration of the sum of $400; one Negro girl called Milly. Signed George Abernathy. Wit. Young J. Harrington and George McKittrick. Proved by Y.J. Harrington before Peter Julien, J.P. August 11, 1803. Recorded 11 August 1803. Fredk. Nance, R.M.C.

Deed Book F: 141
October 12, 1801. Bill of Sale. James Caldwell and Thomas Farrow, of the State of South Carolina in Frederick Nance and Robert Rutherford, otherwise called Frederick Nance and Company, of the aforesaid place. In consideration of the sum of $410; one Negro boy named George about 13 years old. Signed James Caldwell. Thomas Farrow. Wit. J.R. Brown, JQ. Recorded 12 August 1803. Fredk. Nance, R.M.C.

Deed Book F: 146-147
January 8, 1802. Casper Bierly, Sr., of the State of South Carolina and County of Newberry to Martin Bierly of the aforesaid place. In consideration of the sum of $400; one Negro girl named Petty. Signed Casper Byerly. Mary Byerly. Wit. Peter Deckert, John Hipp. Proved by Peter Dickert before Michael Dickert, J.P. April 14, 1800. Recorded 22 August 1803.

Deed Book F: 148
January 8, 1802. Bill of Sale. Casper Byerly, of the State of South Carolina and County of Newberry to Harmon Byerly of the aforesaid place, one Negro boy named Cato. Signed Casper Byerly (mark), Mary Byerly (mark). Wit. Jacob Counts, John Hipp. Proved by Jacob Counts before James McMaster 8 January 1802. Recorded 22 August 1803. Fredk. Nance, R.M.C.

Deed Book F: 149
January 8, 1802. Bill of Sale. Casper Byerly, of the State of South Carolina and County of Newberry to Elizabeth Byerly of the aforesaid place. In consideration of the sum of unknown. One Negro girl named Milley. Signed Casper Byerly (mark). Wit. Jacob Counts, John Hipp. Proved by Jacob Counts before James McMaster, J.P. January 8, 1802. Recorded 22 August 1803. Fredk. Nance, R.M.C.

Deed Book F: 156
March 1, 1802. Bill of Sale. Harbirt Tucker, of the State of South Carolina
and District of Newberry to Stephen Shell of the aforesaid place. In
consideration of the sum of : 100 (pounds of dollars?), one Negro man slave
named Richard. Signed Harbirt Tucker. Wit. George Harbirt, George Shell.
Recorded 23 August 1803. Fredk. Nance, R.M.C.

Deed Book F: 198
August 15, 1803. Bill of Sale. Gasper Burly, of the State of South Carolina
and District of Newberry to John Hipp of the aforesaid place. In
consideration of the sum of $330; one Negro boy named Tom between ages
of 9 and 10 years. Signed Gasper Burly (mark). Wit. John Livingston,
Henry Furr. Proved by Henry Furr before James McMaster, J.P. October 1,
1803. Recorded 21 October 1803. Fredk. Nance, Regr. M.C.

Deed Book F: 204
July 4, 1803. Bill of Sale. South Carolina, Newberry District. Know all men
by these presents that I John Speake Esquire, Sheriff of the District of
Newberry for and in consideration of the sum of $460 to me in hand well
and truly paid by the said Fredk. Nance of the State and District aforesaid
the receipt whereof is hereby acknowledged have granted bargained and
sold and by these presents do grant bargain and sell unto the said Frederick
Nance his heirs and assigns one certain Negro boy named John about 14
years old which said Negro boy taken up and confined in the jail of the said
district aforesaid as a runaway and after bing duly advertised in the state
Gazette of his being confined in the jail of the district and after the
expiration of 12 months legal notice of the intended sale of the said Negro
John aforesaid did on the 2 day of July instant set up and sell the said Negro
to the highest bidder and thus agreeable to an act of Assembly in that case
made and provided for and the said Frederick Nance being the highest
bidder at $440 aforesaid I do hereby warrant and forever defend the title of
the said Negro called john unto the said Fredk. Nance, his heirs and assigns
against the claim and rightful owner or claim of any other person or persons
whatsoever claiming the same. ... John Speake S.N.D Wit. John Anderson,
Elisha Brooks. Proved by John Anderson before John Speake, Esq. July 4,
1803. Recorded October 31, 1803.

Deed Book F: 214
January 17, 1794. We the undersigned named legatees of the late Jacob
Cappleman, deceased, do hereby acknowledge that we have received the
several sums to our names annexed in full of all debts legacies due demands
and accounts on said estate. Wit. William Richards, David Reed. N.B. one
negro wench £45 and one negro child £ 18 a total of £ 63. Equally divided

after the widows death. Signed. Martin Taylor, John Hogg, George Feltman, Frederick Far (mark), Jacob Yonce, (mark), Caty Slike, John Cappleman, Elizabeth Cappleman - each received 9£, 9 shillings, 10 pense.) Elizabeth Cappleman £ 37, 19 s, 8 p. Recorded December 5, 1803. Fredk Nance, Regr.

Deed Book F: 235
December 30, 1803. Bill of Sale. Howel Cobb of the District of Newberry and State of South Carolina to William Moore of the District of Edgefield and State of South Carolina. In consideration of the sum of 124 £ 13 shillings and 7 pence Sterling; 2 Negro woman named Dafna and Chane, also one brown horse. Signed Howel Cobb. Wit John Towles (mark), George Butler. Proved by George Butler before Nathan Abney, J.P. January 2, 1804. Recorded 10 February 1804. Fredk. Nance, Regr. M.C.

Deed Book F: 236
December 4, 1803. State of South Carolina. To all to whom these presents shall come be seen or made known I William Thomas of Newberry District and State aforesaid send Greetings, whereas the aforesaid William Thomas by his certain bonds or obligations duly made and executed and bearing date 6 September 1803 unto the said Jacob Crosswhite of the District of Newberry and State aforesaid planter in the full and just sum of $600 to be paid unto the said Jacob Crosswhite, his heirs, executors administrators or assigns on or upon the 25 December 1805 without fraud or further delay. Now, Know Ye, that the said William Thomas for and in consideration of the said debt or sum of $600 and for the better securing the payment thereof unto the said Jacob Crosswhite his heirs executors and assigns according to the consideration of his obligations and further consideration of the sum of $1.00 to the said William Thomas in hand at and before the unsealing and delivery of these present by the said Jacob Crosswhite well and truly paid the receipt whereof he doth hereby acknowledge ..... sell unto the said William Thomas a tract of land containing 150 acres and the said William Thomas for the better securing of the said Jacob Crosswhite of the payment of the above $600 do grant bargain and sell him the said Jacob Crosswhite one Negro girl named Charlot of about 18 to 20 years of age to have and to hold the said Negro slave unto the said Jacob Crosswhite....4 December 1803... Signed William Thomas Wit. Isaac Davenport, William (J mark) Davenport. Proved by Isaac Davenport January 3, 1804. Recorded January 13, 1804. Fredk. Nance, Regr. M.C.

Deed Book F: 287-288
July 27, 1803. Mortage. The State of South Carolina. Know all men by these presents that I Jacob King of the District of Newberry and in the State

aforesaid for and in consideration of the sum of £164 Sterling money to me paid by Thomas Lindsey, Samuel Lindsey, Esquire, George Well and Abigail Wells all of the District of Newberry in the State aforesaid the receipt whereof I do here by acknowledge have bargained, sold and delivered and by these presents do bargain sell and delivered unto the said Thomas Lindsey, Samuel Lindsey, George Wells and Abigail Wells one Negro man slave named Peter about 25 years of age and also one Negro woman slave and her children the Negro woman named Jane about 28 years of age; one Negro female child named Mima about 9 years and one Negro male child named Sam about 7 years of age and one Negro male child about 5 years of age, to have and to hold the said bargained Negroes with their natural increase unto the said Thomas Lindsey, Samuel Lindsey, George Wells and Abigail Wells their heirs and assigns forever.....27 July 1803. Jacob King. Wit. John Lindsey, Humphrey Wells. Proved by Humphrey Wells before Frendk Nance, JQ. 6 March 1804. Recorded 10 March 1804. Attest., Fredk. Nance, Regr. M.C.

Deed Book F: 293-294
February 28, 1804. Bill of Sale Samuel Wells and Hezekiah Speake of the District of Newberry and State of South Carolina to Samuel Wells, paid by James Law, of the District and State aforesaid. Consideration $350; one Negro man slave named Harry about 21 years of age. Signed Samuel Wells, H. Speake. Wit. Samuel Lindsey, Edmond Lindsey. Proved by Samuel Lindsey before James Law 14 March 1804. Recorded March 13, 1804. Fredk. Nance, Regr. M.C.

DEED BOOK G: 1804 - 1805

Deed Book G: 98
August 26, 1803. Bill of Sale. John Averett of Newberry County, South Carolina to John Harmon of the same place. In consideration of the sum of (unknown amount); one negro boy named Jack, 19 years old. Signed John Averett. Wit. Moses Jacobs, William Harmon. Proved by Moses Jacobs before Peter Julin J.P. October 10, 1804. Recorded October 10, 1804. Fredek. Nance, R.M.C.

Deed Book G: 175
January 3, 1805. Bill of Sale. Stephen Herndon, of the State of South Carolina and District of Newberry to Isaac Davenport of the State and District aforesaid. In consideration of the sum of $650; one Negro woman named Anna and her 2 children, the eldest child named Fanny, the youngest

child name Cela. Signed Stephen Herndon. Wit. Thomas Peterson, James Goggans. Proved by James Goggans before Jacob Crosswhite, J.P. 14 January 1805. Recorded 12 February 1805. Fredk. Nance, R.M.C.

Deed Book G: 198
January 6, 1804. Bill of Sale. John Lark, of the State of South Carolina and District of Newberry to Charles Parkins of the aforesaid place. In consideration of the sum of:$675; three Negroes, Viz., Nance and her two children to wit Austin a boy about 3 years old and Tom about 8 months old. Signed John Lark. Wit. James Fenly, Ruth Black. Proved by James Fenly before Benjamin Long, J.P. 13 March 1805. Recorded 15 March 1805. Fredk. Nance, R.M.C.

Deed Book G: 223-224
March 8, 1805. Bill of Sale. Charles Brooks of the District of Newberry and State of South Carolina to William Moore of the District of Edgefield and State aforesaid. In consideration of the sum of 134 £ 5 shillings; one Negro man slave George, 24 or 25 years of age; 2 feather beds and furniture; one brown may horse 11 years old, one bay horse 6 years old, one Negro woman slave 50 years of age. Signed Charles Brooks. Wit. Benjamin Long, J.P. 19 March 1805. Recorded 22 March 1805. Fredk. Nance, R.M.C.

Deed Book G: 230
September 1, 1804. Deed of Gift. Elizabeth Turner, of the State of South Carolina and District of Newberry to Benjamin Franklin Long, her grandson, of the aforesaid place; one small Negro boy named Isaac about 3 years old. Signed Elizabeth Tuner. Wit. David Turner, Henry Coate. Proved by Henry Coate before Fredk Nance, J.P. 25 March 1805. Recorded 25 March 1805. Fredk. Nance R.M.C.

Deed Book G: 231
September 1, 1804. Deed of Gift. Elizabeth Turner, of the State of South Carolina and District of Newberry to Sally Long, daughter of Elizabeth, of the aforesaid place; one small Negro girl named Ann about 10 months old. Signed Elizabeth Tuner. Wit. David Turner, Henry Coate. Proved by Henry Coate before Fredk Nance, J.P. 25 March 1805. Recorded 25 March 1805. Fredk. Nance R.M.C.

§ § §

Name Index:
(White)

A

Abannon
 William, 18
Abbot/Abbott
Abbott
 Ailsey, 31
 Daniel, dec'd 34, 35
Abell
 John, 96
Abercrombie
 John, 13
Abercrombie, JP
 James, 28, 32
Abernath/Abernathy
 George, 164
 Hugh, 24
 John, 50, 140, 141
 Rhoda, 140, 141
Abney
 Ann, 152
 Mika, 135
 Mikle, 4
 William, 153
Abney, JP
 Nathan, 166
Ackert
 Anna, 99
Adair/Adeair
 Elish, 85
 Elisha, 84
 George, 61, 88
 James, 9, 14, 23
 John, 11, 14
 Joseph, 14, 19
 Robert, 9
Adams
 Godfrey, 128
 John, 93
 S., 118
Adkinson, Sr.
 John, 128
Adkinsson
 John, 79
Alexander
 Jeff, 81

Jesse, 81, 82
Margaret, 81
Algire
 Charistian, 118
Allen
 Charles, 19, 93, 94
 Chas., 80
 Jesse, 24
 Judith, 65
 Judith (See Swan),
  57
 Leair, 88
 Lydall, 8, 13, 24
 Saml., 57, 65
 Sarah, 106
Allen, JP
 Charles, 38
Allen, JQ
 Chas., 27, 35, 45
Allen, QM
 Chas., 61, 72, 83, 85,
  97, 101
Allin
 Lydall, 2
Allison
 Robert, 32
Amburgey?
 William, 110
Anderson
 David, 46, 49, 62,
  69, 93, 94
 Dd., 62
 Gabril, 111
 George, 18
 John, 131, 132, 158,
  165
 Mary, 111
 Saml., 49
 Wm., 111
Anderson, Esq.
 David, 45
Anderson, JP
 George, 7, 10, 27
Anderson, JQ
 David, 75
 Dd., 82
Andrew/s
 John, 123,
 Samuel, 123

Anthony
 Wm., 64
Arnold
 Anderson, 9, 31, 34,
  45
 Benjamin, 9
 Charity, 46
 Ira, 88, 102
 John, 9, 29, 36, 46
 Mary, 65, 66, 72
 William, 16, 42, 75
Arnold, decd.
 Anderson, 103
Arnold, JP
 William, 43, 46
Arnold, JQ
 Wm., 56, 62, 75
Arnold, widow
 Mary, 72
Ashley
 Elizabeth, 96
Atkinson
 Grace, 128
 Henry D., 141
 John, 75
Atkison, Jr.
 John, 129
Atkison, Sr.
 John, 129
Atwood
 James, 59
 Jas., 32
Austin
 Nathan, 4
Averett
 John, 167
Awbrey
 Marthey, 110

B

Babb
 Abner, 103
 Martin, 103
 Mercer, 122
 Sampson, 103
 T. (Thomas), 46
Babb, JP
 Mercer, 116
Bailey

169

Bostick
  Willis, 74
Botte
  Abraham, 66
Bourland
  John, 18
Bowen
  George, 66
  Mary, 95
  Tabertha, 66
  William, 63
Bowen, Jr.
  William, 63
Bowen, Sr.
  William, 63, 95
Bowland
  William, 95
Box
  Abm., 43
  Henry, 52
Boyce
  D., 80
  Drury, 13, 14, 89
  James, 16, 28
  James, decd, 46
  John, 54
Boyce, JP
  D., 54, 55
Boyd
  David, 124, 155
  James, 41
  John, 49, 63, 68
Boyd, JP
  John, 44
Bozman
  David, 142
Bradshaw
  South, 126
Branden/Brandon
  Thomas, 35, 36
Brannon, 39
  J., 49
  James, 50
Braselmann
  Brithern, 154
  Peter, 118, 154, 155
Braselmann & Co., 112
Brasilman
  Drucilla, 118
Brasilman & Co.

Peter, 119
Brd
  John, 85
Bremar, JQ, 159, 162
Briggs
  Jesse, 43
Brison
  James, 4
  John, 33
Brockman
  Amelia, 43, 44
  Amelia, wid, 40
  Job, 40
  John, 17, 40, 44
  John, dec,d 40
  William, 95
Brook
  G., 36
Brooks
  Bartlet, 25
  Bartlett, 25, 26, 28,
    29, 42, 121
  Barttlett, 30, 41
  Betsey Goodman, 41
  Charles, 168
  Chesley, 29
  Daniel, 153
  Dudley, 128
  Elisha, 143, 165
  Zachariah Smith, 129
Brooks, JP
  Thomas, 150, 152
Brown
  Fanney, 104
  J. Roberts, 114
  J.R., 26, 30
  James, 107
  Jeremiah, 143
  John, 104
  Joseph, 64, 110, 115
  Kazia, 115
  R., 25, 42, 114
  Roger, 14
  Samuel, 12, 153, 154
  Thomas, 117
  William, 107
Brown, JLC
  J.R., 15
Brown, JNC
  J.R., 13, 130, 131

R., 126, 135, 139,
    147
Brown, JP
  J., 109, 110
  Roger, 14, 17, 23
  Sims, 158
Brown, JQ
  J.R., 152, 164
Brown, NNC
  R., 127
Brummitt
  D., 119
Bruster
  James, 76
Bruster, DML
  James, 87
Bruster, QM
  James, 86
Bryson
  Elizabeth, 34
  Robert, 23
  William, 23
Bulow
  Charles, 63
  John, 63
Bunnel
  Asa, 62
Bunnel, Jr.
  Titus, 62
Burges/ Burgess
  Elijah, 24
  Joseph, 129
  William, 157
  Wm., dec'd 151
Burk
  Barbary, 43
Burly
  Gasper, 165
Burns
  John, 50
Burnside
  Thomas, 20
  W., 27, 46, 95
  William, 20, 31, 46
Burnside, JP
  W., 28, 38
  Wm., 25, 41
Burnside, JQ
  Wm., 32, 96
Burton, 63

171

Jas., 94
Robert, 50
William, 134, 135,
158
Wm., 8
Burton, S.r
William, 134
Butler
Catrine, 113
George, 166
Henry, 113
Mary, 113
Thomas, 135, 136
Butler, Jr.
P., 160, 161, 162
Pierce, 159, 162
Byerly
Casper, 164
Harmon, 164
byerly
John Sipert, 142
Byerly
Mary, 142, 164
Bylery
Elizabeth, 164
Byrd
Benjamin, 28, 88
John, 85
John H., 88
Purnell Johnson, 88
Thomas, 85
William, 85
Wm., 85
Byson, JP
James, 157

C

Caldwell
Danl., 132
David, 21, 50, 55, 82
James, 29, 30, 37,
41, 126, 164
John G., 158
Joseph, 116, 134,
135, 138
Paul, 111
Robert, 124
Samuel, 48
William, 17, 124
Cameron

Robert, 143
Camp
Benj., 4
Benjamin, 7
Camp, JP
Thomas, 18
Campbell
Angus, 4
Casey, 61
Elijah, 61
Henry, 61
James, 61, 121, 133,
135, 143
Mary, 61
Rob., 76
Campbell, JP
Angus, 4, 6, 13, 20,
30, 35, 42, 48
Caner
Joel, 98
Cannon
David, 82
John, 132, 139, 141
Samuel, 134, 136
Sarah, 139
William, 82
Cappleman
Elizabeth, 166
Jacob, 165
John, 166
Cargile/Cargill
Cornelius, 23, 24
Cornilius, 5
Jno., 18
John, 18, 43
John, Jr. 5
Lewis, 108
Casey
L.E., 155
Casey, JP
Levi, 109
Cason
C.A., 78
Elizabeth, 36
Giles, 30, 31, 36
James, 36
John, 35, 62, 67, 68
John, Sr., dec'd. 36
Joseph, 28, 67, 68
Larkin, 28, 146

Mary, 37
Milly, 36
Rachel, 36
Rebecca, 67, 68
Sarah, 37, 62, 67, 68
Thomas, 37
Thos., 67
Casper
James, 101
Caswell
Robert, 96
Cates
Aaron, 141
Chamberlin
Daniel, 36
Chambers
Thoroughgood, 117
Chamblin
Rachel, 36
Chandler
John, 27, 113, 116,
117
John, Jr. 113
William, 117
Chandler, Jr.
John, 113
Chappel/Chappell
Elizabeth, 153
James, 138
Thomas, 138, 153
Thomas, 153
Cheshire
Benjamin B., 71, 86
Benja B. Jr., 86
Benjamin Burch, 71
Elizabeth Reaves, 86
Hezekiah, 71, 86, 92
Childress, JP
Jesse, 66
Chiles
John, 35
Choice
William, 88
Clack
Charles, 142
Clardy
Hannah, 2
Clark
John, 47, 48, 116
Priscilla, 142

172

173

174

Thomas, 23
William, 27, 66
Wm., 66
Dendy, JP
Wm., 64, 73
Derrah, Jr.
James, 88
Dial
Elizabeth, 58
Hastings, 58
Hasting, Jr., 103
Hasting, Sr., 103
Hasting, dec'd., 103
Isaac, 71, 103
James, 58
John, 113
Rachel, 103
John Jon, 102
Dicker, JP
Michael, 149
Dickert
Peter, 142
Dickert, JP
Michael, 164
Dickson
Elenor, 151, 152
Dillard
Elizabeth, 81
George, 81
George W., 81
James, 113
Samuel, 18
Susanna, 33
William, 33
Dillard, JP
James, 33, 77, 85
Jesse, 82
Dixon
Eleanor, 152
Dobbins
John, 56
John M., 56
Dodd
Mary, 81, 82
Dodgen
James, 114
Oliman, 114
Olleman, 138
Donohoe
Cornelius, 24

Dourah
James, 88
John, 72
Dourah, JP
James, 87
Downs
Jonathan, 7, 9, 110
Joshua, 5, 8, 13
S., 84
Samuel, 84
W.F., 53
William F., 53, 59,
76, 78
Downs,
William F., 70
Downs, JP
Jonathan, 2, 4, 5, 8,
14, 23, 66, 72
Joseph, 6, 8, 9, 11,
17, 21, 24, 29,
34, 35, 37, 39, 57
Downs, JQ
Jonathan, 42, 43, 53,
72
Downs, Jr.
Jonathn., 70
Downy
William F., 94
Doyal
John, 9
Drew
Langston, 22, 23
Dson
James, 153
Ducker
Henry, 103
Ducket
Barruch, 101
Barruck, 102
Henry, 103
Sarah, 77
Ducket/ See Ducker
Duckett
Barruck, 101
Jacob, 20
John, 77
Sarah, 20, 77
Duckett, JP
Benjn., 74
Duckit

Josiah, 155
Dugan
Thomas, 111
Dumas
David, 104
Emeline, 104
Francis, 104
Matildy, 104
Nancy, 104
Nehemiah, 104
Polly, 104
Duncan
James, 54, 74
Dunklin
Irby H., 76
James, 76
Dunklin, JP
James, 51
Dunlap
J., 90
John, 76, 90, 99, 100,
104
William, 49
Durkee
A., 65
Dutten, JP
Wm., 65
Duty
Richard, 5
Duvall
Lewis, 17
Sarah, 112
Duvault
Daniel, 143
Dyer
Hezekiah, 28
Dyson
Abraham, 138
Daniel, 141, 145
James, 55, 141
Jas., 55
John, 152

E

Eagerton
Charles, 75
Earle, CC
Geor. W., 63
East

175

Elizabeth, 64
Josiah, 64
Langsdon, 64
Edward/s
John, 4
John, dec'd.,143
John, 117
Litisha, 117
Margarett, 117
Mary, 4, 117
Mary, widow, 143
Rhoda, 117
Eigleberger
John, 134
Elliot
Thomas, Sr., 13
William, 132
Elmore
J.A., 77
John A., 57, 58
Elmore, JQ
J.A., 27
John A., 53
Elsworth
John T., 160, 161,
162
Ervin/Erwin
Joseph, 27, 148
Ewen/Ewin
Betsey, 52, 53
James, 52
Judy F., 52, 53

F

Fairbarn
Alexander, 11
Falconer/Falkoner
John, 2, 7, 26, 27
Far
Frederick, 166
Farr, Esq.
Samuel, 47
Farrow
Elizabeth, 107
John, 104
Pattillo, 90, 104
Samuel, 47
Thomas, 29, 30, 164
William, 149
Featherston/e

Lucy, 38, 39
Richard, 38
Sarah, 38, 39
William, 38
Feltman
George, 166
Fenly
James, 168
Finch
William, 119, 141
Wm., 116
Finch, JP, 149
Edward, 116, 117,
118, 123, 132,
147
Findley/ Finley
John, 55
Paul, 95, 96
Finney
Agness, 83, 84
Elizabeth, 84
James, 9
John, 83, 96
Martha, 84
Flannagan
Ann Thomas, 33
Reuben, 33
Fleman
Samuel, 24
Fleming
Rob. Jr., 44
Robert, 26
Robt., 80
Samuel, 20
William, 33
Flewallen/Flewalling
Elizabeth, 33
Susannah, 33
Thomas, 33
Flin/Flinn
James, 9
Owen, 142
Floyd
Ann, 127, 128, 130
Ann, widow 131
Frances, 130
John, 130
John, son of Ann,
130
Rebekah, 130

Rebekah, dec'd, 131
Robert, 127
William, 127
Flurry
Joseph, 95
Foote
John, 113
Forkes
Thomas, 1
Foster
Frederick, 142
Joel, 149
William, 35
Foster, Jr.
Anthony, 14
Anty?, 14
Fowler
Charles, 90
D., 91
David, 90
Josiah, 155
Levi, 74, 77, 80
Nancy, 90
Sarah, 91
William, 90
Fowler, decd.
David, 91
Franks
N., 32
Thomas, 52
Friday
Gabriel, 123
Frye
Sibilla, 138
Fuller
Jones, 76, 102
Jones, Jr., 76
Saly, 76
William, 50
Wm., 50
Fulton
Wm., 99
Fulton, JP
William, 62
Wm., 77, 80, 96
Funk
Geo., 55
Furnas
Joseph, 146
Furr

Henry, 165

G

Gable
    Anna, 84
Gain/Gaines
    Betsey 47
    Caty, 151
    Edmund, 150, 151
    Isabella, 151
    James, 151
    Larkin, 47, 93
    Mary Pendleton, 150
    Peggy, 134, 151
    Salley, 150
    Thomas, 132, 136,
        138, 150, 151
Gaines, JP
    Larkin, 56
Gallegey/Gallegy
    John, 24
    Joseph, 24
Galligly
    Joseph, 18
Gallman
    Henry, 144
Gamble
    David, 83, 84
    William, 92, 104
    Willilam, 96
Gant/Gantt
    John, 108
    John, 108
Garlington, 55
    Edwin, 45
    George J., 55
    J., 35, 45, 54
    John, 27, 32, 39, 43,
        49, 50, 52, 53,
        56, 57, 58, 59,
        68, 74, 78, 80,
        86, 87, 90, 94,
        98, 99, 100, 103,
        104, 107
    Nancy, 45
    Wm., 103
Garlington, JP
    John, 67
Garlington, JQ

John, 50, 82, 85, 89,
    102, 106
Garlington, QM
    John, 51, 60, 63, 65,
        66, 70, 71, 73,
        76, 77, 104
    Samuel, 84
Garman
    Mary, 61
    Michael, 61
Garner
    Thomas, 7
Garret/Garett
    Charles, 105
    Elisha, 105
    Houseley, 97
    Jesse, 72, 96, 105
    Jesse, Jr. 96, 97
    Jesse, Sr., 8;6, 87,
96, 97
    Jessey, 66
    Stephen, 50
    William, 57
Garrett, Esq.
    Stephen, 67
Garrett, JP
    Thos., 108
Garvin
    John, 121
Gary
    Thomas, 23, 141
    West, 67
    William, 72, 139
    Wm.C., 72
Gates
    Daniel, 157
    John, 75, 79
    Josiah, 122, 123
Geril
    Thomas, 109
Geril, Mrs.
    Mary, 110
Gerrald, Exr.
    Gerrard, 136
Gibson
    James, 33
    John, 52
    Margaret, 52
    Thomas, 109, 110
    Thomas, Sr., 109

Giddens/ Giddins
    James, 29
G   James (son of James),
        29
Gilam
    Robert, 147
Gilbert
    Caleb, 131
    William, 54
Gillam
    Charles, 131
    David, 42, 152
    Joshua, 147
Gillam, JP
    Robert, 142, 148
    Robt., 119
Gillan, Sheriff
    Robert, 111
Gilliam
    Harris, 131
Gilliam, JP
    Robert, 132
Gillum, JP
    Robert, 120
Gissendence
    Henry, 143
Gist
    Sarah, 35
Glasgow
    Archablad, 132
    Mary, 132
Glen/Glenn/Glynn
    A., 64
    B., 25
    David, 116
    James, 26
    John, 107
    Tryee, 27
    Wm., 22, 31
Godfrey
    Jno., 93
    John, 101
Goff
    Hugh, 102
Goggans
    Abraham, 120
    George, 119, 126,
        140
    James, 120, 140, 168
    Johnson, 120

Mary, 120
Thomas, 73, 120
William, 120
Golden/Golding
  Anthony, 3
  James, 20
  Reuben, 137
  William, 15, 16
Goodman
  Charles, 29, 30
  Clabourn, 31
  Clabourne, 30
  Claiborne, 29
  Daniel, 146
  James, 6, 9
  Joseph, 29, 30, 111
  Maria, 41
  Maryra, 29
  Samuel, 29, 30, 42
  Timothy, 25, 29, 30
Goodwin, Esqr.
  Wyche, 20
Gordon
  Charlotte, 40
  George, 40
  Jean, 40
  Thomas, 110
  Thos., 110
Gordon, JP
  George, 30
Gore
  Michael, 124
Gorree
  John, 115
Graham
  George, 113
  James, 114
  Mary, 113
Graves
  L., Est., 56
  Lewis, 52
  Martin, 56
  Wm., 56
Graves, dec'd
  L., 56
  Lewis, 56
Graves, JP
  Lewis, 24
Gray
  A., 39

Alexander, 39
Alexdr. R., 45
Andrew, 158
Eva Margarete, 133
Frederick, Capt., 136
John, 26, 77
Mary, 77
Peter, 133, 144
Graydon
  William, 76
Grayham
  James, 116
Greelee
  James, 149
Greer
  David, 36, 62
Griffen/Griffin
  Anthony, 87
  Charles, 131, 148
  Edmond, 63, 158
  Horatio, 63
  John 8
  Joseph, 3, 6, 8
  Mary, 3
  Reuben, 139, 148
  Richard, 30, 41
  Sarah, 3, 8
Griffin, JP
  Charles, 55, 123,
    124. 126, 127, 12
    137. 148
  Richard, Sr., 29
Griffith
  Ezekiel, 64
Groom/s
  Richard, 8
Guilder
  Isaac, 124
Gunnell
  William, 46
Gwinn
  Charles, 28

H

Hall
  John, 2
  Nathaniel, Sr., 2

Hammond/Hammonds
  Nancy, 108
  Peter, 54, 55, 57, 108
  William, 55
Hampton
  John, 128
Hampton, JP
  John, 149
Hampton, JQ
  John, 118
Hancock
  Barber, 139
Handy
  John C., 25
Hannah (Little)
  James, 77, 85, 86
Hannah, Sr.
  Robert, 77
Harbert
  George, 150, 165
Harbert, JQ
  George, 151
Harding
  Henry, 73
  Mary, 37
  William, 74
Hardman
  Uriah, 119
Haring
  Henry, 73
Harmon
  Jacob, 149
  John, 167
  William, 167
Harmon, decd.
  John, 149
Harrell
  Jacob, 149
Harrington
  Y.J., 164
  Young J., 164
Harris/Harriss
  Charles, 31
  Jane, 82
  Jane, widow, 82
  John, 82
  John L., 94
  Little B., 42
  LittleBerry, 42
  Polly, 94

Saml., 152
Samuel, 152
Stephen, 67
William, 17, 27
Harrison
John, 144
Harry
Thomas, 80
Harvy
John, 82
Harwin
James E., 141
Haskett
Joseph, 89, 90
Hatcher
Jleman?, 14
Nancy, 14
Hatter
Benj., 81
Hatton
Francis, 150, 151
Hawkins
Peter, 145
Haynie
Maximilian, 110
Hays
John, 119
Hazlet
John, 145
Head
John, 47
Heard
Stephen, 125
Heath
John, 120
John D., 60, 61
Hencock
William, 119
Henderson
Jas., 86
Saml., 16
Samuel, 124
Henderson, C.C.
A., 11
Hendricks
Thomas, 80
Hendrix
Thomas, 55
Henning
Danl., 112

Henrick
Mecajah, 46
Henry
Alexander, 39
George, 152
Nelley, 96
Herbert
Thomas, 118
Herbert, JQ
George, 150, 156
Hern, Sr.
John Fredk., 98
Herndon
Stephen, 167, 168
Hewet
John, 68
Hickman
Adam, 9
Higgins
Francis, 135, 145
James, 82
Hilburn
Levi, 149
Hill
Cason, 145, 146
Isaac, 105
James, 142
John, 142
Joseph, 155
Hipp
John, 164, 165
Histelow
Isom, 17
Hitch, JP
J., 73
Hitt
David, 74
Hix
Edward, 80
Hodge
Hance Hendrick, 82
Hodges
Elizabeth, 83
Frances, 82
Margaret, 83
Richard, 49, 82, 83
Sarah, 83
Wealthy, 83
Hoffmaster
William, 118

Hogg
James, 111
John, 111, 166
Joseph, 111
Lewis, 111
Mary, widow 115
Hogg, JP
Lewis, 153
Holiday
William, 72
Holland
Abraham, 92
John, 103
Mary, 103
Nancy Beasley, 92
Weyman, 92
Holliday
William, 89
Holliday, Sr.
Wililam, 88
Hollidy
Matthew, 72
Robert, 72
Hollidy, Sr.
William, 72
Hollingsworth
James, 102
Jeremiah, 42, 43
Hooker
Edward, 14
Horsey
Abel Jones, 115
Daniel, 115
Sarah, 111, 112, 115
Houseal
Wm., 133
Houseal, JP
Wm., 142
Hudgens
Ambrose, 45, 49
Hueston
James, 143
Huffmaster
William, 117
Huggins
James, 82
Hughes
Mary, 65
Hughey
Thomas, 19

179

Humphrey
Elizabeth, 33
Hunt
Charlott, 81
Samuel, 81, 82
Hunter
Andrew, 111
James, 40, 80
John, 1, 6, 12, 15,
18, 19, 24, 40, 67
Robert, 24
William, 135, 138
Wm., 18
Hunter, JP
John, 5, 6, 16, 124
William, 10, 17
Wm., 10, 13, 23
Hurlbert
William, 95
Hutcheson/Hutchinson
John, 26, 34
Joseph, 3
Hutchenson/Hutchinson,
JP
Robert, 26, 28, 33,
34, 37, 40, 43,
45, 51

I

Inman/Innman
Jahue, 122
Juhue, 122
Irby
Frances, 70, 71
George William, 119
Hennietta, 70
Heta., 70
J.H., 70, 76, 84
James H., 70, 71, 76
Nancy, 70
Polly, 70, 71
Sarah, 71
W., 102
William, 56, 59, 70,
71, 99, 111, 114,
116, 145
Wm., 59, 76, 100,
145
Irwin

James, 21

J

Jacob/Jacobs
Moses, 167
James
Benj., 105
Benj. Dec'd., 105
Benjamin, 86
Isaac, 6
John S., 102, 105
John S.., 106
Thomas, 85
Janes
James, 85
Jay
John, 146
Jeanes/Jeans
Edward, 85
Edward, Jr. 84
John, 54, 74, 84, 85
Joseph, 20
Josiah, 92
Johnson
Abraham, 67, 68
Ann, 67, 68, 153
Benj., 134
Daniel, 128
Elizabeth, 43
Hester, 153
Isaac, 69
Jesse, 69
Johat., 43
John, 43, 94
Jonathan, 3
Levi, 134
Robert, 69, 155
William, 54
Wm. T., 6
Johnston
Elizabeth, 113
James, 136
Jehu, 127
Jonathan, 6
Mary, 128
Robert, 112, 155
Thomas, 113, 127,
128
Jones, 73

A.C.,Sr., 93
Benjamin, 22, 55
Dred, 23, 55
Edward, 79
Frederic, 54
Fuller, NC, 101
Gabriel, 28
Geo., 49
Gibeon, 135
Hiram, 64
James, 19, 21, 22, 23
Jesse, 19, 21, 23
John, 11
Jorden, 19, 20
Joseph, 19, 23, 56,
79, 140, 141
Miles, 21
Nancy, 140, 141
Patsy, 56
Sally, 76
Therisa, 64
Whitmore, 91
Wm., 2
Jowel/ Jowell
Gabriel, 71, 83, 85
Jowell, JP
Gabriel, 59
Julien/ Julin, JP
Peter, 119, 157, 158,
164, 167
William, 136
Julin, Esqr.
Peter, 126

K

Kay
Thomas, 145
Kellet/Rellett
James, 88
Jeane, 28
Jennet, 89
Jennett, 88

Kelley/Kelly
Allen, 73
Betsey, 104
Edwd., 115
John, 104, 121, 122,
153
John, dec'd. 46

180

181

Benjamin Franklin,
    168
Elizabeth, 116
Henry, 116
Polly, 135
Priscilla, 116
Robert, 57
Sally, 168
Long, JP
    Benjamin, 168
    Robt., 65, 80
Loston
    Wm., 139
Loveless
    John, 74, 75
Lowers
    S.B., 80
    Sopia, 80
Lowry
    Polly, 53
    Robert, 53
Luke
    Burrell, 103
    John, 30
Lynch
    W.E., 107
    Wm. E., 107
Lyon
    Joseph, 17

M

MacCary
    John, 122, 123
Madden, 56
    Charles, 63, 68
    David, 12, 28, 72
    George, 22, 56
    John, 63, 71
    L., 38
    Mabra, 12
    Moses, 28, 37, 50, 55
    Widow, 68
Maddox
    Justinian, 30, 31
Mador, JP
    Isaac, 98
Mahen/Mahon
    Bayley, 88
    John, 88
    Joseph, 11

Malone
    Drury, 156
    Robert, 159
    W., 110, 111, 112,
        113, 114, 115
    William, Sr. 116
Maning
    Levi, 144
Manley/Manly
    Jeremiah, 53, 56, 57
    William, 68
Markley
    Abraham, 134
Martin
    David, 107
    Fanny, 96
    George, 117
    Jean, 4
    John, 8, 10, 21
    Joseph, 24
    Margaret, 4, 106
    Nancy, 107
    Reuben, 100
    Shadrach, 12
    Shadrack, 4, 5
Martindale/Martindate
    Joseph, 33
Mason
    David, 23, 138
    Wm., 8
Mathews/Matthews
    Ezekiel, 52
    Jane, 67, 68
    Robert, 53, 57
    Samuel, 52
    Zebulon, 68
Mathews, JP
    Ezekl., 66, 67
Mathis
    Samuel, 10
    Thomas 110
    Zebulon, 10
May
    Doretha, 104
    Dorithia, 104
    William, 104
Mayer
    Benedick, 134
Mayson
    Chas. C., 74

David, 158, 159
James, 120
Job, 159
McCaa
    James, 19, 28
McCambridge
    Jno., 6
McCary
    James, 137
McClannahan
    James, 43
McClictick
    James, 16
McClinto
    John, 19
McClintock
    James, 13, 20, 22, 26
    John, 16
McClintock, Jr.
    James, 16
McClure
    Alexander, 87
    John, 82, 87
    John W., 87
McCoy
    Drayton, 85, 86
    John, 149
    Nathaniel, 13
McCrarey
    Joe, 57
McCrary
    Caty, 60
    James, 60
    Nancy, 60
Thomas, Jr., 57
McCrary, Jr.
McCraw
    Edward, 150
    Stephen, 147
McCreary
    Matthew, 18
McCreay
    Moses, 18
McCune
    Mary, 9
McDaniel
    Jer., 145
    Jeremiah, 145, 149
    Jeremiah, Jr., 145
    John, 149

McDavid
  James, 53
  Jonathan, 53
McDonald
  Donald, 136
McDowall
  Alexr., 34
McElhaney
  John, 128
McGill
  Deborah, 45
McGraw
  Edward, 151
McHarg/McHargh
  John, 45, 54, 57
  Susannah, 45
  William, 55
  Wm., 45
McKie
  Daniel, 120, 126
  Daniel, Jr., 10
McKillar
  Jno., 53
  John, 53
McKiterick
  Robert, 142
McKittrick
  George, 164
McKnight
  Thomas, 87
McLachlan
  Archibald, 53
McLaughlen
  John, 27
McMahan/McMahon
  James, 101, 102
  John, 107
  Thomas, 117
McMahon
  John, 107
  Thomas, 117
McMaster
  James, 164
McMaster, JP
  James, 164, 165
McMorries
  John, 147
  John, Capt., 146
  Nancy, 146
McMorris

J., 140
  John, 135, 136, 140
McNees
  James, 2, 11
  Robert, 2, 93, 94,
    104
McNees, JP
  Robert, 57, 102
McTeer
  Wm., 10, 13
Medley
  James, 56
Meek
  James, 79
  John, 1, 75, 79, 102,
    103
Mehaffy
  Nancy, 88
Meredith
  Henry, 91
  Henry, Capt., 91
  Samuel, 91
Metz
  George, 149
Middleton
  Ainsworth, 69
Milam/Milan
  B., 53
  Bartlett, 44, 52
  Ferrill, 53
  John, 31
  Thomas, 53
Miles
  Saml., 122
  Samuel, 148, 153,
    154
  Thomas, Jr., 47
Miller
  Anderson, 62, 67, 68
  E., 143
  George, 67, 68, 73
  Jacob, 50, 76
  James, 67, 68
  John, 10, 62, 67, 68,
    115, 143
  Jos., 37
  Leonard, 65
  Papa John, 143
  Sarah, 68
  William, 62, 68

Widow of John
  Sarah, 67
Milling
  D.T., 54
Mills
  Alexander, 79
  James, 44
  Thomas, 149
Milner
  A., 94
  Elizabeth, 87
  John, 57
  Joshua, 87
Milner, JQ
  A., 96, 97
Milwee
  William, 6
Mink
  John, 119, 129
Mishouse
  Obadiah, 65
Mitchell
  Elisha, 31
  Isaac, 32, 76
  James, 31
  John, 31
  Mary, 31
  Polly, 105
  Robert, Mayor, 37
  William, 23
Mitchell, JP
  Wm., 30
Mitchell, JQ
  Wm., 27, 31, 37
Mitchersson
  D., 54
  Edward, 7
Mitchussen?, JP
  Wm., 5
Mits
  Adam, 130
Monro
  John, 68, 74
Monry
  John, 73
Montgomery
  Elizabeth, 116
  George, 116
Montgomery, JP
  James, 20

183

O

O'Bryant
   Patrick, 11, 14
O'Dell
   John Prather, 20
O'Flynn, 142
O'Neal/O'Neil
   Abijah, 121, 122
   John, 4, 20
O'Nims
   Thomas, 152
Oliver
   Ah?, 98
   Benjamin G., 89
   Daniel, 91
   J.P., 98
   Permilia, 91
Osborn/Osborne
   Daniel, 51, 52
   Daniel, Sr. 22
   Wm., 30, 31
Oster
   George, 142
Otten
   Jacob, 104, 105
Owen
   Elizabeth, 81
   Hulda, 80, 81
   John, 8
   Susannah, 80, 81
Owens/Owings
   Amelia, 44
   Archibal, 88, 89
   Jane, 89
   John, 44
   Thomas, 92, 104

P

Parkins
   Charles, 168
   Daniel, 128, 157
Parkins, JP
   Daniel, 145
Parks
   James, 80
   Sml., 136
Parks, JP
   Thomas, 54, 64

Pasley
   Robert, 19
Passinger
   Frederick, 144
Patterson
   Charity, 143
Pearson
   John, 54
   Michael, 158
Peister
   Casper, 133
   G. Adam, 133
Pemberton
   George, 153
   George, Sr., 152
   Jesse B., 150
Penington
   John, 13
Perkins, Esq.
   Daniel, 150, 157
Perkins, JP
   Daniel, 140
Pester
   John, 143
   Sally, 143
Peterson
   Thomas, 168
Pettipool
   William, 123
Phillips
   William, 75
   Wm. 102
Pinson
   Aaron, 97, 98
   Abijah, 72
   Alley, 85
   Howard, 87
   Js., 72
   Marmaduke, 54, 72
   Moses, 82, 85
Pitts
   Aaron, 114
   Daniel, Jr. 114
   Edward, 114
   Joseph, 148
   Levi, 149, 152
Plunkit
   William, 133
Pollard
   W., 35

Pollard, JQ
   Wm., 75
Pope
   Elizabeth, 111
   John, 111
Porter
   Tho., 68, 80
   Thomas, 50, 63, 65,
     68, 80
Powell
   John, 32
   Lucy, 104
   Maluchiah, 12
   Milly W., 93
   Nancy, 46, 47
   R., 93
   Robert, 111, 112,
     118, 119, 155
   Robt., 111
   Samuel, 22
   Samuel N., 32
   Tho., 104
   Virginia H., 93
   William, 46, 47, 93
Powell, JP
   James, 47
Power
   John, 29
Prater
   Thomas, 91, 92
Prater, JP
   Jesse, 91, 92, 95
Praytor
   Basel, 98
   Bazel, 98
   Isyah, 98
   Persilla, 98
Prince
   Francis, 128
Pringle
   Jno., 74
   John, 29, 75
Procter
   Phillip, 145
Pruit
   Willis, 116
Puckett, Esq.
   John, 57
Puckett, JP
   J., 40

185

Elizabeth, 92
Henry, 91, 92
Hennery, 91, 92
Johnson, 91, 92
West
Michael, 145
Robert H., 102
Wharton
Pleasant, 38
White
James, 48
Joseph, 145, 146
Thomas, 56
Whiteford
David, 73
Whitmore
Martha, 19
Whitmore, JP
Geo., 33, 38
George, 18, 21, 22, 23
Joseph, 19
Whitten
Moses, 74
Whitworth
Jacob, 34
Wicker
Uriah, 130
Wilkerson
Alexander, 96
Alexdr., 96
Edward, 96
Wilkes/Wilks
Polly, 97
Thomas S., 98
Thomas Jr., 98
Wilkinson
Alexr., 57
Edward, 80
William/Williams
Ann, 57, 58, 147
Col., 3
Daniel, 11, 65, 124, 125, 126, 131
Dan iel, Jr. 11, 15, 139
Daniel, Sr.10, 16, 17, 125
Daniel (dec'd), 29
Danl., 16

Danl., Sr., 15, 16
Duke, 6
Elizabeth, 15, 16, 131, 139
Henry, 103
J.P., 23
Jacob, 59
James, 3, 9
James, Col, dec'd. 2
James A., 8
James Atwood, 3, 8
Jas. Atd., 55
Jeremiah, 113
John, 6, 65
John (son of Daniel, 125
John, Jr. 3, 8, 9, 10
John, Sr., 125
Joseph, 139
Josiah, 57, 58, 65
Josiah, Capt., 65
Judith, 57, 58
Louisa, 57, 58
Lyall, 97
Martha, 57, 58
Mary, 2, 3, 71
Meredith, 145
Natty, 131
P., 147, 159
Providence, 147
Samuel, 131
Thomas, 147
Ursla, 15, 16
Washington, 3, 9, 92
William, son of Daniel , 10
William, Esq..
18Williams, JP
Charles, 88
Providence, 120, 138, 149
Williams, S.D.
John, 125
Williamson
Elisha, 74, 75
Henry, 24
Willson/Wilson
Charles, 111
Frank, 119
Henry, 119

John, 13, 138
Joseph, 64
Mary, 93
Michael, 5
Robert, 155
Thomas, 92
William, 108
Wm., 138
Winn
A., 91
Alexander, 90, 91
Andrew, 64, 94, 100, 106
Daniel, 64
Daniel M., 90, 91
Edmond, 106
Galanus, 27
Gallanus, 64, 105, 106
Withers,
John, Jr. 61
Wolf/Wolfe/Wolff
George, 58,59, 80
J.F., 7, 24, 31
J.T., 52
John Francis , 21
John F., 9, 17, 21, 86, 87
John F., Col., 29
Polly, 86, 87
T.F., 72
Wood
Robert, Sheriff, 41, 47
Sarah, 45
Stel., 18
Stephen, 45
William, 79
Woodson
James, 35
Jas., 35
Word
Charles, 28
James, 55, 56, 58
Work
William, 74
Worthington
Elijah, 140
Elizabeth, 140, 141
John, 140, 141, 149

191

Jude, 152, 153
Milly, 140, 141
Woss
Hennery, 91
Wright
Daniel, 17, 34, 35,
40, 44
Danl., 44
Danl, Esq., 17
Nancy, 31
Sarah, 18, 19, 45
Sarah, widow, 75
Thos., 89
William, 92
Wright, JQ
Daniel, 31

Y

Yarbrough
Hiram, 95
Yonce
Jacob, 166
York
Jonathan, 60
Young, 34, 35
Agnes Lipscomb, 66
Alcy, 77
Archd., 44, 60, 73
Betsy, Mrs., 66
George, Sr., 77
Henry C., 102
James, 10, 12, 13,
15, 16, 25, 26,
28, 37, 38, 41,
46, 48, 49, 56,
107
James, dec'd., 56
Jno. N., 73
John, 104
John N., 73
Richd., 40
William, 12, 66
William Jones, 66
Wm., 10
Young, JP
James, 90, 94, 106

§§§

Name Index
(Black)
Names alphabetically
listed in each type of
deed.

Affidavit
Dave, 5
Negroes taken by
British (not
named), 128

Agreement
Anny, 47
Bet, child of Peggy,
150
Canders, 47
Catren, 47
Delilah, 47
Dennis, 47
Dick, 150
Hannah, 47
Harry, 47
Harry, child of Bet,
150
Jacob, 47
Jean, 47
Jesse, 150
Jiller, 47
John, child of Judy,
150
Jude, 36
Judy, 150
Letty, 47
Masten, 47
Melinda, 93
Micklry, 47
Milley, 47
Nutty, 47
Peggy, 150
Peter, 47
Petty, wife of Jesse,
150
Rachel, 150
Sanders, 93
Sigh, child of Judy,
150
Wigdon, 36
Willes, 47

William, child of
Peggy, 150
Zelphia, 93

Bill of Sale
Aaron, 11, 15
Abb, 27
Abigail, 79
Abraham, 17, 55
Absalom, 12
Absalom, child of
Jinney, 10
Adam, 17, 34, 82,
120
Aff, 35
Agatha, wife of
Toney, 74
Agga, 11
Aggie, 156
Aggy, 15, 16, 125
Aimoy, 2
Albert, child of
Beck, 53
Alice, 31, 59
Alie, 120
Ambrose, 155
Amers, 31
Amos, children of
Toney and
Agatha, 74
Amy, 128
Andrew, 10, 15, 131,
140, 163
Aney, 18
Ann, 46, 137
Anna, 167
Annaky, 112
Annas, 102
Anthony, 120, 124
Aron, 120, 125
Austen, child of
Lucy, 28
Austin, child of
Nance, 168
Barbary, 82
Barnet, 129
Bartley, 15
Bay, 140

Beck, 22, 23, 53, 54, 129, 139, 140, 148
Bell, 82
Ben, 15, 16, 45, 120, 129, 156
Ben, child of Cloe, 153
Benjamin, 27, 34
Benn, 7
Bet, 7, 20
Beth, 21
Betty, 155
Bety, 7
Biddy, 49
Billy, child of Linda, 9
Bob, 123
Bob (called Butt), 42
Bobb, 137
Bond, 120
Brister, 39
Cacob, 48
Cago, 133
Caicy, 24
Cain, 131, 132
Carolina, 158
Caroline, 10, 13
Cate, 129
Cato, 8, 131, 164
Catoe, 132
Ceaser, 22
Cela, child of Anna, 168
Cesar, 32
Champ, 118
Champ, child of Milly, 115
Chane, 166
Charity, 80
Charles, 30, 33, 110, 113, 120
Charlott, 28
Charlotte, 19, 102, 157
Chat, 142
China, child of Peggy, 38
Chooses, 10
Clarissa, 48

Clary, 4, 141
Class, 7
Cloe, 50, 153, 156
Clovis, 11
Collin, 15, 16
Cynthia, 23
Dafna, 166
Dan, 124
Daniel, 120, 138, 142
Daphney, 9
Darkes, 24
Darkis, 129
Dave, 11, 26, 105, 119, 125
Deamond, 10
Deborah, 163
Debro, 131, 140
Dener, 7
Dennard, 30
Derry, 112
Dicey, child of Sela, 9
Dick, 65, 117, 155
Dick, child of Cloe, 153
Dill, 31
Dina, 9
Dinah, 27, 41, 117, 129, 131, 163
Dine, 153
Diner, 140
Dominy, 120
Dorcas, 102
Easter, 10, 15, 16, 125
Easther, 119
Edenborough, 118
Edmond, 50, 55
Edmund, 120
Edom, 11, 15, 16, 125
Eliaz, child of Harriet, 92
Elisha, 129
Endenborough, 137
Eve, 9
Fanie, 105
Fanny, 120, 156

Fanny, child of Anna, 167
Filas, 8
Fillis, 138
Flora, 8
Flora, child of Poll, 27
Fortune, 137
Fortune, child of Susanah, 123
Frank, 33, 37, 117, 158
Frankey, 11, 125
Gabe, 31
George, 11, 31, 57, 82, 122, 125, 131, 139, 140, 145, 163, 164, 168
George, child of Jude, 17
Gideon, 24
Gill, 141
Gorton, 24
Grace, 32
Hagan, 120
Hager, 7
Hagur, 128
Hall, 18, 44
Hannah, 1, 5, 23, 49, 89, 119, 126, 129, 147
Hannah, child of Jinney, 10
Hanner, 158
Happ, 18
Hariot, child of Susanah, 123
Harriet, 92, 122
Harriott, 10, 137
Harris, 125
Harry, 10, 16, 59, 111, 119, 125, 136, 138
Henny, 134
Henry, 49, 89
Hes, child of Nancy, 31
Hister, 39
Hosea, 102

Indy, 102
Ireland, 122, 123, 137
Isaac, 12, 15, 120, 143
Isabell, 10
Isabella, 15, 16
Isbell, 125
Isham, 15, 26
Jack, 10, 13, 15, 29, 59, 60, 112, 125, 167
Jack, child of Milly, 142
Jackey, child of Milly, 115
Jacob, 10, 14, 15, 19, 21, 123, 125, 131, 137
James, 11, 15, 33, 116, 125
Jane, 15, 19, 57, 120
Jane, child of Charlott, 28
January, 7
Jean, 111
Jeane, 82
Jeane, child of Charlotte, 19
Jeffrey, 120
Jender, 10
Jenny, 49
Jeofry, child of Hannah, 24
Jerry, 78
Jesse, 7
Jessu, 120
Jim, 12, 26
Jimina, child of Cynthia, 23
Jingo, 10
Jinney, 10
Joe, 5, 14, 22, 96, 120, 135, 141, 145
Joe, child of Poll, 27
Joel, 138
Joham, 16
John, 8, 10, 11, 15, 82, 95, 96, 103, 125, 149

Juda, 9
Judah, 10
Jude, 17, 28, 30, 82, 112, 113, 125, 129, 135, 157
Jude, child of Hannah, 119
Judith, 7
Judy, 120, 121, 129
Jula, 87
Julie, 82
Kent, 115
Keze, 14
Kitt, 142
Kyzer, 125
Lambert, 140, 163
Lara?, 75
Latt, 15
Leah, 64, 136
Leah, wife of Cesar, 32
Lear, 104
Lett, 125
Letty, 120, 129
Levi, child of Jude, 17
Lewis, 5, 8, 15, 58, 113
Lewis, child of Hannah, 23
Lewis, child of Milly, 115
Lewisa, 95
Lewsy, 118
Lexina, child of Beck, 53
Lid, 15
Lidda, 148
Liddy, 9
Linda, 9
Liney, 96
Litt, 11
Little Fill, 125
Little Phill, 11
Littleton, 33
Lord, 136
Lott, 14
Louisa, 96
Luce, 46, 158
Lucy, 15, 28

Lucy, child of Cloe, 156
Lusen, child of Polly, 57
Lymas, 25
Mack, 131
Major, 123
Man, 16
Margarit, child oh Hannah, 24
Mariah, 57
Mark, 120
Mary, 25, 95, 122, 134, 137
Mary Ann, 37, 123
Mary, child of Phebe, 56
Matilda, child of Peggey, 80
Melia, 95
Melinda, 104
Meriah, 43
Merryman, 90
Mill, 46
Milla, 156
Miller, 34
Milley, 8, 56, 135, 164
Milley, child of Jude, 157
Milly, 115, 142, 164
Minerva, 105, 145
Mingo, 134
Mingo, child of Linda, 9
Moline, 72
Moll, 31
Molly, 120, 131, 140, 163
Monday, 123
Mongo, 134
Morris, 27, 156
Moses, 17, 24, 28, 120, 125, 139, 144
Nan, 133
Nance, 77, 168
Nance, child of Nance, 77
Nancy, 31, 67

195

Suck, 133
Susan, 65
Taid, child of
Winney, 153
Tamier, 53
Tanny, 21
Tina, 3
Tom, 21, 46, 51, 126
Tom, child of Jude,
83
Tom, child of Nance,
77
Toney, 19, 23, 148
Tony, 70
Unnamed, child of
Cloe, 67
Unnamed children
(3) of Phillis,
114
Unnamed (female),
child of Chloe,
62
Unnamed woman,
113
Vaugn, 85
Vina, 40
Violet, 40, 107
William, 64
Winkey, 159
Winney, 130, 152
Winney, child of
Nance, 77
Zilphia, 1

Emancipation

Amey, 155
Andrew, 73, 74
Archibald, 154, 161
Archibald, also
called Archibald
Rox, 161
Ben, child of Jack
and Dinah, 121
Ben, child of Jeffrey
and Judith, 121
Betty, 163
Bob, 144
Cain, 79
Cate, 159
Charlott, 161

Charlotte, child of
Sarah, 160
Chloe, 162
Cloe, child of Jack
and Dinah, 121
Cloe, child of Sarah,
160
Daniel, 155
David, 133
Dick, child of Jack
and Dinah, 121
Dinah, 121
Dinnis, 36
Dublin, 80
Easter, 74, 75
Fanny, child of
Black Sarah, 163
George, 146
Hetty, 71
Hetty, wife of
Humphry, 71
Humphry, 71
Jack, 121, 146
Jeffrey, 121
Jen, 161
Jenny, 161
Jesse, 129
Judith, wife of
Jeffrey, 121
Julias, 163
Lena, 160
Letty, 162
Lina, child of Sarah,
160
Line, 162
Liz, child of Sarah,
160
Lize, 163
Lucy, 160
Lucy, child of Jack
and Dinah, 121
Matt, 65, 66
Mike, 162
Pat, 141
Phillis, 163
Phillis, child of
Sarah, 160
Rachel, child of
Sarah dec'd., 160
Robin, 25

Rose, 155
Rox, Archibald, 161
Sam, 43
Sarah, 160
Sarah, also called
Sarah Threet,
163
Siller, 78, 79
Silvy, 154
Thomas, 161
Threet, Sarah, 163
Tilda, 162
Titus, 72
Unnamed (child),
165
Unnamed children
(2) of Charlotte,
160
Unnamed man, 121
Unnamed woman,
121

Estate Settlement

Alfred, 35
Anarky, 30
Anderson, 58
Anne, 58
Bob, 30
Caesar, 58
Cate, 30
Charlot, 166
Charlotte, 145
Chinea, 151
Cisly, 30
Cressey, 30
Doll, 66
Esther, 30
Fanny, 58
Frank, 30
Grace, 159
Hager, 159
Hannah, 145
Hosea, 90
Isaac, 145
Jane, 30
Jenny, 29
Jinney, 159
Joe, 30

198

201

§§§

Occupation Index

§§§

§§§